The Richer Sex

How the New Majority
of Female Breadwinners
Is Transforming
Sex, Love, and Family

LIZA MUNDY

Simon & Schuster
New York   London   Toronto   Sydney   New Delhi

Simon & Schuster
1230 Avenue of the Americas
New York, NY 10020

First Simon & Schuster hardcover edition March 2012

SIMON & SCHUSTER and colophon are registered trademarks
of Simon & Schuster, Inc.

The names of a small number of individuals have been changed.

For information about special discounts for bulk purchases,
please contact Simon & Schuster Special Sales
at 1-866-506-1949 or business@simonandschuster.com.

The Simon & Schuster Speakers Bureau can bring authors to your live event. For more
information or to book an event contact the Simon & Schuster Speakers Bureau at
1-866-248-3049 or visit our website at www.simonspeakers.com.

Designed by Nancy Singer

Manufactured in the United States of America

1   3   5   7   9   10   8   6   4   2

Library of Congress Cataloging-in-Publication Data is available.

ISBN 978-1-4391-9771-4
ISBN 978-1-4391-9773-8 (ebook)

For Mark

Contents

Part One
THE BIG FLIP

One
The New Providers

The grown-up Hawkins siblings can't tell you why it happened, or pinpoint when, exactly, they noticed the change in their family. Maybe somebody pointed it out at their annual Christmas gathering, or during one of the big reunions the Hawkins family holds every other summer. Or maybe there never was an aha moment. The knowledge just settled in until it became a fact they all knew, but hardly thought twice about. *We have become a family of female earners.*

Which was not how the siblings had been raised.

The siblings—there are six of them—grew up in the Detroit, Michigan, suburbs. Their mother, Marcelle Hawkins, had all six in less than six years, completing her childbearing by the time she was twenty-five and staying home to raise them. Their father, Gary, supported the family by working as an engineer for Ford. He didn't graduate from college, because in the 1960s and 1970s a man working for the U.S. auto industry didn't need to. During his career Gary Hawkins helped launch the Pinto, visited assembly plants and solved their problems, traveled to help open factories in other regions, and as his wife puts it, "had his hand raised" every time Ford needed an engineer to work overtime. His chief regret, in retirement, is how little he saw of the children as they grew.

In contrast to his father, the oldest Hawkins sibling, Danny, graduated from the University of Michigan and married a woman whose earning potential was as high as or higher than his was. Danny took a job in financial services but was reluctant to work the crushing overtime load his bosses expected, so in the mid-1990s he left to become the happy, fulfilled hands-on parent to their two daughters, a stay-at-home father before the term got trendy. According to his own mother, Danny runs a household every bit as well as she did. He shops and cooks with such exactitude that he rarely ends up with leftovers, maintains a budgeting system that involves placing portions of money in a box with sections designated for specific uses, keeps a color-coded family appointment calendar, and has a stair step for each member on which he places packages and other belongings. On Halloween, for fun, he tried doing a statistical analysis of trick-or-treaters to gauge how much candy to buy the following year but decided there were too many unpredictable variables. Over the years, Danny has served as treasurer of the PTA, treasurer of the music boosters, treasurer of the co-op preschool, treasurer of their homeowners association, and sympathizing treasurer of the golf club they belong to. In the evenings he is happy to listen to the workday accounts of his wife, Susan, a senior vice president with the Henry Ford Health System, with her challenges and sharing in her triumphs.

"I have told Susie several times that my job is to make her life easier," says Danny. "And I like doing it."

Meanwhile, Danny's younger sister Leslie works in supply-chain management for a Michigan transportation and logistics company, where she has risen to be part of the top leadership team. Her own husband, Damon, who everybody thought would be a hotshot corporate lawyer and the main breadwinner in the family, instead stepped back to become the secondary earner, working as a real estate broker and becoming the on-call parent for their three children. Like his brother-in-law Danny, Damon cooks, ambitiously; golfs, formidably; drives children to lessons and sports games; cleans house; and is so comfortably domesticated that when some neighbors arrived for a card game and Damon answered the door holding a dust cloth, the neighborhood began calling him "Coco." Damon, who is known for his humor, embraced the nickname and the reputation for housekeeping excellence that goes with it.

Another grown-up Hawkins sibling, Rhonda, had no idea what she wanted to do with her life when she was a young adult. In college, Rhonda changed majors so many times she stopped counting. Eventually she switched to night classes and took a job as a receptionist at Magna International, a company that supplies systems and components to the auto industry. She began working in marketing, got her degree in that field, and did so well that she finds herself—though she is too self-deprecating to allow that this is a big deal—the company's head of global marketing. Her husband, Hank, works in the restaurant business and loves what he does, but scaled back his hours when Rhonda got a promotion that required her to take extensive overseas trips on short notice.

Another Hawkins sibling, Lori, who works in finance, is in a committed relationship with another woman; both contribute monetarily to the household.

The other Hawkins daughter, Shelly, is a divorced mother of two, supporting her own household with a job in the health-care field.

Out of the six adult children of Gary and Marcelle Hawkins, only one—Michael—is in a traditional marriage where he has filled the role of primary earner.

Six adult siblings. Five households supported by women. One generation. One complete economic flip.

It's a profound change in the balance of economic power, a striking role reversal and one that was unplanned, barely noticed, in fact, sneaking up on the Hawkins family when nobody was looking. In a matter of decades, the traditional male breadwinner model has given way to one where women routinely support households and outearn the men they are married to, and nobody cares or thinks it's odd. The Hawkins family—sane, functional, rooted in a midwestern state known for family values—offers a convincing vision of what America is becoming. We are entering an era where women, not men, will become the top earners in households. We are entering the era in which roles will flip, as resoundingly as they have done in this family. You laugh, but that Big Flip is just around the corner.

Not that long ago, in 1970, the percentage of U.S. wives who outearned their husbands was in the low single digits. Some of these women were super-achievers, but more often they were women married to men who were ailing, drifting, unsteady, or unemployable. For generations, female breadwinners were mostly poor women—women whose husbands had difficulty providing. Forty years later, this template has changed dramatically, as the forces that produce female breadwinners have become more powerful and varied. Almost 40 percent of U.S. working wives now outearn their husbands, a percentage that has risen steeply in this country and many others, as more women have entered the workforce and remained committed to it. Women occupy 51 percent of managerial and professional jobs in the United States, and they dominate nine of the ten U.S. job categories expected to grow the most in the next decade.

Part of this ascent is due to the gradual lifting of discriminatory practices that once funneled women into lower-paying sectors and obliged them to quit work when they got married. Part is due to long-term changes in the economy that have chipped away at male sectors like construction and manufacturing while bringing big increases in women's fields such as education and health care. And a large part is due to women's own grit and initiative, evidenced by the fact that women now outnumber men on college campuses in the United States as well as around the world. By the year 2050, demographers forecast, there will be 140 college-educated women in the United States for every 100 college-educated men. Globally, a generation of young women is entering the job market who are better educated than young men are, and poised to become the most financially powerful generation of women in history. In coming years, economists—who study major transitions such as the rise of agrarian society, the dawn of the industrial age, the ascent of the white-collar office worker, the opening of the global economy—will look back and see this as the era when women realized their earning power and, for the first time, outpaced their partners. "The trends are clear," agrees Gary Becker, the Nobel Prize–winning economist at the University of Chicago who pioneered the economic study of families, even predicting that "we could see a day where women, on average, are earning more than men."

In addition to the changes it will bring to the economy and the workplace, the rise of women earners will shape human behavior by challenging some of the most primal and hardwired ways men and women see one another. It will alter how we mate, how and when we join together, how we procreate and raise children, and, to use the phrase of the founders, how we pursue happiness. It will reshape the landscape of the heart. This is a book about how men and women are changing all those things already, and how these changes will play out in the future.

Think the Hawkinses are an anomaly? A fluke? Consider Jessica Gasca, a resident of South Texas who works as a paralegal, supporting a husband and three children. Jessica likes being in the workforce. She prefers it to staying home. So her husband, Juan, watches the children and takes part-time jobs in customer service. "Our kids see me as the father," says Jessica, who has several sisters who also are breadwinners in their households. These women, to their surprise, have emerged as dominant earners in their immigrant Hispanic community, a culture with strong patriarchal values yet one in which women are outstripping men even more rapidly than in the nation as a whole. For many, this creates profound discomfort. "My mom always says: 'All my daughters—I've never taught you to be that way. I can't believe it.' She says that we're providing for the man, when it should be the other way around."

Or consider Alicia Simpson, a psychiatrist, and her sister, Tracy Parker, a banker. Both women are graduates of Howard University, an elite, historically black university in Washington, D.C., where nearly 70 percent of the student body is female. Alicia and Tracy, both in their forties, both mothers, grew up in a male-breadwinning family, and over dinner they tried to remember what they had expected starting out in their marriages, and to understand how it was that they ended up primary earners.

"I always figured it would be a partnership," said Alicia. "Everybody sort of carrying his own weight." For these sisters, the change was so disconcerting that their marriages foundered. Alicia divorced her husband—"I had to push him out of the nest; it was like, either you're going to fly, or you're going to perish"—while Tracy worked through her resentment and struggled to accept her role. "My husband's a great dad and I need him there," said Tracy. "So it was a mind-set that I had to develop."

Consider Rita Radzilowski and her sister, Ginette Trottier, both raised in a working-class family, both college graduates. Ginette, a nurse, married a business analyst who underwent a stretch of unemployment in the recent recession, when his company was sold and many positions were pushed overseas. Around the same time, Rita, who has an associate's degree, a bachelor's degree, and a master's degree—among other credentials—dated a professional brickmason who also lost his job. Neither man graduated from a four-year college. Both face a changing economy where high-paying jobs for non-grads are on the decline. The sisters adjusted by setting their own sights even higher. Rita is preparing to embark on a doctorate and Ginette moved into management and began to consider medical school. It seems clear to Ginette that she may remain the top earner in her marriage—or at least the one with the more reliable paycheck—so she might as well maximize that income as a doctor rather than a nurse. "I want to do it," she said. "I want to make more money. I might as well do it. I know it's a lot of work. I understand."

Or meet Jill Singer, raised on a farm on the outskirts of Boise, Idaho, with the expectation that she would work hard in life but should not expect to earn much for her labor, because earning money was a man's domain. When she was growing up in the 1970s, Jill and her sisters were expected to do agricultural chores alongside their brothers. "By the time we were tall enough to push a lawn mower, that's when we started working," Jill remembers. "But we were also supposed to do inside chores. The boys could come inside and sit, but the girls were expected to do cooking and sewing and mend the shirts." She was raised in the Mormon Church, which—like a number of traditional religions—teaches that the husband provides for, and presides over, the family. Growing up, Jill learned that public space belonged to men and private domestic space to women. "Men were responsible for the 'outside'—income and discipline—and women were responsible for the 'inside'—budgeting for a household, raising the children, staying home and making sure the husband is happy," is how Jill summarizes her upbringing. "I was never led to expect that I would be a primary breadwinner. Ever." Yet Jill now works in construction management and earns twice as much as her husband. Thumbtacked to a bulletin board in her mud room is the church's proclamation on the family, which articulates the man-as-provider philosophy. She doesn't pay much attention to it—believing that it has nothing to do with church doctrine, and everything to do with church politics—and expects any day now to be relieved of her duties as a Sunday school teacher, relating gospel principles to children on the verge of being baptized. She tells her daughters, "Don't believe everything that comes from the pulpit." All three of her sisters, she notes, make the bulk of their family income.

"My parents are so pleased with us," says Jill. "They are tickled pink at how we women turned out."

And finally, consider four young women sitting at an outdoor table in midtown Atlanta, Georgia, on a balmy Saturday in late winter. Two are engineers, one is a banker, and another is an entrepreneur. All are in their early twenties. All earn between $65,000 and $90,000, just a couple of years out of college. In most American cities, single childless women between 22 and 30 make more, in terms of median income, than their male peers, a direct result of the fact that women are now better-educated than men. Of all the major cities where young women outearn young men, Atlanta is number one. Well do these women know the accuracy of that statistic. "I have never had a boyfriend who made more than me," says one of them. Over steak salads and spring rolls, the Atlanta women share techniques on how to make the men they date feel comfortable, and as they talk it becomes clear they are also describing how they make themselves feel comfortable. One likes to let her boyfriend drive her car. She carries lots of petty cash—singles and fives—so she can discreetly pay for tips and parking and entrance fees in a way that seems less obtrusive than flashing around a credit card. "You never actually show them how much money it's costing," she says. "You never want them to be aware of how much work you're putting in."

She adds: "I want at the end of the night for someone not to remember who paid."

Another woman at the table buys movie tickets in advance, and then tells her boyfriend they were given away at work. This same woman recently got a promotion at the consulting company she works for, along with a raise higher than she expected. She struggled to know how to share this with her boyfriend, a manager at a Waffle House who took that job because it was the only one he could find that was near her. She loves her work, and her boyfriend hates his, and the day after her big news he was in tears over how thankless and chaotic his own job is. How do you handle that? How do you celebrate your success when the man you love is floundering? Even when he is supportive and happy for you? And what do you tell people who wonder why you are dating a guy who works at a Waffle House? These are the kinds of questions women find themselves asking. "What's she doing with this guy?" she says. "That's what I imagine them thinking."

This book will look at the many ways relationships are changing as women increase their earnings, overtaking the men in their lives in numbers unprecedented up to now. It will draw on interviews with hundreds of men and women, with a diversity of age and race and backgrounds, people who have one key thing in common: they are living firsthand the profound impact of these major economic changes. People interviewed for this book sometimes spoke individually, sometimes in couples, sometimes in wide-ranging conversations with groups of friends and colleagues. They live in the industrial regions of the Midwest and the immigrant-rich floodplains of South Texas, in college dorms and in trendy downtown areas of major cities around the country. They live in other countries, too, in places as disparate as Denmark and Japan, where the same forces are at work with markedly different outcomes. In Japan, economic power has altered women's behavior so profoundly that some observers believe they have traded personalities with men. And this book captures insights offered by polls and studies, conducted by a range of experts charting women's rise and its emotional consequences. It offers predictions about what will happen as women dominate the classroom and the workplace, in the United States but also globally. It predicts who will marry whom, who will stay single, who will struggle; who will prevail; how relationships will evolve. How sex will change. How children will respond. What decisions college-educated women will make, looking out at a pool of mates who are less accomplished than they are. These are issues that economists and other experts are watching closely as they try to understand the biggest revolution under way in American society since the age of industry gave full expression to the idea that men are the wage earners, and cemented it so firmly that some still believe it to be an immutable law, handed down by God or, alternately, by Darwin.

For sure, things could go badly. As countries all over the world move away from the industrial era model of male breadwinner and female homemaker, there are those who predict a genuine war between men and women: a long-lasting power struggle and protracted renegotiation as women try to get men to provide more encouragement—and do more housework—and men cling to the status and authority they used to enjoy. As more women enter the workforce and succeed, some will find themselves doubly burdened—entrusted with breadwinning responsibilities but awarded few of the perks men have long commanded. A cynic might predict that as more women become the dominant earners, moneymaking will lose its prestige and suddenly there will be nothing so respected as being . . . a stay-at-home father, raising children and tending the household.

Over the years, research and casual observation have tended to suggest that men do not react well when women outperform them. "Men know that women are an over-match for them, and therefore they choose the weakest or most ignorant," observed Samuel Johnson in the 18th century. A number of studies have supported this intuition, suggesting that families with economically dominant women are more likely to split up, in part because men are more likely to stray or retaliate against women who overshadow them. In 2011, a study confirmed that women who win Oscars for Best Actress are at higher risk of divorce, whereas Best Actor winners are not. And now the problem of husbands who feel eclipsed (or outshone) isn't just an issue for the

Reese Witherspoons and Sandra Bullocks of the world. It's an issue for noncelebrities—for English majors, law students, registered nurses, young women starting businesses, you name it. "I think about this all the time," messaged one young woman in an email, expressing how it felt to belong to the first generation of female college graduates who outnumber male graduates, and to look around and wonder whom you will ever marry. One 34-year-old software engineer working in Washington, D.C., said it took years for her to find a man to date who was comfortable with her salary. When she would meet men and tell them what she does for a living, the men would say things like "You must be one of those smart women!" and look alarmed. So she began telling men she was a music teacher, which was technically true, since she is also a violinist, and does some teaching. This worked better, she says, until about the third date, when she told them what she really did. "They would stop calling."

So yes, men can react badly, but the full truth is more complicated, and more optimistic. The negative studies, which confirm fondly held stereotypes about men and women, tend to get a lot of play when they emerge. The media always enjoy a juicy study showing how unpleasant high-powered women are—how troubled their relationships, how bossy and shrewish their calls to the home front, how henpecked and emasculated their husbands. There is a backlashy feel to some of the coverage of women earners, as if it satisfies a deep human need to believe that women when they succeed professionally are doomed to fail personally, and that men will never, ever flourish in the face of female achievement. Google "*Daily Mail*"—the reliably conservative British tabloid—and "female breadwinner" and you will get no shortage of reactionary doomsday coverage. Women will have less sex! They will yell at their husbands! Men will leave them! Heartbreak will ensue, as "a growing band of increasingly successful women climb up the career ladder and financial scale, leaving a trail of broken marriages and relationships in their wake when men resent losing breadwinner status." The idea that women, by winning, are really losing, is popular but it is also—I would argue—simplistic and extremely suspect.

Because, in fact, social norms are changing and so are men's reactions to women earners. Until very recently, sociologists thought women who earned more than their husbands did more housework, to reassert their femininity and conform to social expectations, and that their husbands did less, to reestablish control and masculinity. Now it appears—this just in—that is not true. It is not true now, and possibly never was. All measures confirm that men have been increasing their housework as women have increased their work time. And there are studies that suggest that women actually receive more praise than men do for high earnings. The evidence shows that many men are perfectly able to celebrate their wives' successes and, like Danny Hawkins, give the women they love and admire a full, sympathetic hearing. And young men have different expectations than they did thirty years ago. Men want more time with their children, more flexibility, more of a life outside the office. And what is likely to win them that? A successful, hardworking wife.

While it's clearly true that men in some cases are struggling to get their heads around the idea of being out-provided—and sometimes failing spectacularly, and retaliating dramatically, as you will read in some of the pages that follow—the truth is that many men are happy to share the reins of financial responsibility, or even hand them over. These men correctly perceive that life as a co-earner or secondary earner will enlarge their own pleasures, giving them more time for hobbies, leisure, and children, or for work they find fulfilling rather than lucrative. Increasingly, I would argue, men will *want* to marry a woman who makes more than they do. In some cases, men will want this because they realize it will make their own lives freer and better; in other cases, they'll want it because it seems rational to assume women are favored in a new economy that runs on information, consumer acquisition, and service, rather than industry or hard labor. "When culture runs up against economic trends, usually economic trends win out," says Nobel laureate Gary Becker. By this he means: even if men have been brought up to think they should be breadwinners, and are put off by women who might surpass them, pragmatic incentives will win out over competitiveness and psychological insecurities. Men—smart men—will gladly hitch their wagon to a female star.

The real impediment in the short term may be women themselves. Do women want to be breadwinners with the responsibility and overtime that entails? Can a high-powered woman love a laid-back guy who idles at a lower speed than she does? Some of the evidence suggests: no. Among many women, there remains a vestigial sense that a man needs to bring something to the table besides dinner, no matter how expertly cooked, and that a man who is not generating a salary has reneged on his central obligation. I talked to far more high-earning women who worried that their husbands felt emasculated than to men who actually *did* feel emasculated. Some women struggle with finding ways to appreciate other qualities, besides income, that men have to offer. In fact, women may be further behind emotionally than men. Many resist thinking of themselves as the main provider. "Getting boxed in as the higher earner—it sounds like a lot more work, and a lot less play," one young Ph.D. student I interviewed reflected as she envisioned being the permanent breadwinner in her relationship. It's a wrenching transition, in which the laws of sexual attraction are changing along with the dynamics of the household.

Looking at men's reactions to women's earnings, you could say that men have three options. Men can resist women's rising economic power, even retaliate against it, a reaction vividly captured in much of the journalism and feminist literature of the 1980s and 1990s. Alternatively, men can quit, give up, stop trying: a reaction explored in much of today's coverage about men's anxieties in the face of an economic downturn that has hit them harder than women. But there is a third option—Door Number Three, you could call it. This option sees men rising to the challenge, developing more perfect unions with the women they are intimately connected to; and, inspired by women's example, raising the level of their game. Door Number Three leads to men trying harder in the classroom, competing with women, but in a good way, self-improving, adapting, developing new skills. For women, there are also three options. Women can resent men and focus only on their shortcomings, real and perceived. Or women can hang on to the past, occupying their new role but cleaving to old ones, struggling to retain control over children and home tasks. Alternatively, women can move toward this new vision, expressing gratitude for the many ways men are adjusting, giving ground when they need to, and relaxing into a fuller acceptance of their changing economic role. I'd argue that the third option has been overlooked; that it's occurring; and that it merits more attention than it has gotten.

Because, behind Door Number Three, the future of the female breadwinner—the breadwoman, you might call her—is bright. Women's earning power and the vitality and success it signals will lead to a genuine breakthrough in the relationship between the sexes. It will give women the bargaining power they need to get more help from men at home, usher in a new age of fairness, complete the revolution, push us past the unhappy days of the so-called second shift, when so many men and women were mired in arguments over equity that always seemed to boil down to laundry and dishes. Women's earnings will bring about a new liberation for women but also for men. It will bring about an epoch of fresh realizations and adjusted expectations. Increasingly, couples will even rethink the definition of fairness, and realize that "fair" can have a meaning other than perfect 50-50 equality in all tasks. They will realize that marriages sometimes do work best when the partners occupy complementary roles, doing slightly different things, but what's new is that these roles don't have to be complementary in traditional, gender-bound ways. In relationships, couples will perceive that the goal of absolute sameness is not always workable and not always desirable, either. Each partner doesn't need to be interchangeable, doing exactly the same things, half-work, half-family, dividing the work according to a strict egalitarian notion. Sometimes it really is preferable—and necessary—for one spouse to be the high-powered partner and the other to provide behind-the-scenes support. What's going to be different is that women increasingly will be the ones occupying the high-powered role, and they need to learn to be happy with partners who celebrate and help them.

In the coming decades, there are other developments men and women can look forward to. Men, I predict, will rapidly adjust to the new state of affairs. Pretty soon, we will see more and more men attracted to high-earning, dynamic, and successful women. For the first time, men will start thinking of marriage as a bet on the economic potential of a spouse, exactly as women have done for generations—from the drawing rooms of Jane Austen to the hot tubs of the *Real Housewives* era. A man will look at a woman and think: Wow. Look at her: she's going places. And more and more, it will be men who make adjustments, such as relocation, to support a partner's career.

Meanwhile, women will grow into their identity as breadwinners. Increasingly, they will accept the breadwoman role. Women will change the way they look at men and what traits they find desirable in a mate. They will place even greater value on qualities such as supportiveness (a glass of wine waiting at the end of the day, a chance to unburden), parenting skills, and domestic achievements, not to mention that great old masculine standby: protection. And women will no longer feel that their standing in the world derives from what their husband does or how much he makes. This will relieve a great deal of pressure—cultural, emotional, financial—on men.

Both sexes will be freer to make purely romantic choices—choices that have nothing to do with marriage as an economic partnership. This means more women will marry down; more men will marry up. More women will marry younger men; more men will marry older women. More women and men will marry across racial and ethnic groups. And instead of "matching" on education and earnings, couples will find common ground in an outside leisure pursuit that they can share on an equal footing.

The home front will become more and more masculinized. Men will view the home as the space they can make their own, an adaptation made easier by two decades of American households transforming their kitchens and outdoor grilling areas into performance arenas. "It's just much more fun to be around home than it used to be," is how one domesticated husband put it. "There's just all kinds of stuff."

Women will take to the skies. High-earning young women who remain determined to marry men who make as much or more than they do will turn to more enterprising measures than online dating. Women will use their earnings to travel far and wide, flying from big cities to other big cities, keeping the travel industry afloat and turning the country—the world—into one big marriage market, one giant globally connected dating pool. In countries such as Japan and South Korea, where high-achieving women are still intimidating to men, more subservient—that is to say, poorer—women will be brought from other Asian countries to meet the preferences of men who want to marry someone who will be economically dependent on them. Meanwhile, men in Western nations may opt for mail-order brides, or move and settle in less developed countries with a wife who will take care of them—and take their money.

Contrary to some reports, women will not feel a desperate need to hook up, sexually, as a way to find suitable mates who will commit to them. Some journalists and academics have suggested that so-called hookup culture is the result of high-achieving women rather indiscriminately having sex with the diminishing number of men who share their credentials; that women are offering sex with the hope of snagging a man who will agree to settle down. Not so. It's true that a new generation of women will behave more like men sexually, by having lots of partners, but many of these women will be delaying commitment. Women will become more sexually assertive. They will use their economic resources to find men who are good at sex but also—equally important—good at washing dishes. Sexually, women will feel more free than ever to say no; to determine the kind of sex they are having and how often they want to have it. Oh, and if their lower-earning men criticize them for carrying a few extra pounds, they will happily ignore it.

And contrary to other anecdotal reports, men in the "marriageable" pool will not be looking to extend their promiscuous days. Instead, men will be the ones longing to settle down. Indeed, new studies suggest that men, far from being the commitmentphobes they are often made out to be, may have a greater desire than women for family life.

The pool of Americans who are married will continue to shrink. Rates of cohabitation will rise, as will the ranks of people living alone. Women will be able to afford to wait around and be choosy. But just because a woman might be living alone does not mean she will be lonely. Instead, women will savor the company of friends, although not necessarily in a sexual way. Women do this now, of course, but increasingly the couples at bars and concerts and shows will be women with women. Women will dominate the public square. The public arena will become more and more feminized. Look around you at a restaurant and notice how many of the tables are filled with groups of women—trios, quartets, tables of eight—clinking wineglasses and ordering the filet mignon. More important, women will be less likely to regard a single life as a failed life—and more likely to find pleasure and fulfillment in a life that does not include marriage. Even when in committed relationships, women will want to maintain space for themselves and time for their friends. They will consider clinginess in a boyfriend a major deal breaker.

And within couples, now that it's permissible for men to be stay-at-home fathers and part-time workers, couples will argue over who in the partnership must assume the responsibility of primary earner, and who gets to have the freedom and flexibility that go with being the slow-track partner.

Some couples may struggle, sexually, until men find new ways to recover and assert their masculinity. But this may not be as difficult as people think. Men will craft a broader understanding of masculinity, one that includes domestication but also more time spent on manly pursuits: hunting, fishing, and extreme fitness. Meanwhile, women with lower-earning husbands will work hard to praise them for other kinds of accomplishments. Things that might have been considered "hobbies," if women were doing them, will be granted a higher status when performed by stay-at-home husbands. Family blogs maintained by dads will be considered "book projects."

Women living in cultures and belonging to religions that emphasize the importance of male provision—and female submission—will have to find a way to resolve this tension. Assessing their own prospects in the workplace, and finding them greater than their husbands', women may have to break away from the flock, get permission from their pastors to work, or live in a state of uneasy conflict, in which the reality of their daily life is at odds with the teachings they hear on Sundays. Ministers and pastors will be called upon to supply dispensation for women to be breadwinners, and husbands will "allow" their wives to earn more than they do, thereby maintaining their God-given authority, in spirit if not in fact. These men will preserve their masculinity by designating themselves their wives' handlers and protectors.

The more emotional and logistical support that breadwomen can enlist from their stay-at-home husbands, the more money these women will earn. The workplace, long so skeptical of female employees, will institute some long-delayed changes. More flexibility, yes—one can hope. At the same time, employers will regard supportive husbands the same way they used to look at stay-at-home wives: as crucial domestic backup, a welcome guarantee that female employees will be able to work with as much dedication as men traditionally have. The more backup that employers see women getting on the home front, the more willing bosses will be to invest in the careers of their female stars. Women's earnings will rise. And rise. It will never stop, until . . .

Women marry down, and raise their husbands up.

And that, too, will happen.

Two
The Bargain

It would be hard to overstate the historic nature of women's economic ascendancy. With few exceptions, the world has been ordered until quite recently so that the bulk of wealth and earnings lay under the control of men. What we are witnessing is the gradual but relentless upending of a global tradition in which women were obliged to rely on men economically and to fashion their behavior accordingly. For centuries, women's dependence was seen as not just a necessary ingredient for marriage but the very foundation of the male-female union. Clergymen argued that women's subordination to husbands mirrored humanity's submission to God. Laws dictated that wives could not own property or lay claim to their earnings. Labor unions based their crusade for a living industrial wage on the idea that man was woman's "natural protector." Social commentators declared that being dependent made women more agreeable helpmeets. And every now and then, somebody came along and objected that the deal was not, in fact, such a good one. In 1929, when Virginia Woolf considered the question of which was better for a woman—being granted the vote, or becoming financially self-sufficient—she concluded that of the two, money was "infinitely the more important."

In *A Room of One's Own*, Woolf's brilliant case for women's economic independence, she spelled out her view of what dependency had done over the centuries to women's accomplishments as well as their characters. This is the famous essay where Woolf considers what might have happened had Shakespeare had an equally brilliant sister. In England at that time, she conjectured, the girl would have been denied an education and ridiculed for her ambitions; if she ventured into the world anyway, to seek her fortune and develop her talents, she would have been seduced, consigned to penury, driven to despair and early death. Woolf's essay is a chronicle of rejection and artistic discouragement, but it is also a chronicle of money and the effect of money—or lack thereof—on women's lives and achievements. Even into the 20th century, Woolf pointed out, women's impoverishment meant they remained uneducated and without a robust literary tradition of their own, vulnerable to the insidious psychological undermining of male authority figures who argued that women could not perform as well as men, and who attributed women's deficiencies not to their lack of resources but to an inferiority in their nature. Considering why women had not contributed more to literature and public life, Woolf pointed out that even as kings and merchants donated the gold and wrote the checks to build and maintain magnificent—and historically male—universities like Oxford and Cambridge, women had only lately been able to scrape together funds for a few female colleges. The reason this had taken so long, she pointed out, was because for hundreds of years women had been unable to have their own money.

"It is only for the last forty-eight years that [a married woman] has had a penny of her own," she noted, referring to the fact that married women in England had been barred from owning property or even their wages, under a common law principle that considered a wife's identity to be subsumed into that of her husband. "For all the centuries before that it would have been her husband's property—a thought which, perhaps, may have had its share in keeping [her] and her mothers off the Stock Exchange. Every penny I earn, they may have said, will be taken from me and disposed of according to my husband's wisdom . . . so that to earn money, even if I could earn money, is not a matter that interests me very greatly. I had better leave it to my husband." Here, Woolf made the same argument that economists would later proffer: women, shut out of the world of affairs, saw marriage as the only rational form of employment they could enter into, the best bargain they could strike.

Woolf argued that women's personalities, as well as their relationships with men, were deformed by this bargain. Elsewhere she invoked the image of the "angel in the house": the idealized Victorian wife, saintly, moral, egoless, obliged to flatter and to assume a secondary position in her own household, precisely because she had no resources. "She was intensely sympathetic," Woolf wrote scoffingly of the angel. "She was immensely charming. She was utterly unselfish. . . . She sacrificed herself daily. If there was chicken, she took the leg; if there was a draught she sat in it—in short she was so constituted that she never had a mind or a wish of her own, but preferred to sympathize always with the minds and wishes of others." Women were obliged to repress their needs and soften their opinions to ensure that men would not withdraw their benevolence. In *A Room of One's Own*, Woolf invents a narrator much like herself, who relates how liberating it was to receive a bequest from an aunt giving her a regular income. For the first time, she was able to say and write what she thought, without having to bend her words to meet the sensibilities of male editors and readers. She also found that having money tempered her resentment of men. "I need not hate any man; he cannot hurt me. I need not flatter any man; he has nothing to give me. So imperceptibly I found myself adopting a new attitude towards the other half of the human race."

In the United States, the same pattern of economic dependence prevailed. The most recent edition of *The Researcher's Guide to American Genealogy* warns the armchair genealogist that it is difficult to trace maternal ancestry because women are so rarely included in older U.S. records. "Once a woman was married, there was very little trace of her," the book apologetically notes. While some argue that colonial society was more egalitarian than later industrial eras, in the sense that men and women toiled in the home and were economic partners, the historian Marylynn Salmon points out that the American colonies, each in its own way, followed England's common law, which held that a wife's identity—and property—ceased upon marriage to be considered hers. "After marriage, all of the personal property owned by a wife came under the exclusive control of her husband," notes Salmon, pointing out that a woman's husband "could spend her money, including wages, sell her slaves or stocks, and appropriate her clothing and jewelry. With regard to real property his rights were almost as extensive. He made all managerial decisions concerning her lands and tenements and controlled the rents and profits." Religious colonies like Connecticut and Massachusetts were the most extreme, legislating the Puritan belief in "the wife's submission to her husband's will." If anything, Salmon notes, religious colonies went beyond British law in giving men power over wives' estates, and ensuring male dominance within the family, which was the organizing unit of colonial society. The extent to which colonial women were dispossessed—the extent to which women *were* property—was exemplified by the "wife sale," a ritual inherited from England that sometimes accompanied a divorce. The wife sale is just what it sounds like; according to Salmon, it "demonstrates with graphic precision the inferior status of women in early modern Anglo-American society, for in the most primitive instances the woman was led to market in a halter and auctioned off to the highest bidder." In colonial America, property was the route to prosperity and independence. Not only were most women denied this; among the wage-earning classes, male servants were paid more than female ones, and women were denied the apprenticeships that enabled men to become skilled artisans.

This set in motion a pattern—of paying women less, and shutting them out of skilled labor—that would prevail for the next 300 years. The only exceptions were female slaves, who commanded higher prices than male slaves because of their ability to generate still more slaves. It must be one of the few instances in history where mothers had a higher monetary value than fathers.

In the United States, some observers came to the same conclusion Woolf did: Even when people married for love—and this, along with companionship and family life, was the accepted ideal for marriage—economic dependence warped the relationship between the sexes. In 1898, the writer Charlotte Perkins Gilman, a great-niece of Harriet Beecher Stowe, presaged Woolf's observations in an essay called *Women and Economics*. "We are the only animal species in which the female depends on the male for food," Gilman pointedly noted. Fascinated by Darwin's theory of natural selection, she argued that organisms adapt to their environment, and that for women, men were the environment. Humans could live a more egalitarian existence, she said, but under the influence of culture they had become too specialized. Men were too committed to the world of commerce, women too closeted in the home. She knew whereof she spoke. When she developed depression after the birth of her child, Gilman was ordered by a leading "nerve specialist" to suspend all work and "live as domestic a life as possible," a prescription that traumatized her permanently.

Gilman, like Woolf, was intrigued by the bargain women were obliged to strike in order to live. She was fascinated by the ruses women adopted, the lengths they went to attract husbands, the efforts they made to appear marriageable and alluring. Her analysis anticipated the work of economists, sociologists, and other students of marriage, who even now argue that male-female unions are an exchange in which women "trade" any number of assets—sexual favors, beauty, domestic service—for economic gain. The central question—and one this book will consider—is whether this bargain has been something women were forced into or whether it was one that women embraced. Over all these hundreds of years, have women wanted husbands to be their providers or have they been compelled to put up with it because there were so few alternatives? Does every woman, in her heart of hearts, want to be supported? Does she expect it? Seek it out? And what about men? What do they want in all this?

You could boil down the opposing viewpoints, in a way, to a contest between Marx and Darwin. The Marxist argument would hold that for men, property ownership and control of family income have been a means of oppressing women—a way of obtaining women's labor and domestic services, including childrearing, and ensuring their sexual fidelity. Seen this way, the bargain is one that women gave into unwillingly and under duress. "When [man] became owner of the land, he claimed also ownership of [the] woman," is how Simone de Beauvoir put it. Beauvoir did not let women off the hook, though. In acceding to this trade-off—"the deal," she called it—women gave up a part of their essential selves. "This is an inauspicious road, for he who takes it—passive, lost, ruined—becomes henceforth the creature of another's will, frustrated in his transcendence and deprived of every value. But it is an easy road; on it one avoids the strain involved in undertaking an authentic existence."

In contrast, the Darwinian view holds that this bargain was a terrific arrangement for women, who are biologically constituted to seek a strong male provider who can protect and support the woman and her offspring. The Darwinian argument holds that the reason women's economic dependence prevailed for so long was because it just worked so awfully well for everybody. Women rendered up their looks and housekeeping services, men rendered up their income, their genetic lines were perpetuated into the next generation, children had two parents, marriages were stable, and everybody came out fine. Moreover—this line of thinking goes—marriage over the years has been a bargain that favored the dependent sex even more than the wage-earning one, because it gave a woman a roof over her head and economic protection in the case of divorce or other catastrophe.

Regardless of which view you take, the idea that men should be the wage earners and property owners was for centuries seen as the cornerstone of family life and social order. It seems to have been hard for some to envision why a woman, awarded money of her own, would stay with a man at all. In 1868, when England was debating granting property rights to married women, the London *Times* warned that marriage as society knew it could cease altogether if this happened. "[T]he proposed change would totally destroy the existing relation between husband and wife. That relation at present is one of authority on the one side and subordination on the other," the *Times* wrote, editorializing against the measure. "If a woman has her own property, and can apply to her separate use her own earnings, she is practically emancipated from the control of her husband . . . what is to prevent her from going where she likes and doing what she pleases?"

Enter the Breadwinner

What indeed? What might prevent the emancipation and free movement of women, once wives could own property and keep their wages, as laws passed in the 19th century finally enabled them to do? Well, during the transition to an industrial economy, as more and more households depended on wages rather than farming or property ownership, concrete measures were put in place to ensure that women who did work were mostly corralled into sectors that were lower-paying than men's; that women who did the same job as men were paid far less; that women worked only when they were young and single; that women ceased working—at least for wages—upon marriage; that men remained the source of a family's income and, with that, the final authority in the house.

Readers may feel they know this history, but it's unlikely most people today have a vivid sense of just how thoroughly the workplace, the government, labor unions, and society colluded to make women feel unwelcome in the workplace; to ensure that any wages they earned were supplementary at best; and to reinforce the ideal of man as woman's provider. As the historian Alice Kessler-Harris has painstakingly shown in her book on wage-earning women, *Out to Work*, the prevailing view was that woman's sphere was the home and that she should be made as uncomfortable as possible in the workplace. If women objected, they were derided as "clamorous and unfeminine"—the epithet directed at the leader of a group of organized tailoresses who agitated for fair treatment in 1831. And precisely because women were paid less than men, whenever they made incursions into a "male" field, the cry went up that women represented "ruinous competition" and were destroying men's ability to bargain with employers for a so-called family wage. The view prevailed that the economy was a zero-sum game; that gains for women meant losses for men; that a woman who worked was "taking" the rightful place of a man; that the workplace wasn't big enough for both sexes, a sense that prevails in some arenas to this day.

The point of keeping women out of lucrative work, many historians have pointed out, was to uphold the "domestic code" that prevailed in the 19th century. The code held that it was a man's job to support his household, and a woman's job to keep the home fires burning. Men and women occupied not merely separate roles, but separate spheres. It was now that woman became the angel in the house—a creature of charm and self-effacement, a vision of loving womanliness the husband could return to when his day's work was over. The religious directive of female submission merged with the secular idea that women were morally pure, above and apart from the sordid "bank-note world." Economists have argued that this cult of womanhood developed in response to a world that was increasingly competitive. Pragmatically, men working a long day needed a wife at home to keep the food cooked and the laundry washed and the children tended. Spiritually, a man needed a happy mate to lift his spirits. To ensure she stayed there, it was necessary that a woman's subordination be reinforced from all sides.

To be sure, women weren't the only ones whose behavior was being regulated. Men's behavior was, too. It was thought that having a wife to support kept a man "sober and industrious." A man with dependents to worry about was a man who couldn't afford to be lazy. The conviction grew that a man whose wife was forced to earn income was a man who had abdicated his central duty. Money became the marker of masculine achievement. The title of breadwinner was in part a bone thrown to men to make up for the fact that they were going off to jobs that many of them hated. Ejected from his household, the wage earner was dubiously rewarded with the authority to make decisions and spank children in the period of time when he was home. "Contacts between fathers of urban families with their children were considerably reduced, and the father became a distant personage," observes the French philosopher Elisabeth Badinter. This image of the male breadwinner—powerful, benevolent, yet detached from the intimate daily life of the household—still exerts a hold on us. Even now, 67 percent of Americans feel it is "very important" that the man be able to support his family before getting married, while only 33 percent think this is "very important" for women.

The endurance of this idea is ironic when you consider that it was women who were the vanguard of the industrial movement. As Kessler-Harris points out, in the early 1800s, men and boys were still tied to farm work, so it was mostly young single women who headed off to work in the textile mills of New England. At one point, women outnumbered men in the country's still small manufacturing sector. Early on, some 90 percent of the workforce in New England's textile factories was female. Evidence suggests that dependence was something these young women felt quite pleased to leave behind. Once the mill girls "felt the jingle of silver in their pocket, there for the first time, their heads became erect and they walked as if on air," one worker remembered. "You cannot think how funny it seems to have some money," wrote another, exclaiming, "don't I feel independent of everyone! The [thought] that I am living on no one is a happy one indeed." Briefly, it looked as though the era might bring new independence for women, but it was what Kessler-Harris calls a false start. On average, most girls spent less than five years in the mill, and while there, were paid less than men, and were unable to move up into supervisory positions. As manufacturing expanded, more barriers to women's advancement were put into place, including gender segregation and a lower salary scale for women. There were periods—depressions, wars, accidents—where women's opportunities would expand because men were gone, dead, or both. But their incursion would be followed by an inevitable backlash in which they were derided as competitive and—always—unwomanly.

Outside of the upper and middle classes, the truth was that families often were dependent on more than one earner. Women and children alike contributed to household income among the working classes, but women's earnings were usually generated privately in the home, doing sewing or other piecework. And women's income was persistently seen as secondary. For those women who did work for wages—black women, immigrants, others—an explicit two-tiered wage system was put in place. The government wrote it into labor codes; unions made it mandatory. Women teachers made one-third less than male teachers. Women for most of the 19th century made one-third to one-half what men did. Women were channeled into certain jobs—maids, teachers, seamstresses—as a way to ensure they remained low-paid. A moral code helped justify the segregation: "future motherhood" had to be shielded from the corrupting influence of many occupations, and kept away from men. "Wherever the sexes work indiscriminately together great laxity obtains," noted the U.S. commissioner of labor in 1888. Many professions were seen not so much as being physically tough as spiritually corrupting. In the late 19th and early 20th centuries, protective measures were passed preventing women from doing things like selling liquor. Law and medicine were mostly closed to women in part because women would be exposed to awful truths about human conduct and bodies. Into the 20th century, women were rarely hired as court reporters because the contents of trials were deemed too shocking.

In fact, women might have become family breadwinners much earlier than they did. The economist Claudia Goldin notes that the early 20th century could have been a breakthrough; the expansion of the industrial sector and growth of retail created much new office work, which was regarded as a "nice" job, suitably respectable. In what Goldin calls the "white-collar counterpart of the industrial revolution," offices became mechanized, with typewriters, calculators, duplicating machines. By 1930, women comprised 40 percent of all clerical and sales personnel and one-third of all white-collar workers. And World War I enabled women to make other inroads: while the men were off fighting in Europe, women began to work as bank tellers and even managers. Women were called in to operate stock boards. Not coincidentally, the 1920s gave America the sexually liberated flapper and the women's vote. One woman banker noted that men in finance were friendly to her, but seemed to "have a terrific fear that [women] will eventually take the place of men."

In part because of that fear, the early 20th century proved yet another false start and generated hand-wringing about working wives and their deleterious impact. The freedom of the 1920s was abridged as more employers began to enforce "marriage bars," which were policies directing that married women could not work and single women would be fired when they married. Nor could women move up. In offices, a woman who started as a typist stayed a typist. She would do much better, financially, by getting married, especially since men enjoyed even higher wages once they became husbands. Entrusted with the responsibility of family upkeep, says Goldin, married men were "awarded a premium that is due neither to selection nor to productivity differences. Rather, the premium arises from a social dictum that firms should adequately provide for men's families." Five years into an office career, Goldin points out, the "average man earned 8 percent more than the average woman, after ten years the average man earned

14 percent more, and after 15 years the difference widened to 21 percent." As the historian David Kennedy notes in his study of the Great Depression, *Freedom from Fear*, the "ten million women who worked for wages in 1929 were concentrated in a small handful of occupations." Kennedy notes that women made up about 22 percent of all workers—a not inconsiderable percentage—but the "typical woman worker was single and under the age of twenty-five. Once she married, as almost every woman did, typically before the age of twenty-two, she was unlikely to work again for wages, particularly while she had children at home." Even now, the angel in the house reigned as an ideal: the view remained widespread that employment turned women into not only economic competitors but also unpleasant wives. "The wife who has her own income is thereby rendered a poorer wife [and] feeling independent of her natural protector, she becomes more critical, less lenient to his faults and failings," is how one correspondent put it in a letter to a weekly paper in the early 20th century, explicitly linking women's dependence to the idea that this condition made them nicer to live with. By 1926, the social scientist Ernest Groves was still arguing that when "the woman herself earns and her maintenance is not entirely at the mercy of her husband's will, diminishing masculine authority necessarily follows."

Yet there was no consensus about how much breadwinning men owed their angels in the houses. As the sociologist Viviana Zelizer shows in *The Social Meaning of Money*, money and the meting out of wages were a source of ongoing struggle in marriages. A 1928 survey of 200 upper-class households found that 73 wives received an allowance, while 66 women had money given to them according to their husband's whimsy; the rest had a joint account, or arrangements so haphazard they could not be defined. Women confided how much they hated asking their husbands for money. Some were forced to resort to "sexual blackmail." In 1938, the *Ladies' Home Journal* asked, "Should a wife have a regular housekeeping allowance?" and female readers overwhelmingly said: yes. Yet the higher the husband's income, the less control a woman had over it. Tradition dictated that working-class wives were handed their husbands' pay packets and expected to deploy it (though men often kept a bit back) while upper-class women had no such expectation. In 1923, Zelizer notes, a play called *Chicken Feed,* or *Wages for Wives,* dramatized the injustice. A daughter angry at her father for not giving her mother a regular allowance says to her own fiancé, "Danny, how would you like it if you had a boss and he said—'Look here, Danny, I won't pay you a regular salary. I'll just give you presents when I feel like it. It makes me feel so nice and generous and I like to hear you thank me. And in case you need something, just tell me and I'll see if I think you ought to have it.'" In 1905, a judge sided with a husband who put a rat trap in his pants pocket to stop his wife from rifling them at night for change.

Any lingering whiff of wage-earning freedom women might have sensed in the early part of the 20th century was obliterated by the Depression, which enforced the view that providing was the husband's duty, not the wife's. As Goldin shows, marriage bars were "reinforced and extended" as the workforce attempted to protect male workers by discarding female ones. A federal directive went out saying that "in the face of layoffs [executive branch officials] fire workers whose spouses were employed by the federal government"; usually, the axe fell on the woman. Those women who did work were seen as stealing jobs from men. In 1939, author Norman Cousins proposed a way to end the Depression: "Simply fire the women, who shouldn't be working anyway." Women hired by the Works Progress Administration—the New Deal jobs program—made significantly less than boys. It was when men were least able to fill their breadwinning duties that society made it clear just how crucial these duties were. Working women were terribly stigmatized—and so, of course, were nonworking men.

Within many households, the emotional fallout was immense. Interviewing 59 Depression-era families in the mid-1930s, the sociologist Mirra Komarovsky pioneered the field of masculinity studies. Men told her how devastated they were to feel they had failed as providers. Apart from the relief check itself, the greatest humiliation one man reported was a working wife. "I am afraid the children don't think as much of me now that I am unemployed," another man told Komarovsky. "During the depression I lost something. Maybe you call it self-respect, but in losing it I also lost the respect of my children, and I am afraid I am losing my wife," said another. As women scrambled to find ways of generating income—by, say, taking in boarders—husbands felt helpless and unmoored; they were "in a situation of long-lasting and profound defeat," as Komarovsky put it. "I relinquished power in the family. Now I don't even try to be boss," a man told her. "She controls all the money, and I never have a penny in my pocket but that I have to ask her for it." To be sure, most wives remained loving and some husbands' marital behavior improved. The families most disoriented were those that had been patriarchal to begin with. But not a single man she interviewed was glad to be spared the duty of working. Everything felt out of kilter. So strong was the breadwinning ethos that in 1936, when a young woman named Frances Oldham was hired to assist a pharmacology professor at the University of Chicago, she knew that the only reason she was hired was because he thought her name was male. She felt so guilty that she contemplated not taking the position. Later, married and an official at the Food and Drug Administration, Frances Oldham Kelsey prevented the widespread marketing in the United States of the drug thalidomide, which caused so many birth defects in children born in Europe.

Nevertheless, Kessler-Harris argues that the Depression made a difference in women's attitudes and self-image. Women, even in their jobs as maids or office workers or boardinghouse managers, did succeed in keeping families afloat, and it changed them psychologically. The Depression "solidified their positions as workers," she writes, despite "legislative harassment, newspaper vilification, and social work pressure." So did the Second World War, when for the first time women were recruited into the American workforce with great fanfare, given heavy labor jobs and—crucially—government-sponsored child care that made work feasible for women with children. Historians debate whether and how much the war advanced the cause of women's equality; companies sometimes fired their replacement female workforce so that returning GIs could have their jobs back. But many of the women working during the war continued working after. And here was the war's biggest legacy: when the postwar baby boom set in, it was younger women, eager to start families, who left the workforce, and older married women who entered and stayed. During the 20th century, the proportion of married women working for pay increased "more than tenfold" from "less than 5 percent in 1890 to more than 60 percent in 1990," Goldin points out, and most of this increase occurred after 1940. In the 1950s, Simone de Beauvoir argued that it was earnings that had given women what equality they now possessed. "It is through gainful employment that woman has traversed most of the distance that separated her from the male; and nothing else can guarantee her liberty in practice. Once she ceases to be a parasite, the system based on her dependence crumbles; between her and the universe there is no longer any need for a masculine mediator."

And yet, the postwar period was one of the few eras in American history when the average man could support his family single-handedly and maintain a reasonably high standard of living. It was the high-water mark of the male-breadwinning ideal, as every 1950s and 1960s television sitcom attested. For a really very brief window of time, the expansion of the manufacturing economy and the rise of the white-collar bureaucratic structure and the power of labor unions came together to make a quite decent living wage something even a middle-class or blue-collar man could expect. It was a period of mixed messages. Opportunities for women were emerging and women were discouraged from taking them. Even the most ambitious women were mostly evaluated on their typing.

At home, the idea of women as the embodiment of a higher morality had disappeared. Housewives were not put on pedestals. No one was under the remotest illusion that women were purer than men. Indeed, some saw stay-at-home moms as wielding an awful authority in the home, sucking the life and living out of hardworking husbands. In 1942, in his overwrought but bestselling book *Generation of Vipers*, the author Philip Wylie had invoked the toxic phenomenon of "momism," the diabolical influence stay-at-home mothers supposedly exerted over not only their offspring, but American culture. Somewhat more benign, but still limited, was the popular image of the middle-class housewife as a modern, attractive, and lively sexual partner for her husband, gracing the house with a drink in her hand and nicely tanned in a classy summer shift. Psychoanalytic theory held that women who resented their housewife role, and wanted to work, were maladjusted. Out of this confusion, Betty Friedan would name the problem that defined a generation. She called it the "feminine mystique," but it was in many ways a reincarnated angel in the house: that girlish, complaisant, dependent helpmeet who had haunted and repelled Virginia Woolf.

As contradictory as the postwar era was, it did produce the famous mating strategy—for women—of marrying up. In the middle part of the 20th century, the most effective way for a woman to better her prospects was through marriage to a man who earned more and had more education than she did. In that era, in a cohort of Californians studied by sociologist Glen Elder, more than half of working-class women married men with more schooling. Most middle-class women also married better-educated men. Considering the life trajectories of young adults who came of age in this period, Elder found that these women were more likely than their mothers to enter college—but less likely to finish. Of the women who did go to college, a great number met a husband in their first or second year, then left to get married. Many women worked to put husbands through college and graduate school, burnishing men's credentials while sacrificing their own.

And looks mattered. In the wartime and postwar period, Elder also found, attractive women were more likely to marry up. The benefits of "physical assets" were most pronounced for working-class women, who, he pointed out, often did not have the "mating advantages of a college campus" but were "not necessarily excluded from settings in which to meet well-educated, ambitious men." He posited that working in an office setting as a secretary often enabled women to make an advantageous marriage and provided a happy hunting ground.

From this—the observation that women seemed to be trading beauty for income—academics developed theories showing why this must always be the case. It was in the second half of the 20th century that the view formally developed that marriage represents a trade or bargain. That bargain would become known by a variety of names, among them "exchange theory": the idea that each party approaches marriage with specific resources that will benefit the partner. For women, the resources could be fertility, domestic service, or the kind of good looks that enhance both a man's pleasure at home and his professional and community standing. For men, the resource was usually one thing: wealth.

Any number of disciplines would elaborate on this theme. Among them was evolutionary psychology, which holds that partnering, for animals and humans alike, is about perpetuating one's genetic material. Men and women mate—the theory goes—because each person's gene line is driving him or her to do so. According to this theory, women are more invested in their offspring than men, and since the dawn of civilization have been motivated to ensure their children's survival by finding a strong, wealthy, high-status male who will stick around to protect and provide. Men, in contrast, are not all that invested in each individual child, and would prefer to impregnate as many women as possible. Thus it was in the Pleistocene Epoch—the theory holds—and thus it will be, forever. Ideally, men seek attractive women, under the rough theory that looks and youth signal fertility, while women seek monied men willing to commit to them. This theory is often used to justify infidelity on the part of men: men want sex with as many women as possible but allow themselves to be dragooned into the married state because it is the only way to guarantee a woman's sexual fidelity and make sure the children they are providing for are theirs. It has less success explaining why women are more likely to initiate divorce. But according to this theory, it's not merely a matter of circumstance that women are dependent on men; it is woman's natural biological condition. It is women's preference. Women are the ones who beg for marriage, women are the ones who crave commitment, and women are the ones whose genes cry out for financial dependence.

In economics, a related argument would evolve. In the second half of the 20th century, economists were beginning to look at the family as its own little nation, comprised of warring and negotiating factions. Gary Becker developed the influential theory that households are most efficient, and marriages most stable, when partners take on complementary roles: when men and women "specialize," each bringing a different set of abilities to the marriage. That is to say: marriages work best when one spouse earns and the other stays home. In his landmark book, *A Treatise on the Family*, Becker argued that when one spouse does all the earning, the other is freed to excel at household tasks. Similarly, with one spouse taking care of everything that must be done at home—making dinner, doing laundry, feeding the children, running errands—the other spouse is free to excel professionally. By adhering to a careful division of labor, each partner enables the other to prevail in his or her allotted sphere.

In Becker's initial construction, the wage earner was the man and the stay-at-home spouse was of course the woman. Women, he argued, had a competitive advantage in housework: it made sense for a mother who was breast-feeding to stay home and watch the other children, particularly when families were large. Wage discrimination provided her with yet another incentive to avoid the workplace. If a woman knew her pay would be, say, 10 percent less than her husband's, the couple might make a pragmatic decision for her to be the stay-at-home partner. The husband in this construction was a benevolent despot, assuming spiritual and moral responsibility for his little economy, and the marriage contract was something women demanded as insurance against being abandoned.

Becker's theories helped make the world safe for economists who wanted to explore the bargaining and politicking that go into family life. The idea that complementary roles contribute to marital stability would endure even as it would be fiercely challenged. It would be called reactionary, sexist, wrong, outdated. But Becker saw the flip coming. His book was first published in 1981; in an edition published a decade later, which expanded on his ideas and responded to the commentary they had provoked, Becker—aware that the game was changing in American society—recognized that the tables could turn. Give a woman a slight advantage in the workplace—give the wife, say, more education than her husband—and she might become the one with the greater incentive to work while her husband might have a greater incentive to stay home. Becker pointed out that men were already helping more with housework. If this pitching-in continued, and if women were freed to be more productive in their work life, women might become even more committed to the professional arena. Women might invest more in their own schooling, improve their training and credentials. They might become more valuable workers, better educated, better paid; they might infiltrate men's professions. Their earnings would rise. Eventually, it could be wives doing the wage earning and husbands doing the housework. Were all this to happen, he noted with real interest, "such a development would have major consequences."

Three
The Overtaking

And now here we are. Women make up nearly half the U.S. labor force. The proportion of women ages 25 to 54 who are working or looking for work stands at 75 percent, up from 35 percent in 1950. Of the 66 million women who are employed—up from 30 million in 1970—three-quarters work full-time. Eighty percent of college-educated women ages 25 to 64 are in the labor force. And there has been a radical transformation among mothers. The percentage of women with children under 18 who are employed or looking for work has risen from 47 percent in 1975 to 71 percent. For all the talk about women "opting out" when they have children, today mothers—particularly educated ones—are overwhelmingly likely to be employed. Women's wages have increased significantly in the past three decades, as women have expanded their work hours, battled discrimination, and improved their credentials at precisely the time when the rewards for these are greater than ever. As the economist David Autor has pointed out, the United States and other Western countries are undergoing a massive economic restructuring that is killing middle-skill jobs, outsourcing industrial ones, and requiring a growing number of workers to either accept the few lower-tier jobs still on the premises or take an educational leap into the high-tier ones that pay. It is women who have adapted best to this new world order by taking the good jobs where they are being created.

Among women, the number of hours worked has risen. Women are much more likely to be working full-time, year-round, than they were 40 years ago. As Catherine Rampell pointed out in the *New York Times*, the number of hours worked by the median two-parent family has risen from 2,800 hours in 1975 to 3,500 hours in 2009. This is a 26 percent rise, driven mostly by women.

And if the story of the 20th century was women entering the workforce, the story of the 21st century has been men departing. Back in the mid-1950s, virtually all American men ages 25 to 54 worked. Today, that proportion is closer to 80 percent, in part owing to high unemployment, in part because a growing number of men no longer aspire to work at all. Of the jobs expected to decline most in the next decade, the majority—many in manufacturing—are held by men. The Bureau of Labor Statistics projects that by 2018 men's labor force participation rate will fall to historic lows.

The earning power of wives compared to husbands has risen, steadily and strongly. Wives are breadwinners or co-earners in about two-thirds of American marriages. Among families with working wives, the percentage in which the wife outearns the husband has gone up dramatically, from 23.7 percent in 1987 to 37.7 percent in 2009, the most recent year for which statistics are available, with a particularly rapid rise in the first decade of the 21st century. Gains have been highest for more educated wives, which means breadwinning women are no longer just the wives of poor men. In 2009, the number of married women single-handedly supporting their families rose to an all-time high. Almost 7 percent of wives—nearly 4 million women, up from 1.7 percent in 1967—were sole breadwinners. The share of husbands who were the sole breadwinner declined from 35 percent in 1967 to 18 percent in 2009. Keep in mind, too, that 40 percent of births are now to unmarried women, and that nearly 25 percent of children under the age of 18 live with their mothers but not their fathers. Given these trends, it is only a matter of time before a majority of working wives outearn their husbands. Within a generation, it's also likely that more women, married and single, will be supporting households—especially households with children—than men.

Reversal of Academic Fortunes

One critical role reversal has already occurred. Women are the better-educated sex. They take the majority of associate's degrees, the majority of bachelor's degrees, the majority of master's degrees, and the majority of doctorates. The seeds of this turnover were sown in the 1970s, when women underwent a swift change in self-image and strategic planning. The economist Claudia Goldin has spent extensive time looking at young women's expectations for their lives. The feminist revolution of the 1960s was "noisier," Goldin persuasively argues, but the psychological revolution of the 1970s was more profound. With the widespread availability of the birth control pill, women could more reliably control their childbearing, and had more reason to invest in their futures. Colleges expanded access, the long process of dismantling a discriminatory labor system was launched in earnest, and workplace rewards for college degrees became more apparent. The resulting shift in attitudes really did occur almost overnight. Between 1968 and 1975, the percentage of young women who told survey takers that they expected to be working at age 35 more than doubled, from 30 percent to 65 percent. Women began to choose college majors in ways that demonstrated new ambitions. By the 1980s, far fewer women were preparing to be teachers, and far more were majoring in business and management. The early 1970s, Goldin writes, marked an "obvious" turning point during which the percentage of women applying to medical school, business school, and law school showed a clear, sharp break upward, and the percentage of women preparing for traditional specialties—teachers, librarians, social workers—began to fall. And college-educated women began waiting longer to get married.

Men adjusted in the other direction, as their college going began to decelerate. "The big question that economists ask is: Why are these guys leaving ten thousand dollar bills on the street?" Goldin told me in an interview. "That's what they're doing. You're seeing that in your data. They're leaving the ten thousand dollar bills on the street." Goldin suggests that one contributing cause is that boys mature later than girls do, a disparity that falls hardest on lower-income boys who in many cases "don't have their act together when they're 17, to take the SATs, and 16 to take the PSATs, or 17 and a half to write the college essays," she points out. "But later on, when they're 22, they get the calling."

Women have always had the potential to be high-achieving students. What we are seeing now is the long-delayed unleashing of women's academic abilities, after nearly a century in which their college going was artificially suppressed even as men's was boosted. In the early 1900s, when there was a mass movement to encourage Americans to go to high school, girls outnumbered boys and got better grades than boys did, and women attended college in equal numbers. Back then, however, women who went to college often were making a lifelong trade-off: it was believed that too much schooling made women unsuitable for wedded life and motherhood. "Monstrous brains and puny bodies" was how one Harvard physician described educated women in 1873, declaring that too much intellectual exertion diverted energy from women's wombs to their heads, rendering them infertile. At the turn of the 20th century, female college graduates were strikingly less likely to marry, and those who did had high rates of childlessness, leading to social fears of "race suicide" if too many women became too educated. And of course nobody went to college much, back then, male or female.

The postwar period then saw a divergence of fortunes, as men were awarded incentives for matriculation, chief among them the GI Bill. As Goldin points out, the men who fought in World War II and Korea vastly outdid their fathers and grandfathers in seeking higher education, and college—for men—became more of a middle-class phenomenon. In 1960, 65 percent of bachelor's degrees in the United States were awarded to men. During the Vietnam War, student draft deferments provided fresh motivation, driving men's college attendance to what economists now see was an artificial high. In the 1970s, male college graduates outnumbered female ones by three to two.

But in the 1960s and 1970s, many remaining all-male universities, including the most prestigious, began to admit women—spurred by federal laws and even pressure from male undergraduates who wanted coeducation. Buoyed by an atmosphere of radical possibility, women scrambled to take advantage of the fact that the most sought-after dorms and quadrangles were now open to them. Women drew even with men on American campuses in the 1980s, then began to outpace men with an alacrity that has not abated. Women now receive 57 percent of all bachelor's degrees and account for some 60 percent of graduate school enrollment. They take half of first professional degrees in fields like law and medicine. Among African Americans, women take 66 percent of bachelor's degrees. Native American women earn 60 percent, Asian women 55 percent, and Hispanic women—who belong to the country's fastest-growing minority sector—earn 61 percent. In the black community, the educational gap between men and women has loomed for more than a half-century, in part because African American women suffered so much job discrimination that the only path to something other than domestic service lay through higher education—which led to teaching jobs, if nothing else—and in part because black men, unlike white ones, for decades could expect very little in the way of workplace payoff to a college degree.

But the main catalysts of this current transformation are white women. Between 1970 and 2008, four-year-college attainment among white men ages 25 to 34 rose from 20 percent to 26 percent. For white women in this age range it nearly tripled, from 12 percent to 34 percent of white women. This means that about a quarter of young white men are getting a college degree, compared to more than a third of white women. In "three decades the white male-female gap in college attainment went from positive 8 to negative 8 percentage points!" David Autor has written. At first it was women from more affluent families who bested men in college completion. Now, it's among lower-income Americans that the gender gap is widest. Among all Americans ages 25 to 29, a record 36 percent of women have a four-year degree, compared to just 28 percent of men. By 2019, women are projected to comprise nearly 60 percent of U.S. college and university students, and 61 percent of post-baccalaureate enrollment. The imbalance is so worrisome that in 2011, the economist Laura D'Andrea Tyson floated the idea of some mandatory college for all Americans as a way of keeping men in school.

Focus and Persistence

There are lots of reasons why women outstrip men in school. Some experts theorize, believably, that women have become so accustomed to discrimination they naturally assume they will need more education to be paid an equivalent wage. There was a point, not all that long ago, where a woman needed a 4-year college degree to make as much as a man with a high school education. Like the African American pilots, navigators, and bombardiers who qualified to be Tuskegee airmen, women knew they had to be better trained to get the job at all. Now that the worst discrimination has abated (women still earn less than men at each educational level, but the discrepancy has gotten much smaller), women have a lot of accumulated muscle.

But it's also true that in many ways school has always been better suited to girls, and girls have been better suited to school. This discrepancy shows up early, now that serious academic instruction begins at younger ages. Boys make up 60 percent of the children who delay starting kindergarten, and 66 percent of those who repeat it. They are more likely to be held back a grade during elementary school. While boys post higher test scores in math, girls test higher in reading. From kindergarten through college, girls get better grades in all major subjects, including math and science. Students with reading disabilities, attention disorders, and dyslexia are disproportionately male. Boys are more likely to have trouble paying attention in kindergarten. Girls show more persistence and eagerness to learn, work harder, and are less disruptive. They are more attentive and organized. They like school more than boys do. Boys do less homework and more often come to class unprepared.

And in an area where they once trailed—the rigor of high school courses—girls now prevail. Until recently, girls took fewer and less intense math courses. Now, high school boys and girls take math courses that are equally demanding. Girls are more likely than boys to take biology and chemistry. They outdo boys in taking AP exams and college prep courses. With the exception of sports, girls are more involved in extracurriculars as well as cultural activities in and out of school. Looking at data from a survey of 12th-grade girls, economists Betsey

Stevenson and Justin Wolfers found that young women not only want to excel at home and in school; they want to contribute to their communities. "They care about a broader sense of community than just their nuclear family," says Stevenson.

In a paper written with two colleagues, Gary Becker concludes that women are prevailing in higher education thanks to temperament and work habits—"non-cognitive" abilities. Becker points out that women have more self-motivation; better organization; more willingness to do homework and prepare for exams; fewer disciplinary problems. "[N]on-cognitive skills are the key to explaining the fact that the growth in college attendance in the United States has been an overwhelmingly female phenomenon," Becker and his coauthors write. The disparity starts early. "The better performance in grade school of girls than boys appears to explain much of the growing female advantage in higher education."

College matters more than ever. A college education raises earnings. It raises life expectancy. It is associated with a healthier lifestyle. It raises the likelihood and stability of marriage, and it makes for richer and more productive households. People with college educations invest more in their children.

And education is the most important factor determining who, in a household, emerges as the higher earner. Studying the rise of women breadwinners in Europe, two academics—economists Hans Bloemen of the Netherlands and Elena Stancanelli of France—set out to untangle the characteristics of these unions. They found that in dual-earner relationships where women outearn men, the women's higher education is a central reason why. Other studies have found that in heterosexual and same-sex couples alike, the person who stays home with the children is usually the less-educated partner.

Pressure to Earn

One less-examined reason why girls are prevailing academically is that boys still think they should be working. My interviews for this book strongly suggest—and this is a great irony—that one reason boys are not graduating from college at the same rate as girls is because many boys and young men, especially in the working class, continue to think of themselves as providers. Boys have not lost the industrial era bread-winning mind-set; they want, many of them, to get out into the work-force as soon as they can. For generations, a young man could leave high school and head straight into a decently paying job in American industry. Boys are still playing by those rules, and so are their parents.

Much of the recent attention to younger men has focused on their immaturity and the idea that men in their twenties are hanging around playing videogames and smoking pot and refusing to become serious about life. There may be some truth to this picture, but it's also true that men are dropping out of the educational system because they feel pressure to earn—not only for themselves but also for parents and extended families. And since girls are the ones staying in school—because girls don't think of themselves as providers—they emerge into adulthood better equipped to provide.

Parents may be perpetuating this disparity, favoring girls by giving them more support, emotional and financial. It could be that parents think girls are more likely to need a college degree to earn a living, or that they look at their focused, well-behaved daughters and see a more promising investment, or that they unfairly expect young men to be self-sufficient at an age when they do not expect this of girls. Or maybe parents see a college campus as a more protective environment for girls than living on their own in their late teens and early twenties. Economists have shown that parental attitudes are a key factor in girls' changing fortunes. Some argue, persuasively, that one reason women were given property rights in the 19th century was not because hus-bands wanted their wives to have more autonomy—God forbid—but because fathers were concerned for the welfare of their daughters. Fa-thers wanted their girls to have rights in marriage, and knew economic resources would enhance their standing. As Becker has pointed out, parents make rational decisions based on the universe as they see it. Parents understand that the rewards of education for a daughter are greater than they ever have been. "Although sons and daughters share the same household, historically, they have not had equal access to pa-rental resources," point out two sociologists, Claudia Buchmann and Thomas DiPrete, in a 2006 paper, noting that parents once put a much higher priority on boys' education, but this pattern is shifting and girls may be benefiting more from parental underwriting.

Young men I spoke to felt the inequity. "The father figure tends to want to look after the daughters a little more closely, versus men, it's just—'Well, just go to school, son, do your best, and if you make it you make it. If not, get a job,'" said Jasson Caltzontzint, a Texas man who was forced to drop out of college to support himself, and worked full-time for several years before he returned. It took him almost a decade to earn his bachelor's degree. "What happens with men is, they get easily sidetracked."

His instincts are right on the money. According to a 2011 report by the Pew Research Center, 40 percent of female college graduates say that their parents paid for most of their undergraduate education, while just 29 percent of men could say the same. The 2011 Pew study also showed that the public thinks college is more important for girls: 77 percent of people polled said that women need college to get ahead, compared to 68 percent who think this is true for men.

Repeatedly, women I interviewed spoke of parents who exhorted them to stay in school, to strive for independence, to accumulate savings. "My dad is from Mexico—he's a custodian and my mom is a house-wife," said Annette Alvarado, 29, an elementary schoolteacher who had just bought her first house. "My dad was very strong on me and my sister supporting ourselves. He would always tell us: don't rely on a man, you need to do what you need to do. Go to school and get your degree." When she was in college, Alvarado dated a classmate who dropped out and took a minimum wage job to help support his family. It destroyed their relationship. Her boyfriend would get jealous if she was doing too much schoolwork and neglecting him. He saw her as self-absorbed. She saw him as shortsighted. "We would be arguing back and forth," Alvarado recalled. "All he would do is work. I think I was more selfish— I was just thinking about me. I knew he was going to hold me back, and I told myself: I cannot do this to myself, I want my career."

Another study, conducted at the University of Alaska, confirmed that girls are pushed harder, particularly in the working class. Alaska has the third highest college gender gap in the nation. For every 100 men enrolled in a degree-granting institution, there are 149 women, notes the author, Judith Kleinfeld. To gauge what's propelling students into college—or discouraging them—Kleinfeld, with the assistance of her social science students, conducted interviews among high school seniors, talking about the decisions they made for after graduation. She found that 76 percent of women from working-class families said their parents had encouraged them to go to college, compared to only 41 percent of boys. Moreover, *18 percent of working-class boys were discouraged by their families from going to college.* One boy said his brothers and father encouraged him to go into the trades, saying that an office job was "fruity."

The girls in the Alaska study also seemed to have a much more realistic view of what was needed to prevail in 21st-century America. Girls viewed college as "crucial to their future success," the study points out, and are more likely to have applied to college by their senior year of high school. In contrast, boys justified their lack of motivation by offering up examples of men who had earned a lot of money without a four-year degree. Genius outliers like Bill Gates and the late Steve Jobs (who attended, but did not graduate from, Harvard and Reed, respectively) may have done unintentional cultural damage, convincing boys that college is a waste of their valuable time. Incredibly, Kleinfeld found, boys also thought it would be easy to become a celebrity. "Many of the young men expressed interest in implausible 'dream jobs,' such as designing videogames, owning a recording studio, directing movies, or becoming music stars," Kleinfeld noted. "They had virtually no idea of how to get into these occupations." Girls see the future as it is; boys see the future as they want it to be.

Psychologists have shown that adolescents are prone to grandiosity and that it's crucial for parents to help them align dreams and reality. Parents seem to be doing a better job of this with girls than with boys. I interviewed a number of women whose less-educated husbands and boyfriends seriously aspired to be breakout musicians or game designers; listening to women's complaints about partners with hopes of celebrityhood or quick riches, it struck me that people worry about the effects of celebrity culture on girls, in terms of setting unrealistic standards for beauty. But boys, too, are vulnerable to corrosive fantasies about resembling the stars they read about and listen to, or the overpaid CEOs that are lionized. "Living in the South, I've gone on dates with people who say, 'I'm going to provide for my wife, she's not going to have to work, don't you worry, I'm going to be awesome,'" recounts Liz Thomas, who put herself through college by taking out loans and working in a bridal salon on weekends. "And I'd ask, 'Well, okay, what do you want to do? What's your aspiration?' And they'd say, 'I want to own a company.' And I'm like, 'Great. What kind of company?' and they're like—'I don't know.'" When she hears fatuous promises like those, Thomas—who, at 25, owns her own business as a marketing consultant—runs as fast as she can in the opposite direction. Flor Leal, a Texas woman I interviewed, explained why she didn't marry the father of her child. "He's in a band. Yeah! And he's going to *make it!*" said Flor with heavy sarcasm. "What I've observed—men expect we're going to wait until it gets better, or we're going to wait until I become successful. Why are you waiting? You need to go out and make things happen. What action are you taking to make it better? Like—are you making CDs? What are you doing? I know what I'm doing. I'm finishing up my graduate degree so that I can make more money to provide for my son. So men I think are lacking a plan of action."

In her study, Kleinfeld found that boys were likely to describe themselves as "lazy," even when working hard-labor jobs. This, then, seems to be the new stereotype boys have about themselves, and it's the story that families seem to have about boys. During her interviews, Kleinfeld said she heard lots of narratives from girls that could be titled "The Star Sister and Her Brother the Slacker." Girls talked about their resolutions and achievements, and described brothers who were hanging out and drifting. Maybe it's accurate, but it made me wonder, uneasily, if this is the narrative developing in families. Are parents coming to think boys aren't worth their investment? Because they haven't yet grown up by the time they are 13, or 15, or even 18? At what point does this become a self-fulfilling prophecy? Are families seeing boys' slower progress to maturity as a reason to write them off? Are parents discriminating? Studies also show that boys are suffering from the marginalization of their fathers. In families with fathers who either did not go to college, or are absent altogether, girls used to struggle academically. Now they don't, but boys still do. The "major change which occurred was that girls in [more deprived] households caught up with their brothers and surpassed them," write Buchmann and DiPrete, noting that "females have moved ahead of males in families wherein they once lagged considerably behind—families with low-educated or absent fathers."

"I Never Want to Be Dependent on Anyone": Women's Drive Toward Self-Sufficiency

What this means is the Darwinian notion that women want to marry men who will take care of them has become laughably absurd. As Buchmann and DiPrete put it, the rise in women's college attendance is due not only to ambition and intellectual curiosity, but to women's "growing interest in possessing autonomous resources." Young women want their own money. They are acutely aware of the fragility of marriage and the danger of dependency. Women well know that their future could hold divorce or single motherhood. They know that at some point—early adulthood, late adulthood, in between—they are likely to be self-supporting. Far from displaying some innate biological urge to find a provider who can usher them into a life of ease and bonbon consumption, many women I spoke with seemed obsessively concerned with being self-sufficient. There may be plenty of women who still want to make the wealth-beauty trade-off, or who simply would like to be able to stay at home and raise their children, but there are many, many women who are averse to depending on a man for upkeep. They have seen what happened to their mothers, for whom the marriage contract hardly turned out to be insurance.

Each generation, you could argue, lives in reaction to the generation that came before. In *Children of the Great Depression*, the sociologist Glen Elder shows how boys growing up in the Depression were affected by watching their fathers lose jobs. Tracking these boys into adulthood, he found that as men they threw themselves into the economy of the 1950s. Surveys found that men who grew up in the Depression valued work life more highly than they valued family activities, leisure, or community roles. And these men were pouring their energy into work at a time when an expanding workforce offered boundless opportunity. At the time, Elder points out, the old entrepreneurial model was dying out—before the Depression, many men were small businessmen—and the United States was seeing the dawn of the company man, with large-scale organizations and high managerial salaries. In the cohort Elder looked at, just a quarter of boys started life in the upper middle class, but by the time they were adults, nearly half had attained that category. Much of this occurred through the schooling men received in the 1940s and 1950s. In the families he looked at, 17 percent of fathers had gone to college, while "their sons more than tripled this proportion." Sons of families who suffered hardship during the Depression were not pessimistic; they knew life could be tough, but were determined to prevail.

I see a lot of parallels in women today. Like the boys who grew up in the 1930s and saw what happened to their fathers, women today are close students of their own mothers' fates and financial outcomes. Woman after woman spoke of mothers who felt unable to leave unhappy marriages, mothers who knew their husbands were cheating on them, mothers who experienced poverty after divorce. "A lot of our mothers and grandmothers got married for somebody to support them—my mother had the life that I don't want to live today," said Desirée Mendez, who has bachelor's and master's degrees from the University of Texas–Pan American and is married to Jasson Caltzontzint. Desirée works as a grant coordinator for Rubén Hinojosa, the Democratic member of Congress representing the 15th District of Texas. "She's great, very encouraging, a wonderful mother, but she did totally the opposite of me—she got pregnant at a very young age, started college, never finished, relied on my father for all her income and support, and they divorced. My mother is in her mid-fifties and wondering: Oh my God, where did my life go? I should have gone to college. I should have been more independent."

And it's not just fear of being left high and dry in a divorce. It's a fear of being crushed by marriage, swallowed whole; a fear that marrying a man could wipe out everything they had planned for, endanger their hard work and aspirations. Mandie Gehring, a nuclear chemistry graduate student, has a list of things she wants to accomplish in life—working at a national weapons lab, getting into policymaking, becoming a U.N. weapons inspector—and wants to make sure she doesn't get forced to make too many compromises for the sake of a husband's career. Her fears are not groundless. A husband's long work hours are one key factor that pushes wives from the workforce. So are a husband's high wages. Economists have shown that women often do reduce their own work hours in response to a husband's rising income. Claudia Goldin and Lawrence Katz have done work showing that women MBAs who are mothers and are married to high-earning husbands are more likely to opt out than MBAs whose husbands are lower-earning, or who don't have children. These women end up bailing out to become the COOs of their families, in part because they can afford to, but also because their husbands are working insanely hard to make all that money and the couple needs a manager on the home front to make his career and the family function. But the good news for Mandie Gehring is that economists are beginning to find the same is true for men: men, too, will dial back their own work hours to accommodate a higher-earning partner. A woman who begins her career with a wage advantage over her partner is increasingly likely to keep it.

In Tomorrow's Economy, the Educated People Will Be the Employed People

Through their tenacity, women have improved their prospects more than they realize. By becoming well educated, women have raised the chances that they will be employed, and they qualify for much better jobs than they could have expected 30 or 40 years ago. Laura D'Andrea Tyson has pointed out that in 1970, "only about 22 percent of female workers had attended some college or had a college degree. By 2010, that figure had increased threefold to nearly 67 percent of all women in the work force." Tyson observes that education is a key reason why women's earnings have risen and why "in recent recessions, the unemployment rate for women has been lower than the rate for men." Between 1979 and 2009, she points out, the median real earnings for full-time female workers increased by 31 percent, while men's earnings stagnated.

Moreover, the returns on education have risen more steeply for women than for men. As the Bureau of Labor Statistics points out, at each level of education, "women have fared better than men with respect to earnings growth." Apart from the most highly educated men, most men earn *less* than equally educated men did in 1979, while most women earn *more* than equally educated women did a generation before them. The higher a person's educational attainment, the more likely that person will be employed. In some ways, that's all you need to know. Women are going to continue joining the workforce, and men are going to continue leaving.

Tyson also points out that being kept out of skilled labor and the trades has proved a boon for women in the long run. Fewer than 5 percent of women are in manufacturing and less than 1 percent in construction, she observes: sectors that are sensitive to recession and, in many cases, seeing a permanent decline. Women's higher rates of employment in education, health, local government, and business make them less vulnerable to cyclical ups and downs, making it more common that wives are the ones with the steady jobs, and husbands the ones shuttling in and out of the workforce. We saw this in the most recent recession, during which many women went from being secondary earners to being primary breadwinners in their marriages. The dramatic impact on household earning contributions was made clear in a study done by Kristin Smith, a family demographer with the Carsey Institute at the University of New Hampshire, who found that in 2009 employed wives contributed *a greater percentage of the family income than ever before.* That year, working wives contributed 47 percent of family earnings—very close to half. This percentage has been rising steadily for decades. But the 2009 figure represented a 2 percentage point jump from 2008 and the largest single-year increase in 15 years. A related study by Smith and a colleague underscores just how much wives adjusted to make up for what their husbands lost—entering the labor force, upping work hours, taking jobs they ordinarily would not have considered. In some communities, the flip is now complete, and women are breadwinners as a matter of course. In families where the husband is African American—black men have suffered even higher levels of unemployment than white men—working wives contributed

53 percent of family income in 2008, up from 51 percent in 2007. This means that in black families, women *are* the breadwinners. And in families where the husband earned less than $20,000 a year, employed wives contribute 81 percent of family earnings. Overall, working wives are just a few percentage points away from contributing more than half of household earnings.

For young women, the returns on their educational investment are now becoming clear. In 2010, the consulting firm Reach Advisors came out with its jaw-dropping analysis of U.S. Census data, showing that in most U.S. cities, childless single women between ages 22 and 30 have a median income exceeding that of their male peers. Demographer Andrew Beveridge had uncovered the same trend in a smaller number of cities several years earlier. In the Reach Advisors analysis, the cities at the top of the list of major metropolitan areas—Atlanta, Memphis, Miami, Charlotte, New York, Sacramento, Phoenix—tended to be those with postindustrial, knowledge-based economies, which attract a well-educated population and favor women, and a large minority population. But the cities on the list also include some with a declining manufacturing base, where male blue-collar jobs are being lost.

Reach Advisors' president, James Chung, is fascinated by what he sees as a game-changing cohort of young women. He points out that single women have become prime home buyers, whereas young men are far more likely to be still living at home with their parents. "We don't know what's going to happen to this generation as they move deeper into their lives," he said, "but what we do know is: it's going to be different."

Why the Economy Wants Women

And women have improved their credentials at precisely the time when the economy craves their skills and schooling. The Great Recession and its lingering, jobless aftermath intensified a revolution that had been gathering force for decades, as the Western world moved into the postindustrial era. Between December 2007 and June 2009, men lost three-quarters of the more than 7 million jobs that disappeared during the recession. In August 2009, the adult male unemployment rate stood at 10.1 percent, compared to 7.7 percent for women. While the gender disparity in unemployment rates is no longer quite so stark—women's jobs in teaching and government were hit hard when the recession began to affect state budgets—it's been estimated that in the auto, steel, furniture, and other manufacturing industries, there are at least a million jobs that aren't coming back.

Women are the ones who saw this coming. In a major paper written for the Center for American Progress and the Brookings Institution's Hamilton Project, David Autor points out that changes transforming the American economy include the "polarization" of work opportunities, meaning that jobs are increasingly located in low-skill and high-skill sectors. This means rising wages for workers who are highly educated, falling wages for workers who are not, and fewer middle-skill jobs for anybody. Crucially, Autor points out, women have been better than men at adjusting to the economy's lasting changes. Both sexes have moved out of middle-skill jobs, but women have moved faster than men. The proportion of men employed in the middle-skill sector dropped by 7 percent between 1979 and 2007, while the proportion of women dropped by 15.8 percent. But here's the key difference: at least half of these men trickled down into low-wage jobs, while women surged "dramatically upward" into higher-earning ones. And it's not just fortune that's favoring women. It's planning and perseverance. Women have entered these new fields by "attaining expertise and education in technical and professional fields such as law and medicine, and by gaining skills, experience and seniority on the job through higher rates of labor force attachment," notes Autor. He points out that the same shifts are taking place in much of Europe: a hollowing out in the middle, and the expansion of jobs at extreme ends of the spectrum. Autor dwells on the fact that women have "robustly" increased their college going and men have not, despite the fact that the payoff for a college education is greater than ever. College grads work more hours than nongrads do, they spend less time unemployed, and they receive more benefits, including sick leave, paid vacation, employer-paid health insurance, and pension contributions. "Looking forward, it is clear that females will be the more educated sex for many years to come," he writes, pointing out that real wage growth for women has occurred at almost all levels, while for men, wage growth has taken place *only* among the most highly educated.

Projections made by the U.S. Bureau of Labor Statistics show that women's occupations will be favored in the next decade. Women now make up 51 percent of the professional and managerial workforce, and their penetration at that level is bound to go deeper. The group that will see the most rapid growth is the category called "professional and related occupations," a diverse array of job titles that includes teachers, health care workers, doctors, lawyers, and many other white-collar workers, which is projected to add more than 5.2 million jobs by 2018. Women make up 57 percent of this category. As the U.S. population ages, the field that will see particularly strong growth will be health care. The number one job that will see the most expansion is registered nurses; we'll need a half-million more in the next decade. Teaching—primary, secondary, and special ed—will add more than 600,000 new jobs. There will also be demand for accountants and auditors—about 280,000—who are now predominately female. Employment in "community and social services," also female, will grow by almost half a million jobs. There will be strong growth among market and survey researchers—also female. All in all, of the 10 jobs with the largest projected job growth—nurses, home health aides, customer service reps, food preparation and serving workers, home care aides, retail sales, office clerks, accountants and auditors, nursing aides, and postsecondary teachers—nine are majority female.

Goodbye, Gender Wage Gap

For sure, there are those who don't believe women as a whole will ever be economically dominant. Claudia Goldin feels this will be difficult to achieve until "further changes occur in the home," meaning more input from men and more policies to help them. Many think we won't see it until workplaces become fairer and more flexible. Among the organizations that battle against discrimination and advocate for pay equity—and there are many mature, vibrant groups that now do this—there is understandable unwillingness to declare victory prematurely.

Economists, particularly women economists, who have devoted their careers to studying the effects of discrimination find it hard to envision a world where women overall outearn men, or even earn equal pay for equal work. Many worry that in an era of the breadwoman, wives and mothers will be supporting families on salaries lower than those that husbands might command. In 2011, the Supreme Court denied class-action status to a suit by current and former female Wal-Mart employees arguing that women had been discriminated against in pay and promotions. One plaintiff said in her testifying papers that a man who held the same position she did, but who had less time on the job, was making $10,000 a year more than she was. When she found out and complained to a supervisor, she was told her coworker had a family to support: hence his higher salary. She had a family to support, too, but management was not convinced, giving her a modest raise that did not nearly close the gap. Even now, the mind-set that men are providers and deserve a higher wage by dint of being fathers, lingers. But I would argue that the very fact that these situations receive so much attention, and that attitudes like this are regarded as wildly unacceptable once they are aired (the court did not rule on the evidence itself, but held that the women's grievances were too varied to constitute a class), show just how far we—or many of us—have traveled in our thinking.

It's true that a gender wage gap remains. According to the Bureau of Labor Statistics, in 2010 the ratio of women's to men's earnings was 81.2 percent. This means that women working full-time earned about four-fifths of what men did. The "wage gap" is not an exact comparison of what a female lawyer, say, makes compared to a male lawyer of the exact same age and experience level, working the exact same hours. Rather it compares *all* women working full-time—their median weekly earnings—to *all* men who are working full-time. The causes of the gap are varied: they include the fact that women working full-time work slightly fewer hours per week than men; women overall still tend to cluster in lower-paying occupations; and women haven't yet accrued the seniority many men enjoy. Economists also have shown that a portion of the wage gap remains "unexplained," and is almost certainly due to discrimination.

But while the wage gap is troubling, it's important to look at the direction in which we are moving. The wage gap has shrunk dramatically over the past 30 years; in 1979, women made just 62 percent of what men did. The same factors that have narrowed the gap are likely to close it. One factor has been the decline in explicitly sexist personnel policies like marriage bars and separate job ads for men and women, a gradual eradication of inequity that will continue, thanks to antidiscrimination laws and the advocacy groups that see they are enforced. And importantly, women are accruing seniority, garnering raises, and extending their time on the job. They are also infiltrating men's domains and in some cases taking them over.

And there are localities and sectors where the full flip has already occurred. In Puerto Rico, women already outearn men—in 2009, women's wages were 103 percent of men's. In other regions, women are close to catching up: in the District of Columbia, with a high number of federal workers and a high proportion of minorities, women earn 88 percent of what men do. It's also worth noting that there are professions where female workers make more than male ones. Women food preparers and serving workers make 112 percent of what men do. Women stock clerks, order fillers, bill and account collectors all make more than men. In other professions, women have almost closed the gap: women Postal Service clerks make 94 percent of men's wages; social workers 91 percent. While the gap remains, it's certain to narrow as women move into male fields and become more mature workers.

And the wage gap is narrowest among younger workers. Among 25- to 34-year-olds working full-time, women's earnings were 91 percent of men's in 2010, up from 68 percent in 1979. For workers ages 16 to 24, women make 95 percent of what men do. Some argue that as these women get older and start families, the gap will grow, but there are reasons to think this will not happen. Women are much more attached to the labor force; they are more likely to work during their childbearing years, more likely to make career decisions based on the opportunities available, rather than on the situations of children and husbands. And the wage hit women take upon childbearing is shrinking. The "penalties to family-conducive behaviors have largely decreased over time," Claudia Goldin and Lawrence Katz wrote in a paper presented at a conference on workplace flexibility in 2010.

There are lots of reasons why the maternal wage hit is getting smaller. Many universities are now stopping the "tenure clock," making it more feasible for woman Ph.D.'s to complete childbearing without being penalized. The White House in 2011 announced an initiative to encourage women to enter science and technology careers by getting the tenure clock stopped and permitting researchers to delay grants to take parental leave. Workplaces are instituting more leave and flextime measures. I interviewed a breadwinning mother, Jasmine D'Addario-Fobian, who has bachelor's and master's degrees from American University and now works for the U.S. Justice Department in an office that addresses issues faced by crime victims. Thanks to federal government policies aimed at enhancing flexibility and telecommuting—employees in her division are permitted three work-at-home days during every ten-day pay period, and they can work nine longer days during that period in order to have the tenth one off—she finds herself at home several days each week. When we spoke, this was making it much easier for her to breast-feed her infant son, Ollie, who was being cared for by her husband. In her marriage, D'Addario-Fobian is the one with the college degree, so it made sense for her to be the full-time worker. She was quite cheerful about the arrangement, because her flexible schedule enables her to eat lunch with her family many days, and eases her commute. According to the U.S. Census Bureau, about 64 percent of women are back to work within a year of their first birth, up from 17 percent in 1965.

Where Have All the Male Pediatricians Gone?

Women are still thinking strategically. They are going into fields that will enable them to continue working when and if they become mothers. Some fields have evolved more flexibility than others, and women have gravitated toward them. Women now are 61 percent of veterinarians, 69 percent of psychologists, 61 percent of claims adjusters, 57 percent of medical scientists, 67 percent of financial specialists. As Goldin and Katz point out, some of the largest gains can be found in the "smaller high-end professions." Optometry, once male, now has graduating classes that are more than 60 percent women. Pharmacy graduates are more than 60 percent female, compared to 30 percent in the mid-1970s. Women have greatly amplified their presence in medicine, where there is a low childbearing penalty compared to, say, the MBA market. Among physicians under the age of 45, women are more than half of doctors in the fields of ob-gyn, pediatrics, dermatology, child psychiatry, and medical genetics. They are close to parity in family practice, psychiatry, pathology, public health, internal medicine, forensic pathology, and several others. They are 42 percent of under-45-year-old physicians and half of those who earn MDs every year. The same trend is even more striking in other countries. In Britain, women make up 56 percent of medical students, and the Royal College of Physicians predicts that female general practitioners could outnumber male ones by 2017. Women are 54 percent of doctors under 35 in Britain, 58 percent in France, and an extraordinary 64 percent in Spain.

Goldin and Katz nicely analyze the way women strategize. Colorectal surgery, they point out, offers a predictable schedule thanks to a new technology for doing procedures. So women are becoming colorectal surgeons. Veterinary medicine, which in 1960 was 98 percent male, is another good example of female logic. One reason for women's inroads may be that veterinary medicine is a caring profession, but, Goldin argues, it's also because many vet practices have reduced emergency, night, and weekend hours, which are being taken over by regional vet hospitals and emergency facilities. There is a move to corporate ownership, which allows women to be employees rather than owners. (Owning a practice is more lucrative, but more time-intensive.) Women are now almost 80 percent of graduates from vet schools, compared to 10 percent in 1970. "There is no specialty in medicine that has a greater fraction female and none in which the fraction female has increased as much since 1970," write Goldin and Katz.

Male Flight

The flip in some specialties is also due to what Goldin calls gender "pollution," more starkly described as men's pathological aversion to admitting women into an all-male field—or remaining in a field that begins to seem alarmingly female. Just as white families departed urban neighborhoods in the 1960s and 1970s as black families moved in, so, too, do men flee classrooms when too many women enter. Sociologist Anne E. Lincoln has found that the more women who are in a specialty, the less likely a male is to apply. What's "really driving feminization of the [veterinary] field is what I call 'preemptive flight'—men not applying because of women's increasing enrollment," she said. She pointed out that in 1960, when veterinary medicine was so heavily male dominated, some veterinary schools excluded women altogether. Others had a cap, and admitted only a small number. Once federal legislation made this discrimination illegal, women began entering and men began leaving, very quickly. Male vet students dropped sharply after 1976, and continued dropping even as the profession doubled in size. It wasn't that existing male vets fled the field—it was that men no longer wanted to train for it. The "engine of feminization" is fueled not only by men's lower college graduation rates but also by their "aversion to women students," Lincoln wrote in a study, pointing out that the same has happened in pharmacy. The women pour in, and the men drain out.

"We can use veterinary medicine as a predictor of what is going to happen in medicine and law," Lincoln added in an interview, predicting that these will flip in about 25 years. "It takes decades for a profession to feminize because an occupation that is mostly male is going to have generational turnover as the more senior practitioners retire." So expect a quarter-century from now to see formerly all-male fields—law, medicine—dominated by women. Many journalism schools are also reporting majority female enrollment. And the flip has already happened in psychology and mental health counseling, to the point where, as the *New York Times* noted in 2011, men who want to see a male psychologist or therapist have a hard time finding one. I've also seen this in the pediatric practice where I take my children. Over the decade that we've been going to the same practice, the doctors retiring have been male, and the doctors joining the practice have been female. It has gotten to the point where boys who prefer a male doctor have to wait months to get an appointment for an annual checkup. The five-year-old daughter of a woman I know asked her mother whether men could be doctors, too.

A Motherhood Wage Premium?

It turns out, too, that it now pays to be a mother. For the first time in modern history, mothers in some key professions may enjoy the same earnings boost that fathers have long enjoyed. At the 2011 conference of the Population Association of America, one of the world's leading assemblies of demographers, sociologist Anne McDaniel reported on new data she and Claudia Buchmann uncovered, which showed that in some fields mothers earn more than women without children. It's difficult to gauge from the data why this might be, but any working mother can tell you that people are very productive when they know they have to squeeze in a day's work before child care closes at 6 P.M. In an accompanying paper, the authors underlined just how much women's aspirations have changed. In 1980, the most common professional job for women was teaching. Now it's business. And here is what is most interesting: often there is no clear wage penalty for having children. In the life sciences, medicine, and law, women with young children earn more than women without children, when they controlled for hours worked. In medicine, for example, women with young children earn 9 percent more than childless women. Being "married with young children is associated with higher earnings than being single without children in math and physical science, engineering and computer sciences, life sciences, medicine, law, and business," they noted. Controlling for education, age, and work hours, "women with young children earn more in most elite occupations than women without children."

This was not a result she had expected. But it makes sense, particularly when you take into account single mothers whose families depend solely on their wages. Four out of 10 babies in the United States are now born to unmarried mothers. Single mothers have extremely high labor force participation rates. I interviewed a number of mothers who said that having a child made them more productive and serious. "When I got pregnant, I couldn't party, so I focused more on school," said Diandra Prieto, a married dietitian who had her first child as an undergraduate. Rather than driving her off course, becoming a mother made her more industrious. "I excelled pretty easily," she said.

As women envision themselves as breadwinners, having a child will be motivation to work harder—not drop out. When I asked McDaniel whether mothers might now be experiencing a wage premium, she acknowledged that this was an explanation she considered plausible.

The Opt-Out Revolution—Among Men

Men, meanwhile, are developing an opt-out habit of their own. Just 66 percent of men in the prime working ages—25 to 64—are employed full-time, down from 80 percent in 1970. In 2006, Louis Uchitelle and David Leonhardt wrote a prescient *New York Times* piece on what they called "missing men," men in the prime of their lives who have bid adieu to a life of productive labor. Among those featured was a 53-year-old laid-off steelworker unwilling to take a low-wage job that didn't appeal to him. "I have come to realize that my free time is worth a lot to me," he said. The article noted that many of these men are blue-collar workers without a college education, who "are turning down jobs they think beneath them or are unable to find work for which they are qualified." The war on drugs in the 1980s and 1990s also swelled the ranks of nonworkers, as men—disproportionately African American—found themselves behind bars, often for relatively low-level crimes. The *Times* piece pointed out that these idle men faced higher rates of divorce and had become "unmoored" from family relationships. "A larger share of working-age men are not working today than at almost any point in the last half-century," they noted, pointing out that the same trend is emerging in Europe. In a later, related blog post, Leonhardt noted that for a piece on college dropouts he reported in far southwestern Virginia, he got to know a group of friends, all around 30. "Every one of the women had gone to graduate school. None of the men had graduated from college."

But it's not just working-class and lower-income men who are opting out. During the 1990s, it was the *most educated men* who saw the largest proportional increase in nonworking. A 2004 paper by Jay Stewart, for the Bureau of Labor Statistics, pointed out that "nonwork rates of college graduates and men with some college increased by

70 percent and 57 percent, respectively," in that decade. He also found that many nonworking men spend much of their free time in "leisure activities and sleep"—unlike women, who when not working for pay, do productive things like child care and housework.

But many men, rather than slacking off, are fulfilling a desire to be more involved fathers. A 2008 workforce survey conducted by the Families and Work Institute found that since 1992, the percentage of men under 29—so-called millennials—who want jobs with greater responsibility has dropped by 12 percentage points, from 80 percent to 68 percent. This puts them about even with younger women, 65 percent of whom want more responsibility—up from 54 percent in 1997. Again, men are trending down and women are trending up in terms of eagerness to advance. Moreover—and this is important—there is no longer any difference between mothers and nonmothers at work: both want more responsibility. In 2008, the desire of younger mothers for jobs with responsibility was at its highest point—67 percent—since they first started asking the question.

The survey also found that men and women are both less likely to say that men should earn the money and women should take care of the children. The change has been greater among men: in 1977, 74 percent of men expressed this belief, whereas just 40 percent think so now. Fathers spend three hours with their children on a workday, compared to two hours in 1977. Younger fathers spend 4.1 hours each workday with their kids. The percentage of men who say their partners take more responsibility for child care dropped from 58 percent in 1992 to 46 percent in 2008.

And men are suffering from the work-life stress that has for decades exhausted women. The percentage of men who feel torn between the demands of home and work has also risen, from 34 percent in 1977 to 49 percent in 2008, compared to women's 43 percent. The experiences of men and women—the wash of conflicting emotions that working parenthood makes inevitable—are converging. In fact, the report notes, "fathers in dual-earner couples are now significantly more likely to experience some or a lot of work-life conflict than mothers in dual-earner couples." No wonder more and more men are dropping out: men now feel more work-family stress than women do, likely because the workplace is even more inflexible and unforgiving for fathers than it is for mothers.

The collective impact of all this is clear: women's earnings really could eclipse those of men. The "dramatic change in labor force participation of women is one of the most important transformations in the economic and social worlds during the past generation," Gary Becker posted in 2010 on his blog. "American women are starting new businesses at a much faster rate than they did in the past, and the number of female heads of large companies, although small in number, has been growing." When I talked to him, Becker said that the most likely scenario—the sector where we could see a flip in earnings first— is looking at full-time female workers compared to full-time males. Other economists say that this becomes more likely when you take into account median salaries, rather than average ones. The median is the point at which half of all salaries are above and half are below; taking median salaries blunts the impact of the huge Wall Street outlier salaries that still go to men.

A World of Educated Women

These changes are not confined to the United States. In the European Union, as a *Newsweek* article pointed out, "women filled 75 percent of the 8 million new jobs created since 2000." In Japan and Britain, single young women make more than their male counterparts. In South Korea, the employment rate of women in their twenties is higher than that of men. Women are 25 percent of breadwinners in U.K. romantic partnerships, and the percentage is about the same in France. And women around the world are outdoing men academically to an extent that few people realize. It's reasonably well known that women are now a majority of university students in the United States, the U.K., Canada, and many developed nations, but—here is the real news—women are the majority of university students in most countries in the world. Women are 61 percent of college and university students in Mongolia, 53 percent in Botswana, 62 percent in Saudi Arabia, 60 percent in the

United Arab Emirates. Women are a majority of students in higher education in most of Central and Eastern Europe—Georgia, Albania, Latvia, Macedonia, Poland, Slovakia, and Slovenia. They are 58 percent of university students in Kazakhstan, 57 percent in Kyrgyzstan, 53 percent in Iran, 65 percent in Kuwait. Advocates for women's rights tend to focus on countries where strong fundamentalist forces work to keep girls out of classrooms, and while this is important coverage, it can obscure the fact that elsewhere women are not only occupying classrooms but also dominating them.

For decades, organizations like UNESCO, the World Bank, and the Organisation for Economic Co-operation and Development (OECD) have been pressuring countries to increase schooling for girls, and the campaign has had an impact. The trend toward globalization has prompted countries to build their university systems. Countries understand that to thrive in the global economy they need an educated workforce. Women have been the ones to take advantage of this expansion. Like their counterparts in industrialized nations, girls in developing countries do better than boys in terms of grades and outcomes. According to Anne McDaniel, countries where women are thriving in higher education tend to be those with more egalitarian gender ideologies. This becomes self-reinforcing: as women gain more education, they demand more egalitarian marriages. More egalitarian marriages influence the culture and propel more women into education. As more women get educated, more women are likely to work; when more women work, more women are likely to seek education. Fields of study available to women expand. Women have more access to positions in the labor force and politics.

And while it's true that in some countries, such as Iran and Saudi Arabia, there still isn't much in the way of an earnings boost for women who are college-educated—because women are shut out of much of the workforce—their rise in numbers is bound to have an impact. Around the world, there are movements for enfranchisement and property rights for women. Anju Malhotra, a vice president at the International Center for Research on Women, said that in the last five years policymakers in many developing countries seemed to her to show a new understanding that adding women to the workforce doesn't mean men lose their jobs. To the contrary, it's what permits economies to grow and expand.

Many overseas development groups are investing in women. This is due in part to new research suggesting that when women control household resources, they are more likely to use money for the benefit of children and families. In households, women are more likely than men to play the role of benevolent despot that Gary Becker described. MIT economist Esther Duflo has done groundbreaking work showing that in South Africa, women who received a government pension used it to help their granddaughters, and the health—and literal physical height—of girls was enhanced. Similarly, economist Shelly Lundberg and colleagues found that when a family subsidy in the United Kingdom was paid to women, the result was an increase in expenditures on children's clothing. This spending pattern accounts in part for why, as women become more educated in developing countries, child mortality falls. Adding women to the economy helps the economy and it helps individuals. "The World Economic Forum has estimated that closing the remaining employment gender gap in the United States would increase U.S. GDP by up to 9 percent," noted *Newsweek*, quoting Harvard business professor Nancy Koehn: "I think women are really going to shake up the workplace over the next 15 years. This is just the beginning of a tsunami of change." Women in developing nations are more likely to describe themselves as "ambitious" than men are. The *Newsweek* piece pointed out that in Brazil, where 60 percent of college graduates are women, the economy's growth rate in a recent quarter was 9 percent.

Wives, as a result, have a whole new value for their husbands. To the extent that married men's finances have improved in the past decades, wives are the reason. Unmarried men are the ones who have suffered a blow to their standard of living. According to the Pew Research Center, husbands are increasingly likely to be the chief economic beneficiaries of marriage, thanks to the earnings women bring with them. This is an unprecedented development and it bears stopping, for a moment, to get your head around. Let's review this fact again. Husbands are increasingly likely to be the chief economic beneficiaries of marriage. The Cinderella story has been rewritten. The old order has been overthrown. Men are becoming the dependent sex. Keep in mind: men have *always* benefited more from marriage than women in terms of health and psychological well-being, which may be one reason wives are more likely than husbands to seek divorce. Now men benefit more economically. So who has the greater incentive now to get married? Men or women?

Four
The New Rules of Mating

Women in college dorms now routinely sit around debating whether they would be willing to date—or marry—a man who did not go to college. It has become an ordinary question, one of those idle yet urgent self-examinations that arise when women are looking toward the future trying to figure out how their lives will unfold. Women fresh out of college ask one another the same question. "A friend and I were talking about deal breakers," recollected Kate, a Boston University graduate who works for a nonprofit in Washington, D.C. The first item that came up—the main quality that would disqualify a guy as dateworthy—was lack of a college degree. "I just would not go there," she said. She worries that this sounds elitist. But she has tried it and it did not go well. "He was a veteran—a pretty young veteran of Iraq. He's a nice guy, but we just clearly had nothing to talk about. He didn't even vote. I was like: You were in Iraq, and you don't vote?" She reflected, "I feel like the way my life is, what I say and do—there's just a threshold that I think college creates that I wouldn't go under." This is a problem for thousands of women surveying the romantic landscape and seeing a dearth of men as well schooled as they are. And it's new. When I was in college in the 1980s, my roommates and I sat around talking about our futures, too, and what we wondered was how we might have families and careers of our own, given how high-powered the men we knew were. Among the many things we worried about, whether there would be enough male college graduates to go around was not one of them. But it also never occurred to us that we might ask a husband to stay home or that he might want to. It never occurred to us that a man might be willing to privilege our career over his.

Nor did we wonder what the point of a man is. Women now ask this question. "A guy no longer is a necessary thing," observed Betsy Soler when I talked to her. At 20, Soler was a senior, already making $70,000 directing the social networking program for Florida International University in Miami. She didn't have a boyfriend, and wanted one, but she stopped every now and then to ask herself what for. "I almost feel like guys aren't necessary anymore, and it's kind of a terrible thing," she reflected. "I'm not sure what you do. I guess you keep hoping that you meet this guy who is Prince Charming—who has a great job, as you do, and is I guess aspiring as you are. But it almost seems impossible." With that, she summarized the modern female quandary: Now that I am self-sufficient, what do I need a man for? Remind me: Why would I want to get married? And within marriage, how would our lives unfold? And assuming that I would like a man to go out with, where would I find him?

Good questions, and they show how disorienting women's economic rise can be even for the women enjoying it. There tends to be disagreement among academics over what men and women want in a mate. But it is safe to say this: during the second half of the 20th century, both men and women came to prefer partnering with someone from the same educational and socioeconomic background. Women no longer expect to marry up—to be Princess Diana, young and naive, attaching herself to an older, better educated husband. We want to be more like Kate Middleton with Prince William; those two went to the same university, took comparable degrees (actually, she did a bit better), and are the same degree of good-looking. We want to be attractive and wealthy and for our spouse to be those things as well. We want to be Sheryl Sandberg, COO of Facebook, married to Dave Goldberg, CEO of SurveyMonkey. We want to be a gorgeous and wildly successful Internet entrepreneur married to a gorgeous and wildly successful Internet entrepreneur. Women have not been trading beauty for wealth, not for quite a while. Women have been trading beauty and wealth for beauty and wealth. In a sense, as sociologist Andrew Cherlin points out, we have always wanted spouses who resemble us, but "matching" once meant marrying someone from your religion or ethnic culture. It was common, in the 1950s and 1960s, for a Catholic woman who did not have a college education to marry a Catholic man who did, because what mattered was being Catholic. To marry outside your religion or culture was considered risky. Now we match through education or lack of it. Education, for many, *is* our culture.

This is a development with real social ramifications, not all of them good. It is one reason social and income inequality have become exacerbated. As men and women with high earning potential seek out one another, people with less education pair up or—more likely—don't marry at all, and the economic rift between Americans grows wider. Once, when women did marry up, marriage had a social leveling effect. These days, marriage widens the growing division between the have-nots and the haves.

This trend toward matching may be one reason why lately even the Darwinian argument has been revised. A new theory among people who look at evolutionary incentives for partnering is that Early Woman did not trade her looks and fertility in return for provision from a strong and high-status male. Instead, Early Woman was herself an energetic and competent provider. With her foraging, Pleistocene Mom brought in as many calories as Pleistocene Dad—maybe more. The biological anthropologist Helen Fisher argues that what we are seeing is a return to the way humans used to live. She points out that during our hunter-gatherer phase, women were not exactly hanging around the encampment waiting for men to haul in a freshly killed woolly mammoth. To the contrary, women were the reliable bringers-in of sustenance, going out every day to find roots and berries their families could survive on, while men trickled in periodically with the odd but delectable hunting prize, the occasional piece of protein that was roundly applauded. She argues that we are seeing a return to the original human pattern, where women were co-providers.

She also argues—and here is where the Marxist and Darwinist arguments converge—that it's been a disadvantageous 10,000 years or so for women. Inequality between the sexes arose, she points out, when we stopped foraging and started farming, transitioning to an economy based on dominion over the land. The plow was invented, and it became men who felled the trees, men who prepared the fields, men who headed off to markets and came home with the local equivalent of money. "It's women who get the second-class jobs of picking and weeding, and you see in agrarian societies around the world a whole shift in the power between men and women, men becoming the quote 'head of the household,'" Fisher said. But in a knowledge economy based on information and service, women have an advantage they haven't seen for millennia. "College is built for the female brain. What do you do in college? You sit. You read. You write and you talk." Fisher argues that we've moved forward to the past, and that this is hard for men and women alike. "It's an adjustment for both of them. We've got 10,000 years of a belief system to shed. Nobody knows how to do it."

The thing is, matching has become difficult, at least for women, in a world where women are better-credentialed than men. Up to now, the evidence has suggested that brilliant, high-achieving women will be the ones left out: the two most recently appointed Supreme Court justices, Sonia Sotomayor and Elena Kagan, are dynamic and dazzling and single. Former U.S. secretary of state Condoleezza Rice periodically finds herself grilled on why she never married, most notably in a 2011 television interview with host Piers Morgan, who asked her with startling condescension if she was "high maintenance." "Do you hold out hope?" he inquired, patronizingly. It may be true, what Samuel Johnson said about men not wanting women who will overmatch them. Some speed dating studies have found that men are attracted to women who seem as smart and ambitious as they are, but are put off by women who seem smarter and more ambitious.

But there is growing evidence that men are changing their minds, and coming to understand the clear advantages of having a well-educated, highly paid partner. And the more well educated and highly paid, the better. A powerful body of work shows that women, as they become more educated, become more valued as wives. So it's plausible that, more and more, the highest-achieving women will be the ones who get snapped up. There are economists who argue that one reason women joined the workforce is because men, especially younger men with working mothers, *prefer* wives who earn. For women, it's clear that being college-educated is no longer a liability in the marriage market; it's a marked advantage and a predictor of marital stability. It's also beginning to appear that men, not women, are the ones seeking commitment. For the dating website Match.com, Helen Fisher did a study with evolutionary biologist Justin Garcia and social historian Stephanie Coontz, looking at what single men and women want in life and romance. They found that as women become self-sufficient, they want space and independence; men are quicker to fall in love, more drawn to family life. This rebuts the original argument of the evolutionary psychologists, who held that intimacy was more important to women, a way to bind men to them and ensure the provider would stick around. Women have become more like men, and men like women—assuming that there was ever really that much of a difference. "I think the idea that men just want to disseminate their seed and women just want to have babies is bullshit," said Justin Garcia. "Everybody wants it all, at different times."

"The Person I Marry I Have to Admire"

But what my interviews with scores of educated young women suggested, pretty strongly, is that women still want men to be their equals. Women who did go to college tend to be very skeptical of men who did not. Women want a man they can love—of course—but they also spoke, over and over, of wanting a man who is on "my level." This held true for women of all races and regions and classes and education levels. Occasionally women couched this in terms of earnings—"I want someone who makes more than me or at least equal to me," said Nikia Williams, a 35-year-old electrical engineer in Detroit—but more often, they spoke of qualities like intellect and drive. "I want to date an equal," is how Elizabeth Fuller, a UCLA graduate working in the New

York technology sector, put it. Women see being college-educated as a proxy for being motivated and interesting. They want a man who is not boring; a man they don't have to explain things to; a man who has similar aspirations and interests. They want a man they can *talk to.* High-achieving women live in a culture of achievement and want men who inhabit the same reality.

"I briefly dated this guy, a first-year med student, he was fantastically gorgeous, seems a great guy on paper, but not interesting. I need a guy who is really interesting," said Kim Allen, a law student in Washington, D.C.

Drive is also crucial. To be attracted to a man, women felt he needed to be moving forward. "It's about always trying to be a better version of yourself," said Michelle Mendonça, a woman in her early twenties who works in finance. "I find that somebody's lack of desire— their contentment to stay where they are and not move forward—it's not attractive." When she is looking at profiles on Match.com, she says, "I make sure they have a college education. I want to make sure a guy is driven. There's always something you can be striving for."

Mixed in with this was reluctance to support a man, economically, in any long-term, major way. Being the permanent provider was something that did not interest the women I talked to. They could entertain the idea of earning somewhat more, but did not aspire to be the sole earner. "We are all so incredibly independent that we know we're always going to take care of ourselves," said Meredith Hopps, an Atlanta engineer, describing herself and her circle of friends. "We don't want to have to take care of anybody else."

Most profoundly, women spoke of wanting a man they could look up to. "The person I marry I have to admire," said Wendy Rodriguez, who came to the United States from Mexico when she was 14 and was planning to go to law school and, from there, to make a career in immigration law. She would only consider dating a college graduate. "Not because I'll have a better life or economic status. But because I have to admire that person."

Helen Fisher, the anthropologist, doesn't think this is surprising. For thousands of years, women have grown used to looking upward, grown used to expecting that their partner would—or at least should—

be motivated and achieving. "It's a time of dramatic adjustment for both men and women, a kind of adjustment that we really haven't been required to make in 10,000 years," she pointed out. "This generation is going to have to rise to the occasion. All these women are not going to be able to find a really high-powered man," she says. "For millions of years, women have wanted a partner who helps provide. We're a pair-bonding animal. We raise our children as a team. However, there are many ways that a man can provide without having a lot of money. I've always said, as women's roles expand, men's roles get to expand, too."

The Millionaire or the Policeman? Hmm.

You can see popular culture working through this. Hollywood is furiously producing movies in which high-powered women struggle with ambition, wealth, and the effect these have on men. In *The Devil Wears Prada*, Anne Hathaway's journalist-protagonist and her cook-boyfriend are both getting started in New York careers; the more Hathaway's character pulls ahead, the more conflicted her cook-boyfriend feels about her. The price of success becomes even more apparent when her boss, the awesome fashion editor Miranda Priestly, played by Meryl Streep, calls home from the Paris fashion shows to find her husband has left her. In *Morning Glory*, Rachel McAdams's hyperactive TV news producer is lectured by Harrison Ford's aging newshound about the dangers of workaholism and the havoc it can wreak on family life. Indeed, the exhausted male executive dispensing wisdom to the up-and-coming female is almost, now, a trope. In *Up in the Air*, George Clooney's character's fear of commitment is a warning to the perky but ruthless young woman executive who is on the verge of superseding him.

How can a man be sexy when he's in an inferior position? Screenwriters are trying to figure this out. In *The Proposal*, Sandra Bullock plays a book editor who is domineering and feared by everybody including her assistant, played by Ryan Reynolds. In order for Reynolds's character to become a believable love object, it is necessary for them to take a trip to his parental estate in Alaska, where he is shown to have ancestral wealth that outstrips hers. It helps when Bullock is thrown from a boat and must be rescued. And in the end, it is necessary for him to get a promotion so that he can be near her level.

But other films show couples finding an equilibrium that permits the woman to remain in charge. In *The Young Victoria*, Emily Blunt plays the queen after whom an age was named, confronted by men who want to rule through her or control her. The only suitor who genuinely wants to see her govern is Albert. At first, she holds him at arm's length, arguing that she wants to find her own way. But when court intrigue proves too treacherous—when there are too many men who want to dominate her—she realizes she needs him as her mediator. Obliged to fit into her court, he becomes a househusband; passionate about honest accounting, he takes on the running of the royal household. But the movie makes sure to convey that Albert is still masculine in every way that matters. When Victoria is fired at by a would-be assassin, Albert leans forward and takes the bullet. She doesn't need a provider, but she does needs a protector, and this—I would argue—is a clue to how couples in the future will manage their roles.

Marry up? Marry down? Don't marry? In *Bridesmaids*, a big-screen vehicle for *Saturday Night Live*'s Kristen Wiig, her character finds herself torn between the attractions of a classic alpha male and those of a police officer whose humor and Irish accent are about all he has to offer. In an opening scene, she is having energetic but not that satisfying sex with the rich alpha male, played by Jon Hamm, who afterward tells her to leave. She must weigh his asshole charms against those of the cop, who actually wants her to stick around after they sleep together and urges her to open a new bakery after her old business failed. His eagerness repels her, until . . . it begins to attract her. Throughout, what you see is Hollywood asking: What can a man give the woman who has everything? In what way, if at all, do the sexes need each other, now that the old economic bonds have been broken?

Two Options: Marry Down, or Don't Marry

Women have two options. All women could follow the example of African American women, who—not necessarily of their own volition—are increasingly estranged from the married state. Black women are the most enduring example of the economic flip and its romantic consequences. They are more likely than white women to earn more than their male partners, and more likely to be better-educated than their husbands. They also have become much less likely than white women to be married. The black middle-class female—affluent, attractive, funny, smart, unpartnered—is a staple of fiction and self-help literature. As academics like Donna Franklin have pointed out, the African American family has been divided by racism and economic inequality since the time of slavery. Black women have had to work at higher rates than white women because their husbands' wages were lower than those of white men. Black women rarely had the luxury of staying home. Partly as a result, Franklin points out, black women have tended to be more assertive in marriage, something that also resulted in their being unfairly stereotyped as "matriarchs." Yet African American women are often exhorted to restore to men the authority the culture has taken away. In recent decades, African American men have taken an enormous economic battering. Partly in response, observes the sociologist W. Bradford Wilcox, churches and the larger community urge women to treat men as the household leader, as a way of binding men to family life and giving them "identity and purpose." Yet the dissonance has led to unhappiness for both sexes: black husbands are more likely to be domesticated but don't necessarily feel good about it, and black women don't like having to do the domesticating or, alternatively, pretending to be submissive. "The more a traditional gender arrangement is lifted up by the community," Wilcox points out, "the more that the new economic realities make it challenging."

In this context, does marriage make sense? More than 70 percent of African American children are born to single mothers. Almost seven out of ten African American women are single. "Not since slavery have black men and women been as unpartnered as we are now," writes law professor Ralph Richard Banks in his 2011 book, *Is Marriage for White People?* As Banks points out, "college-educated black women are twice as likely as their white counterparts to be unmarried." Blacks are twice as likely as whites to divorce. So this is one model for adjusting to the economic flip, and it's right outside the door.

Gay and lesbian couples offer a different model. Same-sex couples are more willing to partner outside their educational, racial, and other traditional boundaries than straight couples. They are less concerned with matching, partly because they are "matching" in the realm of sexual orientation. And gays and lesbians are freer from ideological gender baggage; if one partner finds himself cooking *and* cleaning up, he is less likely to have steam coming out of his ears than your typical straight woman, who is prone to obsess about household parity. Gay and lesbian couples are better at figuring out how to organize households in ways that play to each other's strengths. Disparities in earnings can be an issue but partners are better at keeping them on the table. These couples, even as they seek the protection and legitimacy marriage conveys, suggest that intimate partners with mixed education and earnings can find equilibrium. Interestingly, lesbians—who know from an earlier age they are unlikely to be stay-at-home mothers—tend to earn higher wages than women overall. Meanwhile, gay men—knowing they won't be old-fashioned *Leave It to Beaver* breadwinning fathers—have tended to earn slightly lower wages than men as a whole.

So far, both the African American and the same-sex models are prevailing. In the United States and many European countries, there has been a striking rise in the number of women and men who are delaying marriage and a rise in the number of people not marrying at all. In 1960, 72 percent of adult Americans were married. Today, the percentage is just over half—an all-time low. In 1960, 68 percent of Americans in their twenties were married, compared to just 26 percent now. Cohabitation, meanwhile, has risen dramatically.

But there also is a new pattern emerging. Women are overcoming their reservations and marrying down. Women are partnering with men who have less education than they do. The kind of man women think they will be attracted to, and the man they end up falling in love with, often turn out to be different. A number of women subtly altered their aspirations even as they were talking to me, downgrading and revising. "They don't have to be equally educated—they don't have to have an engineering degree or they don't have to have a master's degree, but [they need to have] some form of education," said engineer Christi Nesmith. "Or at least be intelligent. And have a desire to succeed." Nowadays, a woman is more likely to marry down than a man is. In 2007, 28 percent of American wives ages 30 to 44 had more education than their spouses, compared to just 19 percent of husbands. Among college-educated women, 36 percent—more than a third— were married to a man who was not college-educated, an increase of 6 percentage points since 1970.

The question—for people entering into relationships under these conditions, and for existing couples where the woman is pulling ahead—is what these unions will feel like. Up to now, studies have suggested that marriages in which wives are better-educated than husbands may be more likely to dissolve, perhaps because they hold opposing views about raising children and running households. Sociologist Annette Lareau has shown that working-class parents tend to be more authoritarian but also give children more space and freedom. Upper-income parents tend to hover more, and discipline more lightly. For couples with mixed education levels, this creates fertile ground for disagreement. "We've talked a lot about discipline—he tends to be a lot more about spanking," said one wife I talked to who had been spanked as a child, but owing in part to her education now rejects that strategy. "I'm like, no—I've told him that so many times." Betsey Stevenson, chief economist for the U.S. Department of Labor and a long-time student of earnings and marriage, fears unions in which women have more education will be more fragile.

I would argue that these partnerships will work best when couples find a realm of common endeavor outside work or school. Couples will find a separate place to feel they are matching. "I don't think my husband is not smart," said one woman I interviewed. She teaches English and philosophy at a high school for gifted students. Her husband is an electrician. "Does he read all the Shakespeare I have, and the Socrates and Plato?" she said. "No, but I don't understand a lot of his electrical work, either. I'm teaching a seminar on death and dying and grieving, and he doesn't have any problems talking about that. That part is not a problem for me, and it doesn't seem to be a problem for him." This couple found common ground in the intensity with which they both value their children and stable home life—and, not incidentally, in the fact that they went to high school together, and have shared memories and a shared group of friends. Other couples will find common ground in leisure and hobbies.

But there is no question that a new element of competition has entered relationships between men and women. What we are seeing is not a return to the origins of human civilization. Women are not going back to being foraging co-providers. They are bringing in the protein. They have become the hunters. So the real question is: What will happen deep inside these unions now that women are crossing categories, competing and winning where men once prevailed? Can relationships withstand this competition? And what happens when women are winning in a domain—income—that is stark and easily measured?

Looking back at the history of the workforce, you could argue that men have exhibited a psychic horror of competing with women. Barring women from men's fields of endeavor was sexist and wrong, sure, but it also may have entailed a degree of emotional self-preservation. It is hard to feel you are directly competing with the person you love and live with. The big employment sector shifts—fields going from male to female—suggest that the sexes move almost like schools of fish, flashing in and out of crevices and coral reefs, endeavoring to stay out of one another's territory. Now we're in each other's space. When women enter the realm of earnings and prevail, there are bound to be reverberations. How will couples manage the potential for secret competition and overt one-upmanship? Will men give up? Retaliate? Will breadwomen carp and hector? Or will women mourn the freedom and flexibility they once enjoyed? I would say: yes, yes, yes, and yes. Couples will need to find a way to manage competition. Some men will manage it by trying less hard in the workplace and finding other realms of achievement. Others, seeing women achieving and thriving, will ratchet their performance upward rather than downward. Men will raise their own game—just as women once did looking at men. Men will compete with women, women with men, and the upshot will be more equality and higher achievement. We'll make each other better. We'll play to our strengths. Money does change everything, and there are a number of ways that truth is about to play out.

Part Two
THE BACKLASH

Five
Competition and Undermining

As Women's Earnings Rise, Some Men Will React Badly

The Rio Grande Valley, at the tip of Texas, is a citrus-rich floodplain that spreads out along the north bank of the river, west of the Gulf of Mexico. The Valley, as people who live there call it, comprises the cities of Brownsville, Edinburg, and McAllen, as well as smaller communities and *colonias*, which are unincorporated neighborhoods settled by immigrants and low-wage workers, somewhat hodgepodge and often devoid of infrastructure, like drainage systems and even indoor plumbing, but illustrative of the dreams that pull people to the United States. In one *colonia* not far from Edinburg, a home has been constructed on stilts—to avoid the flooding that washes through the neighborhood—and topped with crenellations. It looks oddly like a castle, which is what it's meant to resemble. According to local inhabitants, the owner promised his sweetheart that when they moved to America, he would build a castle for his princess. The provider ethos emerges in places you wouldn't necessarily expect to find it.

Though historically agricultural and poor, this part of the United States is not a backwater. A rapidly growing region, it has international airports, several institutions of higher learning, and scores of big-box stores: Target and Sears and Marshalls and Kohl's and Barnes & Noble, a stream of cheap retail outlets aimed not just at the local population but also at Mexicans who come north to shop. One of its flagship institutions is the University of Texas–Pan American, a branch of the UT system that ranks very high nationally in awarding degrees to Hispanics. Women outnumber men in the freshman class at UTPA, and the imbalance grows as students move toward graduation. When I was researching this book, I contacted alumnae at coed universities that are majority female, to find out what life and love are like during and after college. I was flooded with emails from UTPA graduates: young Hispanic women who are amassing degree after degree, bettering their prospects even as they live in a community that is still, as they describe it, pretty strongly macho. One of these was a 26-year-old woman named Claudia Vasquez. Her experience mirrors that of any number of women, in any number of regions, whose partners felt threatened by their success and retaliated in a similar way. In the category of men reacting adversely to women's higher earnings, her story seems a good place to start.

Claudia, smart and sociable, grew up outside Edinburg in a one-floor house her parents built by hand, adding sections as they could afford it. Her mother and father were both born in Mexico. Claudia's mother was sent at the age of nine to the United States to work as a maid in a local household, and her father did migrant farm and construction labor. As adults, both her parents worked. Claudia can remember as a child sleeping in the car while her mother worked an early morning factory job, assembling components for audio systems. She hardly remembers her father, who was killed on a construction site in Houston when she was little. Raised by her mother, whose schooling stopped in the first grade, Claudia did extremely well academically. She took college-credit courses in high school and won scholarships to continue on to the university. She met her future husband in middle school, where they played in the band together. They went to different high schools, but met up again at UTPA and started dating.

Of the two, Claudia recalls being more focused. She majored in social work, and entered the new-employee training program in a local Child Protective Services office while she was still a student. Two days after graduating from UTPA, she began a full-time job with CPS. Her fiancé—by then they were engaged—was slower off the mark. After they graduated, he spent a couple months trying to decide what to do with his psychology degree. As their wedding date approached, she urged him to make a decision, and suggested he consider her agency. He was accepted into CPS as well, in a different unit, and began training to become a full-time employee.

Claudia from the start made more than he did. Her social work degree earned her a salary premium, and she had gotten her training out of the way in college. In terms of seniority this put her just a few months ahead of him, but that and her credentials were enough to keep her earnings, always, a nose higher. She realizes now that "he always felt like he had to play catch-up to me. I was always two steps ahead. By the time he felt he had caught up, I got ahead again."

At first Claudia had no idea her husband was feeling competitive with her—or that he felt he was losing. But not long into their marriage she noticed his behavior became colder, more distant. She suppressed her dismay, thinking it was first-year jitters. He would make remarks about her appearance, telling her she had gained weight and was no longer good-looking. In retrospect, she sees, the chill intensified when a new employee—a woman—was brought in and Claudia's husband was assigned to train her. He began spending a lot of time with the new hire. Coworkers started talking, but Claudia tried to ignore the water-cooler comments. Every now and then she would mention the new trainee to her husband, but he told her it was her insecurities talking. Then came a Friday night when he said he had to work late. As midnight came and went and he hadn't returned home, she knew it wasn't a child abuse case that was keeping him. She called his cell phone, but it was turned off.

Getting into her car, she headed for the coworker's place. When she pulled up, "I saw his vehicle," said Claudia, who recounted this scene as she sat in a hotel restaurant, unhappily picking at a sautéed chicken breast. I spoke with Claudia on a Saturday, her day off, and she was wearing a silky teal-colored shirt with ruffles, a black suit jacket, and a star-shaped crystal pendant that her mother made for her, along with matching crystal earrings. Claudia's black hair was shoulder length and glossy, her manner a little stiff, but more relaxed as she talked about what happened. Uncertain what to do, she pressed the last number she had called on her cell phone, which belonged to a friend having an at-home movie-night party. The friend and several others piled into a car and headed over to help Claudia if she needed it.

Sitting in her car outside the other woman's apartment, Claudia still wasn't sure how to react. Since she couldn't reach her husband, she sent the woman a text, asking, if he was there, to have him call her. "After that, he walked out of her home and she was there by the door. He hugged her and gave her a kiss." Parked at the curb, Claudia flashed her lights. When he saw her, he came over. To her surprise, he went on the offensive. "He was yelling at me: 'You're making that poor girl in there feel like she's causing problems between us!'" recalled Claudia. She went into social worker mode: she told her husband she was sorry if the other woman felt victimized, but she wasn't married to the other woman—she was married to him. "What I told him was—I don't want to be forcing you to be with me if you don't want to be with me. If you'd rather spend time with this person, that's fine, but just say it—don't say you're going to be working." Her calm, she said, infuriated him. He told her later he would have preferred it if she yelled back. Instead, she rolled up her window and drove home, not wanting to aggravate him further. Later, she realized she was more worried about managing his feelings than examining her own. "He had changed so much with me, months prior to that. I tell my friends, I went through my grieving stages earlier, when I was with him and trying to salvage it."

Back at work, Claudia was called into a meeting with a supervisor, who wanted to know if she was okay. Claudia was mortified, but understood that her marital crisis had become a workplace issue. "Basically everybody found out what had happened. Most of the people in supervisory positions are women, and they called me in and spoke to me separately." Her husband also was called in. "My husband says they ganged up on him—they reminded him that the first year with a state agency is probationary."

That was two years ago. Though she still sometimes refers to him as "my husband," Claudia filed for divorce. As luck would have it, her ex-husband's division was relocated from a nearby office building into her own, so they now work a hallway away. On occasions, he has used their infrequent encounters to spell out her shortcomings as a wife. The main problem, he told her, was that she was outperforming him. "He didn't feel he was good enough for me. I was too smart; he couldn't get away with certain things. I would call him out." He told her she corrected him in conversations, a remark that surprised Claudia—when she thought she was responding to a point he had made, he felt he was being admonished. He told her that when he was learning his job, she "would be the one that would help him, and explain things to him," whereas with the coworker, he got to do the explaining. "He could kind of show off whatever he knew. He didn't feel he could show off with me." He was still seeing the other woman. "He says, 'Now I'm the one who's two steps ahead of her, instead of feeling that I had to catch up with you.'"

Claudia doesn't know how much her salary advantage derailed her marriage, but she does know this: her ex-husband had the online password to their bank account, and wouldn't give it to her. "He would know what I would spend, but I wouldn't know what he would spend." Looking back, she realizes, his attempt to manage their finances was part of an effort to manage her. "He needed to have control of who my friends were and what I was going to spend money on." Once, she did ask for the password, and "he got very upset. We had a huge disagreement over it. That was when things were already falling apart."

And it's funny, she said, thinking about money. She now was engaged to a man she met at an auto repair shop where she took her car to get fixed. Her new fiancé, who works in the parts department, does not have a four-year college degree, but he's working on getting one, so as to catch up with her. He, too, worries about feeling inferior. And he is always trying to pay for things, to equalize the imbalance. "I'll tell him no, don't give me money, but he'll hide it somewhere at my house." He paid for her car to be fixed, and tried to give her money when her mother's house needed repair. "He says, 'You can save your money—I'll pay all the bills, give your mom what she needs.'" When they get married, he aspires to support her. "His goals are to have a job that doubles—that would act like my salary plus his—so that when we do have children, I don't have to work."

The thing is, Claudia doesn't want to be supported. She doesn't want to be a stay-at-home mother. She would like to have children, but has plenty of free day care in the form of her own mom. "I think I would go crazy if I didn't work," she added. "My work is so stressful, but I love it. In my undergraduate and graduate career, the professors would tell us: if you survive one year in Child Protective Services, you can do anything. I've been there for four years and I just can't see myself going somewhere else." She has already obtained her master's degree, and is working on her therapist's license in case she wants to open her own practice. And she never wants to have to ask a man for money. All of this, she knows, could lead to conflict with a husband who wants her at home. "Especially because of the nature of my work, where every day is different, you never know when there's going to be an emergency."

Her fiancé also worries that she is insufficiently affectionate; she doesn't behave, emotionally, the way he's used to women behaving. "He'll say that I'm cold," she said, perplexed. "I'll say that I'm not cold, but I just don't want to be leaning on you for four hours. I'll do the cuddling, but an hour or two hours. I'm not into the whole four-hour thing." Unable to finish her lunch, she asked for it to be boxed up for later, and then sat there, thinking. "We were talking about it the other day. He's had, like, two other relationships prior to me. He said, 'I know I'm not good-looking, but my other girlfriends would be all over me.'" She reminded her fiancé that those were women whose affection did not prove reliable. He agreed, but it's obvious that her profession makes him feel insecure. "He's like, 'I know I'm being needy, but can you give me a hug?' He'll say, 'I never felt this way about anybody else before—the way that I love you.' He's told me, 'I know your job is different from mine, and you're more in contact with attorneys and judges and this and that, you're so beautiful, so why wouldn't you go with them instead of me?'" Her fiancé worries when her work takes her into bad neighborhoods. He calls to make sure she's okay. He wishes she would talk to him more about her job. "If you want to talk about parts, we'll talk about parts," she will say, and: "Am I supposed to worry that you'll be at work and a part will fall on top of you?"

"He's the one that wants to talk," she reflected, puzzled. "I've told him, sometimes I feel like I'm the guy in the relationship. I say: 'You're the one that wants to be clingy.' At that point, when we're having these discussions, I'll tell him: 'Why do I have to be the guy?'"

"I Would Rob a Bank Before I'd Let My Wife Earn More than I Do!"

Claudia's narrative—betrayal, confrontation, crisis—was one of a number of narratives related by women describing relationships that turned competitive when they began outpacing their partners. Women described boyfriends and husbands who became cold or insecure or controlling or—this was a common theme—argumentative. Men challenged them on decisions that didn't warrant arguing over. The swift deterioration of Claudia's early marriage highlights the insecurities that women's earnings do seem to awaken in some men, and suggests that in the years ahead, there will be—as the *Daily Mail* likes to put it—broken hearts, and even street-side confrontations. Tensions go far beyond the friction caused by arguing over housework; they travel deep into identity and power and self-worth. And they can be a problem for younger couples who you might expect to have more evolved attitudes. One executive I interviewed brought up the topic of spousal earnings at a meeting in her office, and was astonished when a colleague in his twenties exclaimed, "I would rob a bank before I'd let my wife earn more than I do!" Thinking about it, she reflected that his wife worked for the same company, and was doing better than he was. "I'm going nowhere at this place," she had heard him mutter. And in 2011, a writer named Aaron Gouveia blogged for the "Dads" section of the website maintained by the Good Men Project, a media project dedicated to defining "modern manhood" and what it means to be a good man. In his post, he confessed how much he hated being outearned by his wife, who is a banker, and how ecstatic he felt when he landed a job that enabled him to outearn her. "The first thought that popped into my mind was: 'THANK GOD I'M MAKING MORE MONEY THAN MY WIFE!'" he acknowledged. He was uncertain why he felt that way, and not proud of it. He wasn't just glad that he had a good-paying job; he was very specifically glad that he was making more money than his wife.

So you can expect this in the coming decades: some men will react badly and even histrionically when they feel they are losing a competition they have never before had to enter. "A lot of guys don't want you to be that successful," points out Christi Nesmith, the engineer. "They don't want you to be independent." Her insight is borne out by a number of studies showing that when wives outearn husbands, the risk of divorce rises. In the past three decades, the literature on women's earnings has accumulated and it is, like much research, wildly mixed. But a number of studies do suggest that relationships are more likely to see a decline in happiness when women's incomes rise above their husband's. In 2003, researchers in Finland found that marriages where women outearned their husbands were at a higher risk of divorce. In 2009, researchers in Germany confirmed this, publishing a study in which they tested the validity of Gary Becker's theory that marriages do best when one spouse is economically dependent. The Germans found that Becker's theory does hold true when men are the ones earning—these marriages do tend to be stable. But when the roles flip, and the woman outearns the man, the likelihood of divorce becomes "substantially higher."

In the United States, in 2010, sociologist Jay Teachman elaborated on those findings. Like other researchers, he found that initially women's employment stabilizes marriages. This is an important point. A number of studies have found that family stability is *enhanced* when women contribute earnings, for the obvious reason that more affluent families have an easier time paying bills, more money for leisure pursuits, less anxiety. But that may be true only up to a point. Teachman found that problems start once women began to earn more than 60 percent of household income. There may be a tipping point: a level of female earnings that men are happy about, and a point at which they become unnerved. Not surprisingly, the men most bothered are men to whom money, as a marker of success, is most important.

And in 2010, Christin Munsch, a Ph.D. student in sociology at Cornell University, looked at marital cheating. She found something similar to what the German researchers found. Women dependent on their husbands are, generally, faithful, while dependent men are more likely to stray. In general, it's important to remember, cheating was rare. Like that of the Germans, Munsch's study confirmed that the economic dependence of wives does seem to make marriage more stable. But the dependence of husbands had the opposite effect—it blew some of them wide open. In an interview, Munsch allowed that it's irrational for economically dependent men to put their marriages at risk by cheating, but there you are. Life is not always rational. Love, certainly, is not rational. Money definitely is not rational. For some men, successful wives become living reproaches, and they rebel.

There are different explanations for why this happens. Marital therapists who specialize in power dynamics argue that men—who are naturally competitive in the workplace—sometimes feel women are competing with them, when in the women's minds they are not competing at all, but simply trying as hard as they can. "I can think of many, many examples where the woman is just doing something [such as working and earning] that she perceives as for the family, and the man perceives it as competition, or telling him what to do, or some kind of judgment about his competence. That's such a strong part of masculine socialization," says Carmen Knudson-Martin, a therapist who teaches at Loma Linda University and coedited a collection of studies on gender and power. Mira Kirshenbaum, clinical director of the Chestnut Hill Institute, a therapy practice in Boston, points out that there are specific factors that make women's earnings feel threatening to men. The potential for discord is exacerbated, she says, when men and women work in the same field; when one or both are competitive; when the man is insecure; or when the man lacks an outside realm of endeavor in which he feels competent and accomplished. It's also problematic when partners committed to one another before the woman's career took off—or before the man's began to stall—or when one, or both, come from a traditional culture which holds that the man should provide. The greater the number of risk factors present, the more destabilizing women's earnings can be.

Meanwhile, different academic disciplines have their own interpretations. Sociologists tend to attribute these tensions to hundreds of years of cultural expectations. When women outearn men, they argue, both men and women feel so freakish that they bend over backward to restore the old sex roles and create the appearance of conformity. Veronica Tichenor, a sociologist at the State University of New York Institute of Technology, published a study in 2005 showing that women breadwinners often do not accrue the same perks that breadwinning men do—no Barcalounger in front of the television, no sense of entitlement, no extra authority over vacation and spending and where the family lives. Her work suggested that women overcompensate for their new stature: instead of making the most of it, they spend a lot of energy deferring, placating, minimizing their achievements, and transferring authority back to their husbands. Seen this way—the argument goes—gaining income actually makes women lose power.

But economists (and some sociologists) tend to disagree; they look not at the negative influence of cultural expectations but at the positive influence of having money. As such, they offer a more upbeat assessment of why women's earnings sometimes lead to divorce. It's not necessarily that the women's money is poisoning these marriages; rather, money could be enabling women to leave a marriage that is already poisoned. This is known as the "independence effect," and it's sometimes offered as the reason why divorce escalated in the 1970s, when women began working in substantial numbers. Jay Teachman thinks the independence effect probably accounts for why his study showed an elevated risk of divorce when women exceeded the 60 percent mark: women who hated their marriages were finally, blessedly, able to leave them. A stable marriage isn't the same thing as a happy marriage. And in the long run, economists have shown that higher earnings for women translate into more bargaining power, not less. The economist Fran Blau has shown that men began helping more around the house when a critical mass of women began working, and that even husbands of stay-at-home wives do more housework than they used to. A rising tide has lifted all boats. And the Pew Research Center found in 2008 that wives who outearn their husbands do have more decision-making power in the home—"especially over major purchases and household finances"—than men who outearn their wives.

When it comes to marriages that are still adjusting to the Big Flip, I would say that both sociologists and economists carry part of the truth: yes, women's earnings may make some couples feel uncomfortable and stigmatized, but at the same time, earnings give women more power. They allow a woman to leave a marriage that's rotten and give her more confidence and authority.

The Psychology of the Individual

There is another field of research that, I would argue, even more powerfully helps explain the subtle emotional dynamics that can derail marriages like Claudia's. This involves not gender roles or domestic bargaining power, but what the valet Jeeves, in the P. G. Wodehouse series, liked to call "the psychology of the individual." The field of psychology has also made an effort to understand the new competition that affects unions between men and women, and in some ways provides the most satisfying explanation of its effect. Chief among these is a branch of psychology that looks at "social comparison": our all-too-human tendency to compare ourselves to other humans. We are not only a competitive species but a relentlessly and sometimes pointlessly comparative one; we gauge our success by looking around to see how other people are doing. Happiness, for humans, is often relative. We notice how others are faring, and only then do we know how we are faring and whether or not we are happy about it. This instinct will be hard to leave behind, because it has nothing to do with changing social norms and everything to do with stubborn and unconscious truths about human nature. We may believe we are fine with the spectacular success of somebody we are close to, while deep down we are resenting and even trying to thwart it. Spouses up to now have been spared the constant comparison that can happen when both are working and earning, and now some are experiencing it acutely.

One of the pioneers of social comparison is Abraham Tesser, a psychologist at the University of Georgia, now retired, who helped develop a theory that we build our identity by measuring our accomplishments against those of other people. We shore ourselves up through ceaseless little comparisons with others. The people whose performance affects us most, psychologically, are people with whom we identify—a friend, maybe, or a college classmate, or somebody who comes from the same hometown—who is striving in a realm that also matters to us. When both of these criteria are in place—we identify with the person, the person is doing something that we are *also doing*—it can be destabilizing to see that person doing it better. A stranger can win a Nobel Prize and we may feel happy, or just mildly interested, but if a close friend gets a promotion, we feel something more complicated. We feel happy but also oddly bad. This person is like me, we think. So why didn't this happen to me?

Tesser's theory works like this: If my best friend is a violinist and I am a pianist, I don't mind that she's great and I'm mediocre, because we are striving at distinct endeavors. Her success, in fact, reflects well on me, because I am honored to know her and lucky to have her as a friend. But if I'm a violinist and my friend is a better violinist, then I am simultaneously happy for my friend and disappointed in myself. However—and this is important—these things are happening subconsciously, and I may not know it. I may think I'm happy for my prize-winning violin-playing friend even as I'm comparing her performance to my own and feeling incompetent and unhappy and making the occasional passive-aggressive comment. "If you ask people—how do you feel about your friend doing well, they'll say I'm thrilled and delighted," Tesser says. "But if you watch their face, they're not thrilled and delighted."

Tesser did experiments that bore this out. He set up scenarios where friends were set against each other in a competition, and afterward, "if you tell them this other person outperformed you in an area you don't care about, you'll see a pleasant emotion on their face. If you tell them this other person has outperformed them on something that's important [to them], you will see their face register negative affect. It happens quickly, and without awareness. You can't do surveys. You can't ask people. What you can do is watch for signs of either distress or happiness."

While his initial work looked at friendships, Tesser found that the same phenomenon can corrode relationships between family members. Siblings, married partners, even parents and children. To be sure, we take pleasure in the success of loved ones. "It's a source of pride that your wife does well, that your husband does well, that your friend does well," says Tesser. But we want these people to be succeeding at a task that is *not important to us.* When our wife or husband or best friend is doing well in a field where we are also striving, taking joy becomes harder. As Tesser and colleagues noted in one paper in which he looked at romantic pairings: "When couples find themselves part of the same 'team,' but also competing along some dimensions, the potential for complex reactions exists."

"People Are Obsessed with What Other People Make"

In the years since Tesser and others developed the theory of social comparison, people who look at workplace behavior have found that this same phenomenon holds true on the job. We compete with co-workers, and salaries are a natural point of reference. "People are obsessed with what other people make," says Lamar Pierce, a business professor at Washington University in St. Louis who is intrigued by how it destabilizes us to find out somebody is making more than we are. Money has a peculiar effect on the psyche. It is a clear, cold marker for success and a stark, obvious metric for comparison. This is well known to corporations and other employers, who have learned that it can be disastrous for morale when salaries become public, particularly in workplaces where pay is awarded by merit, as opposed to, say, a government grading system or recognized union scale. When people do learn what colleagues make, enormous problems can ensue. Employees who were happy, and felt they were doing well in their jobs, compare themselves to other employees who are being paid more, and feel discontented and resentful. People don't just get angry with management. They get angry at each other. Colleagues view each other as enemies, unfairly favored. Factory floors become unsafe.

And, as with Tesser's experiments, this holds especially true when the other person seems like us. A black employee will be more threatened by the higher salary of another black employee; a woman by the pay of another woman; an immigrant when someone from the same country seems to be doing better. The most salient comparisons are those we make with people with whom we identify. And here's the problem for marriage: now, more than ever before, your spouse does resemble you, and your spouse is likely to be striving for the same thing—a high salary—that you are. This is the inherent problem in marrying someone with the same degree or credential set. And because many companies do work hard to keep salaries private, the salary of your spouse may well be the *only* salary you know. "You live with this person, you know exactly what they make, you know exactly what *you* make, and if at all you feel badly about this, it's accelerated, day in and day out, if you wake up every morning and look at this person," Pierce points out.

This is why Aaron Gouveia of the Good Men Project was obsessively focused on outdoing his wife. Not anybody else. His wife. His wife was the person he wanted to beat. Similarly, in 2011, when National Public Radio profiled a husband and wife who both endured a spell of unemployment, and when the wife was the first to find full-time work, the husband, Brian Barfield, commented of his beloved Jennifer: "Every dollar she earns is one more under my nose that I didn't."

Not only are couples using each other as a point of salary reference; a growing body of research suggests that the comparison is harder on men than it is on women. Measured against the way things used to be, the world at the moment looks better for women—comparatively—than for men. A 2010 paper coauthored by Pamela Tolbert, a professor at Cornell University's School of Industrial and Labor Relations, and Ronit Waismel-Manor, with the School of Behavioral Sciences at Netanya Academic College in Israel, found that wives who earn the same as their husbands are more satisfied with their careers than wives who earn less. Meanwhile, husbands who earn the same as their wives are less satisfied with their careers than those in traditional couples where the man earns more. In both cases, the researchers conclude, "spouses use each other to assess their level of career success." But here's the crucial gender difference: wives feel good when they draw even with their husbands, because this is not something women have achieved much up to now; men feel bad when they are not outperforming their wives, because they are used to thinking this is how it should be. Similarly, in 2011, a psychological study found that young men assigned to read census data enumerating women's academic and economic gains over the past half-century experienced anxiety because they were measuring their own gains and feeling bad about it. Women reading the same data felt better. The women were comparing their performance against that of women before them and feeling elated. Men were comparing themselves against that of women today and feeling depressed. Given all this, it's easy to see how money can introduce destabilizing new dynamics of competition into intimate relationships.

Opt Her Out

For better and worse, Abraham Tesser found, we have evolved means for coping in these situations. Some of the accommodations are benign and helpful, while others can be corrosive. Among the benign adjustments: If I am feeling eaten up by envy about how badly I am doing compared to my friend, one coping mechanism is to cede the field; quit the pursuit. If it bothers me that my friend is better than me at the violin, in order to preserve our friendship (and my own sanity) I might give up music and take up tennis. We can shift our sense of what is important to us and find something else to work hard at. Tesser's research has shown that this is exactly what occurs in successful marriages: as the years go on, spouses avoid the friction of competition by staking out their own terrains of endeavor. They specialize, build niches. Within marriage, one spouse is designated the chef, and the other one becomes the cleaner-upper. In academic couples that work in the same field, husband and wife make a mutual decision that one is the better teacher and one is the better researcher. Spouses find ways to differentiate their talents. One might even move into a new discipline. Tesser has done work with couples and finds those most satisfied with their marriages are those that have managed to divvy things up. Some theorists, looking for an evolutionary basis for these psychic shifts, argue that this may have been what allowed humans to become pair-bonding creatures to begin with. Instead of competing, we divide up fields of labor; and just as Gary Becker argued, we become dependent and complementary.

Moreover, Tesser found that this happens as relationships deepen and grow. Studies done with dating couples found that they haven't yet made these emotional adjustments, and don't yet feel any pleasure in the other person's achievement, either. Thus, the question of who is good at what, particularly in an arena that matters to both, becomes a "kind of romantic battleground early in relationships," Tesser and his colleagues wrote in one study. Thinking about Claudia, the young woman whose husband cheated on her with a coworker, it's notable that her relationship was still in the early, battleground stage.

But here's the problem with money: it's a universal measure of success. Even when partners migrate into different specialties, they might still compare salaries. This leads us to the second method of coping. Instead of separating from the task, if we begin to feel too bad about ourselves, we can separate from the other person. We can go. Leave. Divorce. Seek out a new, less-threatening partner, just as Claudia's husband did. We can choose to pair up with somebody who makes us feel better about who we are and how we are doing, rather than worse.

Or we can invoke option number three. If you can't quit your job and you don't want to leave the marriage, Tesser points out with a laugh, "you can really screw the other person."

This is known as undermining. Among friends, in a psychological experiment, it might involve giving your friend clues in a guessing game that will cause her to provide the wrong answer. In a marriage, it might translate into finding small, insidious ways to make your wife feel bad about herself—or even to impede her success. Even a man who is benefiting from his wife's higher salary might subtly work to prevent her from succeeding too fully. Gary Becker, in *A Treatise on the Family*, acknowledges the irrationality that creeps into economic decision making. Envy, he allows, can cause people to work against their own interests. Siblings can turn on one another and destroy family fortunes because they are jealous. Greed gets sacrificed on the altar of other, even darker emotions. This helps explain why some men retaliate against high-earning partners—why a man might applaud his wife and quietly work to make her life more difficult.

The most extreme example of undermining is for a man to nudge his wife out of the workplace altogether: to make the domestic climate so unpleasant that she departs the field of competition. This is what worries Lamar Pierce, the Washington University professor who has studied the psychological impact of salaries. In recent years Pierce has become especially interested in how salary competition plays out in marriage, and he fears it does not play out well. As a business professor, he is not all that interested in marital happiness—he is interested in labor force productivity. He is concerned that women may be going to such lengths not to outperform husbands that they leave the workplace altogether. "The biggest cost of income comparison in marriage is not what happens when your wife outearns you," Pierce told me in an interview. "It's all of the decisions husbands and wives make to avoid this." His concern arises in part from conversations with female colleagues: one told him that in salary negotiations she made sure to negotiate a number that did not surpass that of her husband to keep peace in the house. "When I talk to couples from outside the United States—particularly Asian colleagues—they say look, you have no idea how big of a problem this is in other countries," Pierce relates. "A lot of my female friends stopped working. It's not okay for them to outearn their husbands, so they just stayed home."

This is an important point to ponder, and it's an underlying motivation that does not often get discussed in the conversation about opting out. When we talk about women who opt out, we assume these are women who choose to do so: either they want to be stay-at-home mothers, or they are so frazzled by trying to balance work and family that they choose family. And some women opt out because even though they would prefer to be working, their wages are so low that it's not possible to find affordable child care that would make it worthwhile for them to take a job.

But some women, Pierce suspects, opt out because they feel pressured by their partners. I think he's right. In one interview, I was talking with a female breadwinner who mused that her own ambitious sister stayed home, unwillingly, at her husband's insistence. "She did it under duress." Pierce is worried that because of this strong-arming, our culture is losing talent. His concern is that if some men do act to neutralize high-achieving spouses so the women won't reflect badly on them, and if women do dial back their careers as a way of placating these men, the American economy will be poorer for it: poorer from the judicial opinions she might have written, from the business she might have started, from the medical discoveries she might have made. It strikes Pierce as not unlike what we have lost by discriminating based on race. "You wonder how many African American physicists there were in the early 20th century"—or would have been—had discrimination not prevented so many from fulfilling their promise. The same goes for religious discrimination. When Jewish applicants were excluded from the Ivy League by quotas, he points out, many Jewish students enrolled in his own institution, which has benefited from their presence and philanthropy. Discrimination has costs not only for the victim but also for the perpetrator.

The problem for women is that they cannot relocate to escape the consequences of competition and retaliation, unless they leave marriage. And when you look at the rising number of single mothers and other unmarried women—when you look at the fact that barely half the adults in America are now married—it's reasonable to ask whether women's desire to escape this kind of spousal undermining may be hurting the marriage rate. If it becomes too difficult in a marriage to handle the pressure from a partner who wants you to ratchet down your own performance, or who subtly refuses to help you, then one solution for a woman is to remove herself from relationships rather than remove herself from her job.

"I Wanted to Continue Being the Breadwinner"

In South Texas, I had coffee at a Barnes & Noble bookstore with Elizabeth Delgado, who at one low point in her life had been a single mother subsisting on welfare. After giving birth to her first child in her late teens, she sensed it would be a bad idea to partner with the father, and didn't marry him, and it took her a while to become self-reliant. But she persevered, graduated from college, and became a high school teacher, working for an educational consulting firm and doing test preparation. She even bought a house. Then she married another teacher, and they had a child together.

Elizabeth wanted to keep working after she had the baby. "I had been the breadwinner in my family for five years, so to me—I wanted to continue being the breadwinner. It was a matter of pride. Going from welfare to being able to help my family, making more than $40,000 a year—it was a source of pride for me." But her husband insisted she stay home. She did, for one year. She hated being away from teaching, in part because she didn't want to fall too far behind him. She, too, felt competitive. She understood that money is a form of control, and it became clear he was controlling; he would call her whenever she went out to meet with a friend or to visit her mother. When she did go back to work, it created tensions: she made more than he did. "He did mention that I was getting more than him—I know it was an issue," she says. "I know it bothered him." He told her she was "too ambitious." They are now divorced, and she is a single mother once more.

The daily diminishment can be both subtle and overt. One professional woman described to me an esteemed colleague: "I've never seen [her husband] accompany her on anything where she's speaking, or getting an award—nothing." Another spoke of a colleague, prominent and highly respected, whose husband "completely devalued her job. He had no idea how recognized or regarded she was." A man could make his wife feel bad about herself by ignoring her accomplishments or by telling her she has gained weight and isn't sexually attractive. He could take up with another woman who makes him feel better about his achievements and makes his wife feel worse about hers. He could become distant and uncooperative. He could refuse to attend office parties or help her advance. He could say niggling little things in public. He could provoke fights the night before she has to leave on a business trip. He could complain when she takes business calls during dinner. He could refuse to move for her career. I talked to a woman who at the beginning of her career worked as a broadcast engineer for the U.S. military. She married another soldier and quickly proved herself the more competent worker. Her husband left the military; even when he was jobless, he refused to move when she got an offer to head up a recruiting office. She quit when he wanted to move back to his hometown; once there, he still couldn't get a job, and she rebuilt her career and dumped him.

For many couples, the currents running back and forth as they attempt to adjust to the Big Flip will be contradictory. Men—like women—can be supportive and empathetic, and, at the same time, they can be discouraging. Ambivalence is an important word to keep in mind. In 2008, Souha Ezzedeen, a professor of human resources management at York University in Canada, published with a colleague a study in which she showed how this emerges in marriage. In the paper, Ezzedeen explores the valuable support many women do receive from husbands. She interviewed 20 executive women, some of whom earned more than their husbands, and found that the majority were wonderfully affirmed by the men they had married. The support they felt most grateful for was listening and being emotionally attentive. These women missed housework help if it wasn't there, but if husbands were providing help around the house and were also being supportive, the aspect the women felt most grateful for was the latter. They appreciated unburdening themselves to an intimate companion willing to buoy their spirits. "He was listening all the time," said one wife, whose husband got her through a period when she was dealing with a hostile boss. "And I mean he was a shoulder to cry on. I just can't imagine having gotten where I was without him."

But several women reported that their husbands were both supportive and undermining. These women said that "their husbands embarrassed them in public by mentioning their absence from home and that their husbands refused to accompany them to work-related functions." They said their husbands were aggravated when they had to travel; one said her husband was proud of her, but considered her career and income to be secondary to his. Ezzedeen concluded that "supportive and undermining behaviors are not opposites but independent behaviors that can coexist." For men who value money, it's possible to like the money your wife is earning and to hate it. It's possible to feel happy and competitive. It's possible to send all sorts of mixed messages. "He loved the gold credit card," one New England businesswoman I talked to reflected. She had built a thriving seafood-packing business, surpassing—greatly to her surprise—the business achievements of her husband. "And he resented me for it."

Cars Will Be Totaled

For women, being the target of ambivalence will be chaotic and confusing. It's a hard way to live, never knowing whether you're to be praised or punished. I spent several hours one morning with 52-year-old Daphne Adams. Gray-braided and low-key, Daphne was wearing reading glasses and a comfy black unitard as she lounged in the spa and nail salon she runs in a rambling commercial building on the outskirts of a midwestern rust-belt city. The waiting area provided ample evidence of her resourcefulness and work ethic. In addition to lotions and nail polishes, cabinets at the front offered scented bath salts she makes herself. There were tiny drying fans everywhere, and a popcorn maker, and a soda machine, and all manner of beauty products including dyes for the "hair down there," by a company called Betty Beauty Inc. Daphne told me the story of a client who dyed her pubic hair some bright blazing color, and met her husband at the door wearing nothing but a matching feather boa. The next time the woman came into the salon, she reported that the resulting sex had been so successful that her husband bought her a new car. Proof that the wealth-beauty trade-off lives on!

Domestic life hadn't gone so well for Daphne, who is capable of buying a car on her own. In addition to her undergraduate and master's degrees in business administration, she is a licensed respiratory therapist, a professional guardian, a licensed nursing home administrator, and a notary public. She recently got licensed as a manicurist and esthetician and natural hair colorist, for good measure. Daphne has been a breadwinner most of her adult life. When she was younger, she married a man she'd known in college, but discovered that even when he told her he was working, he wasn't. She did what she thinks too many African American women do: she carried him. She agrees with those academics who argue that black women have worked hard, maybe too hard, to protect black men from the discrimination and negativity they encounter; that despite being subject to a double dose of discrimination themselves, black women have sought to make up for the status the world took away from their men. "It's the mothering in us," Daphne said. "Wanting to make everything right. Trying to make things nice and comfortable for the man. It's like—we fix it. We need to fix things. I think that's pretty much been our downfall." She got out of that relationship and supported her boys on her own.

Ten years ago, Daphne began dating a man she met online. He had gone to the same magnet high school she did. He seemed to be a person of integrity and she felt he would be a good role model for her sons. But he, too, had an underemployment problem, so she brought him into her business. At the time, she was working as a guardian for sick and elderly people, taking cases from probate court. She paid him a salary. He lived with her and contributed to the expenses. She worked hard not to exert too much authority at home. "I was tired of always being in charge," she said. "When we were working together, I was the primary decision maker, but when I got home, it was: okay, you make the decisions and I want to just sit back and follow." But he was reluctant even to pick which restaurant they would go to. Then he stopped contributing to the expenses. Eventually, guardianship got too stressful—she was always working—so she handed her cases over to him and started the spa.

The problem was, he hadn't been able to make a go of the guardianship business. She was obliged to pick up the house note, the car note, everything. He told her he was depressed. Then he took her Cadillac—her company car—and came home without it. He told her it was in a ditch, and the damage wasn't too bad. She went to find it and learned that he had hit another car—fortunately there was no one in it—flipped it, and smashed it up pretty thoroughly. And now he was refusing to speak to her. "He's been going around the house not saying anything," Daphne marveled. "This morning I had to ask: What have I done to you recently to make you so hostile?"

It turned out that her boyfriend's feelings were hurt because she had stayed out all night hosting a bridal spa-party that was supposed to involve 45 clients but ended up attracting more like 60. She figured she couldn't turn away the business, not in a recession, so she worked all night and the masseuses and manicurists stayed and she earned enough to pay the monthly mortgage payment. "When the party ended at five, I climbed up into the massage chair to get some sleep." He was mad at her because she didn't call. "What I'm trying to do and accomplish," she concluded, "has created quite a bit of animosity with my companion. I've noticed that competitiveness for a long time."

"Baby, You Google": Some Men Will Just Give Up

Of course, there is another way to escape the ego assault of self-comparison: give up altogether. In the face of rising female earning power, some men will choose capitulation. Men will compare themselves to women and think: Okay, if she's doing so well, then there's nothing left for me to do, really. Think about those growing numbers of prime-age men who are no longer working or looking for work. A significant number live with a spouse. Some of these men, rather than forcing wives out of the workplace, may be leaving it themselves. Ceding the field. It's over, babe: You win.

Big mistake. If a woman feels a man has given up—if she feels he's leaving everything to her—this creates yet another opportunity for disaster. Look back at Daphne Adams and how she wanted her non-contributing partner to make some decision, any decision, when they were at home. Sociologists might argue that this has to do with gender roles and that she was trying to shore up his manhood or conform to stereotypes, but it seems plausible that she was just trying to restore some equilibrium: to level their relationship. She wanted to respect him. There is something in a woman that does not enjoy looking down on her partner. I talked to women who felt the men in their lives were trying less hard specifically *because* they, the women, were striving. "It's like: She's got this covered, so I don't need to do anything," is how one dissatisfied wife put it. I talked to women, including young ones, who thought men were rudderless because they no longer felt performance pressure. These men had been raised to think of themselves as providers; since women were capable of doing that on their own, men had become demoralized. So they had quit.

Women hate this. People want relationships that are level. They want some sort of equality, some sort of matching. A social comparison study published in 2008 confirmed Tesser's findings that we can feel disturbed by "upward comparison"—we can feel personally diminished when our spouse is better at something, particularly when it's important to us, even if the spouse's success makes us feel good about our partnership. But the 2008 study also showed that what we really don't like are downward comparisons. If anything, we may dislike that more. Those of us who are not intent on dominating our spouses—and most of us aren't, male or female—don't actually enjoy it when our spouse is underperforming in an important arena. It may be an ego boost, briefly, to be a better cook or cleaner or earner than your partner, but in the long run it can mean you have to do all the cooking and cleaning and earning.

Elena Diaz, a whip-smart 22-year-old who works at a dialysis clinic in Harlingen, Texas, stood out among the women I spoke to who felt distressed by nonperforming partners. The first time we talked, her husband, she said, was teetering on the brink of joblessness. The two had met in college, where at the outset he seemed more studious than Elena. They had a child together, and, somewhat to her surprise, becoming a mother made her more disciplined and academic. Hispanic women in South Texas have discovered an intriguing solution to the work-family balance problem: many women have children young and are able to draw on their extended families—mothers, grandmothers, aunts—to watch the children. Women get childbearing out of the way early and escape having to take a wage hit in mid-career. Yet even as Elena began to apply herself, her husband began to lose his own focus. He barely managed to graduate, she says, and did so only because she signed him up for classes and sat him down and made him study. After college, he took a job as a salesman. By the time Elena and I met in person, he had already lost that job for nonperformance.

"I'm kind of losing hope in men; it's like picking the least juvenile man," said Elena, crossing herself before she began her breakfast taco. Tiny, with long brown hair, a peach sweater, and eyeliner that curled up at the edges, she reflected that the men she knew had been raised by fathers who were providers first and foremost. The culture had changed so rapidly, and women had surpassed them so quickly, that men were unable to imagine a new mission. They had lost their sense of adult purpose. So they had stopped being adults. "My husband and his friends, they just love being bachelors—they love to hang around and smoke pot and play videogames. I really think it's a subconscious fear of failure."

Elena and her husband now had two children together. Marrying him, she now saw, had been a mistake. Not long before we met, she called him from work to make sure he followed up on some job leads, and as she rattled off their conversation, it resembled the kind of doomed exchange a mother might have with a super-recalcitrant teenager. "I'm in the office, and I said, 'What are you doing?'" she related. "He says, 'Walking the dog.' I'm like, 'Okay, so how did everything go today?' and he's like 'Good, good.' And I'm like, 'Okay, what did Olive Garden say?' He said, 'They're going to call me back.' And I said, 'Did *you* call them?' and he said, 'They're going to call me back.' I said, 'That's not very professional. What happened with UPS?' He said, 'I don't really think I'm going to go with UPS. I'm going to shoot for FedEx.' I said, 'It's not about what you prefer—it's about what you can get. I made it clear in the morning that you have to do both.' He said, 'I don't know where UPS is at.' I said, 'Baby, you Google. Dude, you go online, and Google it and get an address.'"

The conversation went on in the same vein; he assured her he had applied online to FedEx; when she asked for his password and login, he made up some words and numbers and she plugged them in and couldn't log in and that's when she knew that he hadn't applied to anything. "He started laughing, and said, 'I'm going to do it right now, babe.'"

"He didn't do anything all day long—not even his laundry," she said. "I hold his hand through life. It's pretty exhausting." She saw him as a liability rather than an asset. "I'm paying the $800 rent; his car, which is $200, insurance, light, Internet, gas," she enumerated. When she had threatened him with separation, he assured her he was happy. "I'm like, 'Of course you're happy! I do everything!'" So she kicked him out.

Still, she felt responsible for his welfare. She was thinking she should find him a psychologist. "I don't even know if it's a psychologist thing. He needs a personality transplant. I don't know. I feel bad for him. If I leave him, his life is going to totally suck."

Elena also worried about her son growing up without a male role model. She was trapped in an environment where it was going to be hard to find a partner who matched her. But she didn't want to leave the area. She likes having family nearby, and friends, and beaches. When we finished breakfast, I wondered what the future held for her. "Our mothers were pushing us so hard to get educated; many of them had bad experiences with men," she reflected. "And then the men on the other hand can't grow a pair. They're just taking longer—the women are doing it and the men aren't. They think they don't have to. Then by the time they're 27, they say, 'I'm single, nobody wants to date me, I still make $8 an hour. Maybe I should go back to college!'"

"I Get Up Early and Make Coffee"

It's important to point out here that for many—probably the majority—of men who feel unsettled by women's higher earnings, the primary emotion aroused isn't envy or resentment or anger or competition or deflation or paralysis. It's guilt. Most men don't resent women earners, or retaliate, or quit trying. What men do, though, is continue to place intense pressure on themselves to earn. Men still think of breadwinning as an obligation. Men feel they should contribute as much as or more than women do, and blame themselves when they can't. This, for men, is probably the greatest reason they struggle with women's earnings. Men have changed their minds about what's okay for women, but not about what's okay for men. If there is a double standard, it's that men are easier on women, in terms of expectations for earnings, than they are on themselves.

Sociologists Ilana Demantas and Kristen Myers illuminated this mind-set when they interviewed a group of men who had been laid off during the Great Recession. Many were being supported by wives or girlfriends. These men were full of appreciation for the women they lived with. They understood how valuable it is to have a partner who loves you and will stand by you in a crisis. "It's a blessing that my wife works and makes good money," one interviewee told the researchers, who presented their findings at a conference in 2011. "If I was living on my own, I would be in serious trouble." To show their gratitude, these men were helping in any way possible. "I pick up the slack around the house more because I feel like it is the only way to repay my duties," said one. Another said, "I get up early and make coffee every day for Colleen before she goes to work. I don't even drink coffee, but I make it for her. She gets to sleep a little longer."

Reflecting on these findings, the study authors ventured that men have come to a psychological crossroads. The economic crisis presented them with "a unique space" in which to reconsider everything they believed about women and earning up to now. We have come a long way since the 1930s: during the Depression, women who found ways to support their families were resented not only by the culture but also by the very people they were supporting. Boys who took jobs to help out were accorded the head place at the dinner table, while mothers who did the same were remembered bitterly by their own offspring. Not any longer. "Our respondents valued women's work as essential to the survival of their family," they noted. "Instead of expressing resentment toward the women upon whom they relied, these men expressed gratitude and respect for women's paid work."

But the men in the study still felt they should be contributing. They were deeply shaken by their inability to provide, and sometimes wept when they were talking to her. In that sense—men's expectations for themselves—we do not seem to have come so far. "You kind of feel almost worthless," one man told the interviewers. Another commented, "It makes you, or at least it did me, feel like less of a man."

The truth is, if men are troubled by women's higher earnings, often it's only because men worry they have fallen short. Some fear their wives will leave them. If they aren't bringing in income, what are they bringing?

This is one reason why women bend over backward to give authority back at home. For women, trying to find a way to help a partner feel better—and help him expand the definition of providing—is a more common challenge than being actively undermined. It was a challenge for Jennifer Hoppenrath, in her mid-thirties, who works as an "information architect," designing user interfaces for everything from dishwashers to fighter jets. She enjoys her work and feels lucky to be in a field that's thriving. "My field is going so good: companies were like, oh, come work for us," reported Jennifer, who was getting offers even as her husband lost his job as an account manager in sales during the economic downturn. Newborn baby in tow, they moved from Seattle to Austin when her company relocated her. When I interviewed her, Jennifer reported that her husband was being endlessly helpful—he got up with the baby in the middle of the night, he oversaw the cross-country move. Even so, he worried that he wasn't of enough use to her.

"I remind him that he does provide," she said. "He does all these things. We moved across the country— Oh my gosh, he did all the packing. It's just amazing the amount of work he did. He really works full-time. He often gets less sleep than I do. I'm like—you *are* working. Just because you're not contributing financially." She also felt it was hard for him to see her field flourishing as his was tanking. He told her: "I'm willing to take a massive cut in pay and can't seem to get those jobs—and here you are, you've got people throwing offers at you." It wasn't that he was envious or resentful, she said. "I think he does feel like: 'Hey, I just had a child, and should be providing.'"

Six

Let Go, and Lexapro

Women Can Be Competitive, Too

This is probably a good place to acknowledge that the old bargain was not always so advantageous for men. Breadwinning is hard and often thankless and unpleasant, and it's not necessarily a privilege. Women have been discriminated against in the workplace—no question—but it seems fair to say that women up to now often have been freer than men to enjoy time with children and, if they want to, the joys of a job. Women, or many women, have had the luxury of choice. Even now, about half of men say their wives can do what they want: work, not work, work part-time, it's okay with them, because they feel earning is their responsibility. It also seems reasonable to ask whether bread-winning does bestow more authority upon men, and if so, what that authority consists of. What did it ever consist of? When I was growing up in the 1960s and 1970s in a Virginia railroad city on the border of Appalachia, most fathers I knew were small businessmen and lawyers, and most mothers were housewives. In retrospect I'd say the women had no problem spending their husbands' money—occasionally they hid an extravagant purchase under the bed—and the men had no more authority than the women. Less, probably, because they were so rarely there. The mother of a friend of mine was known as "the General." The fact that she earned no money did not prevent her from being the supreme ruler of the family unit.

The evidence is mounting that men are increasingly on board with the changes in women's earnings. Some may resent women who supplant them as providers, but most do not. To the contrary, men are grateful and they are trying hard to make their gratitude apparent. So expect this: in a breadwomen's world, women will experience their own share of resentment, competitive feelings, and ambivalent emotions. In the short term, it may be women who are most unsettled by the new world order. Women will resist, postpone, and deny the idea that they have become the new providers. Women will envy husbands who are at home, cooking and watching the children. Women will hoard authority. They will not be as nice about all this, perhaps, as they should be. They will complain that men can't do anything correctly. They will text too many domestic reminders and to-do lists. At the end of the workday, they will walk through the door and come face-to-face with men eager for conversation. They will ask men to back off and give them space. They will enjoy more bargaining power in their marriages, but won't always enjoy the actual bargaining process. They will struggle to preserve their own sexual attraction to men even as they strive to remain feminine and pleasing. They will feel taken aback by partners who seem overdomesticated. They will lie about their accomplishments to men they are interested in dating. They will cling to the hope that all this is temporary. They will feel, in their heart of hearts, that something is wrong. The fact is, men have made a lot of progress; the question is whether women have come as far.

Women, like men, have lately experienced an accelerated version of the domestic upheaval caused by their own rising fortunes. As the Great Recession sped the transformation of the American economy, many wives abruptly were forced to leave their old lives behind, taking jobs to replace the ones their husbands lost. Overnight, women abandoned comfortable roles as stay-at-home wives and secondary earners, catapulted into a reality that for many will be permanent. They found themselves teleported, you could almost say, into the life women will be living from here on out. The degree of recalibration this required could be seen—among many other places—in an airy room overlooking the St. Clair River, in Port Huron, Michigan, which I visited in the late summer of 2010. One of the mightiest engines of the industrial age, Michigan has been suffering the loss of high-wage factory jobs for a decade. In 2009, the unemployment rate in Port Huron—an industrial city northeast of Detroit—peaked around 25 percent. By 2010, it was still in the low 20s. Driving into town, I saw on one building an advertisement announcing cut-rate crematorium prices for "death care in changing times." Factories were shuttered, and the only new enterprise anyone could think of was a business that demolished foreclosed homes.

The airy room was a jobs bank, operated by a statewide entity called "Michigan Works!" Located on the sixth floor of a municipal building at the edge of the river, the room had a dozen or so computer terminals and a sweeping view of Sarnia, Ontario, across the water. The day I visited, eight or ten men were seated at the terminals. The men were unemployed. To qualify for benefits they had to apply for new jobs, and to apply for jobs they had to draw up résumés, and to draw up résumés, they had to formulate objectives, thinking up key words describing a job they would be willing to take. To do that, many had to come to terms with the fact that they did not know how to navigate the nuances of computer programs. They were stymied by having to think up a word narrow enough to describe an actual job, but broad enough to ensure that good jobs didn't get ruled out.

"The objective is the hardest part," reflected Tammy Schmitt, one of several Michigan Works employees stationed in the room to help men master the new method of applying for work. In much of industrial America, the old method worked like this: if you were male and your father worked at a plant, the day after you graduated from high school your dad took you to the plant, and you stayed there until you retired. There was no computer, no jobs center, no sending off résumés into the void of the digital hiring universe. Nor was there an expectation that women also would be applying. "In the 1950s and 1960s, when people were getting these jobs, women stayed home," said one supervisor at the jobs bank. "I grew up in suburban Detroit, where half the parents worked for GM and Chrysler. Most of the women stayed home, even in blue-collar families."

What you could see in this room were men stunned by the loss of those industrial and heavy labor jobs, which they often hated but which gave their lives meaning and forged their adult identities. Now they were being escorted into the knowledge economy only to find that women had traveled there before them and become familiar with the landscape and competent at the tasks. "The men struggle more than the women with the computers," Tammy observed, surveying the room for anybody who was floundering. It wasn't that the men were afraid of machines. To the contrary, most were skilled machinists. They could fix anything, but were unaccustomed to using a keyboard and a mouse. "If it was considered more of a tool, it would seem more masculine," Tammy reflected. She bent to help a man with tattooed hands and a skinny ponytail that was braided in a curious way, not exactly braided but differentiated with elastic hair ties. As she watched, the man with the tattooed hands formulated his objectives, typing in "welding" and "machine work" and "factory work."

At another terminal, a young man was assisted by a woman who appeared to be his mother, or an aunt. He was so hesitant and took so long that the woman shoved him out of the way and began typing for him. "All right—this is where we go," she said, typing in his skills. "Concrete. Bridgework." The young man was wearing a T-shirt that said, "Safety. It's a team effort!"

At another terminal, a man also had brought a woman along to help him. Often, the men came to the jobs bank flanked by women, whom they jokingly referred to as "my secretary" or "my moral support." This one looked to be a wife or girlfriend. She did not look very morally supportive. "That is exactly what I was showing you!" she snapped. Then she, too, seized the keyboard and started typing. "Dan's Excavating," she said, typing in the name of his last employer. She had reading glasses hanging from a chain, and they swayed from the force of her irritation. They had come in to update his file, and when they rose to leave, she declined to be interviewed. "It's for him," the woman said with some disgust. "Not for me."

Nearby, a man was typing his name. His wife had assisted him on an earlier visit, and he was having a hard time coping alone. "I don't understand what's going on here! My wife put it in here, and—" said the man, who was exasperated. The exasperated man was wearing jeans, a beige polo shirt, and glasses. He had short gray hair. "Capital C-H-A-U," he said, then paused, having gotten ahead of the program.

At another terminal, a man was typing, slowly, with the index finger of his left hand.

Tammy Schmitt circulated, offering help and encouragement. Reading glasses perched on top of her short blond hair, Tammy was wearing a black and white patterned dress she found at Target that looked as sleek and professional as anything at Ann Taylor. Like every woman staffing the room that day, she understood all too well what the men were going through, and what their wives and girlfriends were also likely feeling. Her own husband, Stephan, had worked in sales for a major industrial machine manufacturer, but lost his job when the company closed its regional branch. Before that, Tammy had been the secondary earner in her marriage. Now she was supporting them both on a salary considerably less than Stephan's had been. For Tammy, the shift brought new stresses and intensified others. She had always been the voice of fiscal reason, the marital partner who nixed exorbitant purchases. Now her role as naysayer was amplified, and she worried about foreclosure. She was not alone in her anxieties. Virtually all the staffers in the computer room that day were women, and all knew what it was like to support a laid-off husband. Not far from Tammy was Nancy Martin, whose husband had lost a job in the lumber industry when the housing market collapsed. For years, Nancy had enjoyed poring over blueprints and attending parties to celebrate the opening of vacation home developments he had been involved in building; now she had taken a second, weekend job at Home Depot to pay his health insurance. Not far from Nancy was Shelley Lukasak, whose husband also worked in the machining field. Like every woman I spoke with, Shelley remembered the exact date her husband got the bad news: April 29, 2009. Up to then, she had worked ten or fifteen hours a week at Gymboree, a schedule that enabled her to be a stay-at-home mom for their children. When he was thrown out of work, she went to work full-time at the jobs bank. Having him at home did not go well. She ate a lot of burned dinners and resented the fact that she wasn't the one cooking. "It was very stressful for both of us," she said. "My control wasn't there." Listening to her, another staffer remarked that when her brother-in-law lost his job, her sister had to go on antidepressants.

"I told my sister: Let go, and Lexapro," the coworker remarked. "It's not 'Let go, and let God' anymore. She got on the Lexapro and it seemed to be better."

"You have to get on something," Shelley reflected. Her husband had been recalled to his old position, which was a good thing but still didn't mean they could go back to their former arrangement. The economy was too uncertain, so Shelley had kept her full-time hours. It wasn't ideal. Still, it was better now than it was when her husband was home and she wasn't.

"I was jealous," she said, arms crossed, looking out at the computer room. "He had my life. And I wanted it back."

Newsflash: Men ARE Doing Housework.
Women Stunned, Reeling.

Shelley's comments summarized the mind-set of many women: I'm not sure this new life is the life I wanted. As new economic changes take hold, men—despite the guilt and anxiety they are feeling—will experience a curious sense of psychic enlargement, while women will feel their options have shrunk and constricted. Women outearning their husbands will feel territorial and more than a little bitter. And laid-off men will not be the only men staying home: like their wives, these men are part of a larger and more long-lasting movement. A study presented by sociologist Karen Kramer at the 2011 Population Association of America conference found that in the United States— as elsewhere—there has been a steady increase in men staying home not because they have to, but because they want to: because they think it might be nice to have the life women have enjoyed. After every recession, Kramer and her coauthor found, there is a permanent upward blip in the ranks of stay-at-home fathers, whose numbers have doubled in three decades, rising from 280,000 in the late 1970s to more than half a million now. Stay-at-home dads made up 1.7 percent of the population of married fathers in 1976–1979, and 3.3 percent in 2000–2008. And this is a conservative estimate, looking only at men with at least one child under 18 who have no earnings at all and whose wife works full-time. Men relegated to the home discover they like it. In coming years, women will come to terms with the fact that men have invaded their space and are thriving in it.

"Husband have envied their wives, absolutely," reflected Linas Orentas, a downsized auto industry program manager who agreed to be interviewed when he came into a different, Detroit-area jobs bank. Orentas, a precise man who was wearing a neat button-down shirt and slacks, articulated what has long been men's own work-life challenge. "You want to spend more time with your kids, but you don't want to be seen spending so much time that it looks like you don't have a work ethic." For him, work-life balance had become simpler, because what it consisted of now was life. "I'm at home, washing, cleaning, cooking, doing all of those duties I've always enjoyed, frankly," he confided. "Our kids' favorite day of the week was always Sunday morning, when Dad made pancakes. Now I say I got promoted from one day a week to seven." Like many men I talked to, he found housework easy; his only challenge was that he tended to read the directions on the laundry detergent bottle way too carefully, approaching it as a task that needed less to be rid of than mastered.

Brad Speck, an affable assistant director at a jobs bank in Livonia outside Detroit, was familiar with this emotional journey, having traveled it himself. When he was younger, he worked in a factory making the wooden shelves on which Beanie Babies are displayed. It was repetitive, meaningless work, and he couldn't stand it. When he lost his job in the 1990s, he found himself the hands-on parent for his two young children. The first day, he realized he did not know how to diaper a baby. He had not changed a diaper on their older child and apologized to his wife for not having helped her. As time went on, he said, "I made supper, I did all those things that were foreign to me. I started baking—I can make cinnamon rolls like nobody's business." Being laid off changed his priorities. He got an offer to operate a pizza franchise, but felt the hours would be too demanding and wanted to continue attending his children's sports games. So he opted for the jobs bank and a more manageable, family-friendly career in human resources—a female sector. Other men, he said, will come to the same place. His prediction came true faster than he might have expected. As the recession eased slightly, men's employment picked up as men began to infiltrate female domains like nursing and teaching.

Spending time in recession-ravaged, permanently recalibrated Michigan, I also had to wonder whether some men were holding out from taking new employment because they were savoring the forbidden pleasure of being home. The day after I met Tammy Schmitt in the Port Huron jobs bank, I visited their home to talk to her husband, Stephan, who seemed to be giving free rein to his inner househusband. At 2:45 P.M. he had the ingredients for country-fried chicken assembled. Genial, extroverted, he is a mechanical engineer by training and temperament, and it pleased him to approach cooking with the foresight and attention to detail that he brought to sales proposals for industrial machinery. To the left of the cooktop he had set up a draining station on which the chicken could rest after cooking. The Crisco was out and on the counter, and so was a bowl in which he was thawing boneless skinless chicken breasts—not the best cut for fried chicken, but he wanted to use up what they had in the freezer.

"I'm so much unstressed," Stephan told me, bustling around the kitchen island of the Dutch colonial whose yard—neatly cut, bordered with well-tended perennials—also showed the results of his zeal. He had lost his company car, but hardly missed it; there was a motorcycle in the garage that was more fun to ride. "I never was before so healthy and happy." Far from resenting Tammy for being the breadwinner, he said he fantasized about Tammy taking a second job so she could support them. He was kidding, but only sort of. What he wanted was to win the lottery. He was sure a new job would come along soon—he had a couple of prospects—so he considered this period an interlude. Every day, when Tammy came home, they would take their yellow lab, But-kus, for a walk, then Tammy would sit at the island and drink a glass of wine while Stephan made them supper. A native of Germany, he had been in the United States for more than a decade, working in sales to automotive companies. He and Tammy met in St. Louis, and moved here when his division was transferred. The work was high-pressure and he did not miss it. If Tammy could support them, he could devote himself to what had become his true calling: the culinary arts.

"If I would not have started my passion for cooking," the recession would have been much more debilitating, he said. He had even started pulling together his own cookbook in a loose-leaf binder. On one side was a folder in which he kept recipes he wanted to try, including a baguette recipe from Julia Child, a tricolor farfalle with creamy mush-room sauce, and a Tuscan-style Porterhouse steak. He found recipes by watching cooking channels or searching the Internet. If he tried it and it was good, he'd put it on the other side for permanent inclusion. Bacon-Dumpling Soup made the cut; so did Kansas City Sweet and Smoky Ribs. "I'm going to end up with a library of dishes which I feel are signature dishes, which would be worthy potentially to be served in my own restaurant," said Stephan. "Some people have a fantasy league in football. I'm thinking about my own restaurant."

So in this household, Tammy Schmitt at the end of her own workday was presented with the unexpected challenge of a husband who seemed, in some ways, slightly too well adjusted to being home. Stephan's cooking takes some fortitude to face on a regular basis. She is a small woman, who stays in shape by power walking—having re-cently undergone radiation treatment for breast cancer, she was pre-paring to participate in a 60-mile walkathon for the Susan G. Komen Foundation—and "it's hard having a heavy meal every night." She also found it disconcerting having Stephan home all the time, much as she loves him. When he was working and traveling, Tammy got used to having evenings to herself where she could curl up and watch *Grey's Anatomy* and eat nachos for dinner. Now Stephan was there, always there, eager to talk when she walked through the door. At the end of the day, she said, "I have to tell him, whoa, dude, back off."

Women Will Have to Learn to Appreciate New Qualities in Men

As women become primary earners, some will be unnerved when they walk through the door and find men eager to serve them. For all the noise over the years about men's duty to do housework, men now may be embracing domesticity more readily than women embrace the vision of them dusting and mopping. In the past year or so there has been a startling revision among academics who study the housework question. Until recently the notion was popular, and widely accepted, that when women earn more than men do, men do less housework, and women do more, as both genders try to conceal the fact that they are not conforming to the roles society has established. The best-known articulation of this was Arlie Hochschild's 1989 book, *The Second Shift*, whose title came to serve as shorthand for the idea that women, when working and even outearning their husbands, are burdened unduly with household labor. In the book, she also suggests that men who earn less than their wives are the least inclined to pitch in with housework. Other studies pointed toward the same idea, and the women-who-earn-more-do-more thesis was born. It came to be known as "gender-deviance neutralization": couples who are deviating from expected behavior find ways to compensate and restore the old balance of power.

But that idea has been called into question. In 2011, Oriel Sullivan, a sociologist at Oxford University, published a careful analysis of the by now vast array of scholarship on men's housework contributions versus women's. Her findings challenge the idea that couples double down on gender conformity when women earn more than men. Sullivan shows that findings in some earlier studies were based on a tiny subset of families; that the data may have been misinterpreted; that everybody glommed on to the theory in part because it was delicious and felt right. What the newer scholarship is finding is that men are doing more housework than they once did; that we may not be at parity yet, but we are getting there; and that working-class men are in the forefront. In part this is because in upper-income households where both spouses work, help can be purchased. In lower-income ones it can't. Somebody's got to do it. And men are stepping up. In short, Sullivan says, there has been a "clear adaptation over time by men to their wives' changing employment situations."

In an accompanying essay, the distinguished sociologist Paula England examines why the gender-deviance idea spread despite its shaky foundations, and graciously takes some of the responsibility. She also says that Hochschild's book, while vividly and accurately evoking couples' very real and often miserable tensions over housework in the 1980s, "fostered a basic misconception" by conveying the idea that women have two shifts but men just have one. Recent U.S. data, England points out, show that "husbands average slightly more" total work per week, when you add in paid and unpaid work. To be sure, this is not the case in all families: The second shift is worst for mothers of preschool children who are employed full-time. But men have a second shift, too. Over time, she argues, the "big picture" is the long-term rise in women's working; the fact that women's own housework hours have diminished; and that men's have risen.

And men still bear the brunt of breadwinning expectations. Another 2011 study, conducted by Paula England, Liana Sayer, and two colleagues, found that when men lose their jobs, wives and husbands alike become more likely to leave the marriage: "Men's breadwinning is still so culturally mandated that when it is absent, both men and women are more likely to find that the marital partnership does not deserve to continue." Women want men to help with housework—no question—and are happier in relationships when men do. But for now, they also expect men to earn. For now, housework parity is what many women want from men—not full conversion.

Once upon a time, men with a domestic side felt they had to hide it; there is a hilarious scene in Susan Faludi's 1991 book, *Backlash*, where she is interviewing a noted antifeminist philosophy professor at his home, and he is desperately trying to conceal the fact that he has been cooking with his son. No longer: while reporting this book, I was talking to a labor economist who mentioned that he and his wife had a toddler, and "and if either of us stayed home, it would be me." When I asked why, he said it was because his wife liked office culture, whereas he was happy messing around the home. Given that more and more men are unashamed to say this, the question becomes: How appreciative are women, really, for the help men are providing? How appreciative should they be?

"I Was Looking for Sort of an Equal Partner"

The questions are surprisingly hard to resolve. For former stay-at-home mothers, it can feel threatening when men invade their domain and prevail. But for women who embrace a professional identity, it's not always easy, either. Many women have worked so hard to escape what they see as a constricting housewife's role that it's disconcerting to see a male partner embrace those same duties, particularly when this happens suddenly. It can be unsettling to find that the hard-charging executive you were initially attracted to has become—well, different. Hard-charging, still, but in a new arena. On one trip to Michigan, I talked to a Detroit area executive, Deborah Wahl Meyer, who was still a little bemused by her husband's transformation. I made contact with her through a networking group called Inforum; when the director asked a group of women if anybody would be willing to talk about outearning their husbands, most of the women at the table with her were reluctant, Deborah reported, for fear of bruising their husbands' egos and airing marital laundry. But Deborah was willing, because she thinks the changes are good even if they aren't easy.

An ambitious executive whose career has taken her all over the world, Deborah was never interested in being a stay-at-home spouse—nor in having one, either. "What I was looking for was a partner who's engaging with me at the same level," she said—a man whose executive metabolism was as high as hers is. When she met her husband, they both had high-level careers in Southern California. It was easy to maintain dual fast-track jobs as long as they were childless, but when they had a son, and her husband's career hit a rough patch during the bursting of the dot-com bubble, their easy egalitarianism "began to unravel." Deborah became the leading spouse and he became the trailing one. She was offered a high-level position at Chrysler—a move significant enough to win her a mention in the *Wall Street Journal* and one of those pen-and-ink portraits—and they relocated so she could take it. She eventually moved on to a top role at a housing development company. Meanwhile, her husband was still trying to penetrate the Michigan job market, so he was caring for their son. And cooking. Definitely cooking.

"For both of us, it's not really what we are looking for, and that provides a lot of tension; I was looking for sort of an equal partner," said Deborah—who, like Tammy Schmitt, was a little bewildered by the cornucopia of cooked offerings bestowed upon her every evening. "My husband is an amazing chef; he is great and he cooks me dinner and it's so wonderful and generous," she said. She wasn't ungrateful, but she was reeling a bit from seeing her galloping gourmet succeeding at domestic tasks she had never mastered. "He's great at keeping order, good at discipline and routine for my son, he is far better at that than I would ever be. I don't enjoy doing it," she reflected. It was not an easy transition for either of them; they both felt resentment at times, she said, but were making an effort to talk about how the terms of their implicit marital contract had changed.

To a certain extent she was relaxing into her role. And beginning to understand the benefits of the old-fashioned division of labor. When she got home at end of a long day, her husband had the chores taken care of, and she did not feel the need to redo them. "I feel a lot more able to sit and relax when I come home—I think, I was working all day, I deserve to hang out and read my magazine. I don't expect to be waited on. I'll do my part, but if I don't feel like getting up and doing the dishes, I'm not going to do it."

Our initial interview took place over the telephone. When I met Deborah in person several months later, she seemed more acclimated to her new lifestyle. It was winter when we met for early-morning coffee; she was cheerful and rested, wearing a casual-Friday outfit of jeans and an elegant tailored jacket. The night before, she had come home and there was a gorgeous fire going, and music on, and her son was peacefully reading, and dinner was ready. It was the kind of scene a working girl could get used to. "His culinary skills," she said, "have reached new heights."

"You Just Spent a Whole Bunch of My Money Without Telling Me": Women Will Experience Secret Spasms of Feeling More Entitled to Their Earnings Than Their Spouse Is

But just as women begin to feel that maybe it is okay to luxuriate a little bit when they get home from work, the question arises: How much luxuriating is fair? Women have long argued that men were wrong to claim the special chair in front of the television, wrong to think their paycheck bought them out of sorting socks. How much leisure and authority are female breadwinners entitled to? What privileges, exactly, *does* money buy? In the coming years, women will struggle to decide what rewards, if any, derive from their earnings. Women will wonder whether they deserve perks in return for being breadwinners, and in their heart of hearts, they will answer: Yes. Yes I do.

In obvious ways, the Big Flip is tough for men and women in conservative, so-called red state communities, which are more attached to old-fashioned gender roles. But the flip is not as easy as you might think for people in blue states who regard themselves as progressives. When you cast aside a belief system—when you reject the idea that breadwinning accords privileges—you have to build a new belief system from scratch. I talked about the unexpected difficulty of doing this with a mechanical engineer named Rose, a married woman in her mid-thirties. It would be hard to find a woman who has worked harder to divest herself of gender stereotypes than Rose has. As an undergraduate at a prestigious East Coast university, she took women's studies courses and joined a group called the Freedom from Gender Society, devoted to dismantling conventional notions about the sexes. She has been working all her adult life, and never expected to be supported. After college, she got a master's degree and has never known a spell of nonemployment.

Along the way she partnered with Michael, a man who also sees himself as forward-thinking, who is equally well educated and opposed to outdated stereotypes. When they first started going out, he was doing sophisticated linguistic work for a telecommunications company, but when much of that began to be exported to other countries, he saw the handwriting on the wall, went back to school to get his own master's, and emerged from grad school to confront a big gaping hole where a job market used to be. He spent a year unemployed except for tutoring and other jobs he could get on the side. Both Rose and Michael were stressed about this; when I interviewed him, he was doing as much housework as possible: cooking, cleaning, shopping, litter-box-emptying, you name it. "See? Really, I am still useful!" he said, a little plaintively. He wished Rose wouldn't worry so much about the pace of his job hunt, and that she would understand you can't send out résumés 24 hours a day. She, for her part, was reeling from the financial responsibility that descended upon her faster than she had expected. They had wanted to wait to get married until they could afford a wedding and invite all their friends, but when Michael lost his health insurance, they decided to marry quietly—so he could get on Rose's policy—and announce it later.

Gender-free though she aspired to be, Rose found herself faced with a host of unresolved dilemmas. Before they got married, she had loaned Michael some money. Should he continue updating that Google spreadsheet tracking the interest payments he was supposed to be making? Or should the debt be forgotten? Did he now owe her nothing? And would they ever be able to afford a home of their own? They live in northern California, an expensive housing market; they were still in a group house with roommates, which is not the worst hardship in the world, but kind of a bummer for newlyweds. Rose would vent her frustrations in comments to a sex blog called Fig Leaf, confessing that it wasn't that she wanted her husband to earn more than she did—she just wanted him to earn more than he was earning at the moment, so they could afford a place of their own.

Rose was also experiencing the burden, familiar to men, of knowing that more people than herself depended on her income. She was learning what it felt like to have dependents, and to understand she couldn't change jobs on a whim. She couldn't quit or relocate or experiment. Employed in the aerospace industry, she was feeling a little bored, and vulnerable in the volatile economy. Under other circumstances she might have been inclined to look for a position she liked better and felt more secure in, but she figured she needed to strive to keep the one she had. So she did what men have typically done; she worked harder. "I put in a lot of extra overtime hours," she recalled, "and volunteered for travel assignments that I might not otherwise have." It paid off. Her next performance review was stellar, an experience, she found, that "makes you feel better about your job."

Yet Rose also wasn't sure what privileges, if any, all this hard work entitled her to. As the breadwinner, was she entitled to anything? If so, what? And what obligations did she owe to her husband? If she volunteered for travel assignments to show her bosses how gung ho she was, should she call home first and run it by Michael? She found herself signing up for travel without always clearing it. And when he did get a new job, this raised more questions. Since Rose was still earning twice as much as he was, should she continue to let him do the bulk of the housework? Or was she obliged to pitch in more, and make sure it was 50-50?

So here is yet another quandary. Given that women all along have argued that men should do more when they get home from the office, does this mean women who are higher earners have an obligation to do the same? Even when the husband is better at the tasks? Freedom from Gender Society, any thoughts?

And every now and then, Rose admitted, she had to bat away a feeling that these were *her* earnings he was spending. Michael was usually the person who took their cats to the vet, and on one visit while he was still unemployed he okayed an expensive procedure without asking her. "I was kind of upset about it," she reflected. "I don't know if I would have expected him to ask my permission, but at least tell me before spending it. I did kind of feel like—you just spent a bunch of my money without telling me." If they had both been working full-time, and he decided to spend a thousand dollars on a vet bill, "I would have been like, okay, that's your money—spend it on our cat, whatever."

I talked to more than one female breadwinner who admitted to the occasional uneasy feeling that the money she earned was "my" money as opposed to "our" money. Another wife I talked to, a lawyer in Washington, D.C., is married to a consultant who took the slow track. Having him at home has worked out wonderfully for both of them. Yet even given their careful egalitarianism, the wife acknowledges secret, almost illicit proprietary feelings about her income. "I have friends where it's the man who's earning more money, and the woman says to me, 'He gets really upset when I want to redecorate the kitchen,' and I'm supposed to be very sympathetic to the woman because I'm a woman," she reflected. "But I also understand the territorialness—the territoriality of: I did earn the money. I understand the husband's point of view much better than I would like to. I understand the feeling that 'I've earned it.'" The lawyer is aware that feeling more entitled to the money she earns is contrary to feminist principles and to the sharing inherent in a marital partnership. "If I caught myself feeling [that way] I would censor it, but I think it's there—it's there from the culture."

"Why Even Ask Him": Women Will Make More Decisions Unilaterally

Some women are skipping the secret ambivalence stage about spending and going straight to feeling that their paycheck entitles them to more say over decisions and resources. In late 2010 I interviewed the two Michigan sisters whose partners had suffered recessionary setbacks. One, the nurse Ginette Trottier, related that her husband lost his job around the same time that they got married. Up to then, he had been a business analyst making over $50,000. Abruptly, he lost his house to foreclosure and wiped out his retirement money trying to save it. "As bad as it could get, it got," she recalled cheerfully. From the start, she was paying the credit card bill, utilities, food bill, etc. "I've been doing that so long that I got used to it," she said when I talked to her. An energetic, upbeat woman, Ginette was padding around her house in stockinged feet, wearing jeans and a flowered long underwear shirt, hair tied back in a ponytail with a barrette on top. Even before they bought the house where they live now, she said, "It felt like I was paying everything."

Their new home had been purchased in her name. She was working as a hospice nurse and found her work satisfying and stimulating. It also was her experience that being the homeowner and moneymaker did give her more standing, and endowed her with the right to make unilateral choices. "There's a lot of decisions I've been making," she said, gesturing toward a sectional sofa in the living room, which she selected. They have one daughter together—two years old, she was prancing on the sofa while we talked—and she has an older daughter from a prior relationship. The last three nights, she had been Christmas shopping by herself, picking out presents for the girls without consulting him. In part this was because her husband was away a lot, working in a hockey shop and picking up other work here and there, but it was also because she didn't want to argue. "It's just, why even ask him," she said, preferring to avoid confrontation.

Making decisions wasn't something she was happy about. Before, she would have asked his opinion about the presents. But in their straitened circumstances, conversations about money were so stressful that sometimes it was easier to shop alone. "His sense of his own masculinity has changed," she said. "He'll say, 'Oh, we can't afford that,'" and I'll say, 'I'm going to get it anyway.' We've had a lot of fights that way, too—he'll say, you're going to get your way anyway, so I'm not going to say anything."

She did make concessions. When they were house hunting, her husband preferred a tan colonial in a subdivision of newer homes. She didn't have a strong opinion—the market was awash in options, many of them foreclosed properties—so she agreed. She let him pick out the flooring, and ceded the dispute over granite counters (her choice) versus Formica (his, because it is cheaper). Yet even in these instances, she was the one with more decision-making authority, in the sense that she was "letting" him have what he wanted. "I knew that in the long run I would be paying for it," she said. Her paycheck gave her the opportunity to sacrifice her preferences. Having money to bestow—being the magnanimous one—is a privilege in and of itself, one that women up to now have not been familiar with. Similarly, not having money to bestow is humiliating. The prior Christmas, her husband gave her a card with $100 inside. Opening it, she blurted, "Hon, you don't need to do that—you don't have money to do that!" It led to a terrible argument, and Ginette made a note to herself never, ever, to dismiss his generosity.

It seemed quite possible to her that she would remain the higher earner. Some recession-era women earners might get their old lives back, or some version of their old lives, but Ginette was pretty sure the life she was living was the life she would continue living. Her husband does not have a four-year degree, she said, and felt reluctant to go back to school and get one. "He was never really a school kind of guy." She, in contrast, has two undergraduate degrees: one in photojournalism, another in nursing. She was moving into management and considering going to medical school to become a medical examiner. Working in a hospice had made her familiar with death and dying. "I think it would be more interesting to be a doctor—where you're opening up bodies, actually looking at the blood vessels," she says. "I know I can do it. Then we wouldn't have to worry. I could take care of him. I just—I mean, I feel bad he cashed in his 401(k). He has no retirement." In her early thirties, she thought about retirement incessantly. The idea of easing her husband's lot was a major part of her motivation.

And if she did become a doctor, she continued, her husband could devote himself to coaching youth ice hockey, a calling he loves but one that's not well paying. It would suit her fine if she was supporting him and he was doing something he enjoyed. The day I interviewed her, he was out on a punishingly cold day pouring cement on a construction project. He raised their daughter during the first year of her life, heard her first word and saw her take her first step. He was doing laundry and had started cooking meals. He made dinner from a recipe on the back of a Campbell's soup can. It was dry but she told him it was wonderful. He was endeavoring in every way possible to remain valuable to her. And she did value him. Like Rose, Ginette was assuming a genuine breadwinner identity: absorbing that she could be the permanent primary earner, ramping up her performance at work, and rising to the challenge at home by figuring out a way to support a husband and two daughters and thinking about how the person she loved could do work he found fulfilling. Back when they were dating, she said, her husband was generous and paid for everything. In two short years, their roles had completely shifted.

While we were talking, Ginette's sister, Rita Radzilowski, came over to chat. She was in a similar predicament. Her boyfriend, a brick-mason, got laid off, and didn't go to a four-year college, and wasn't planning to, she said, whereas Rita has a string of degrees that she was planning to augment by enrolling in a doctorate program and becoming self-incorporated. On a Sunday afternoon, she was carefully groomed and professional-looking, with stylish rectangular glasses, blond hair swept on the top of her head, a gray top and black scarf. Rita felt that there were many aspects of her own relationship affected by the fact that she was doing better than her boyfriend. And she, too, was wondering whether paying should give her more say. If they went on an outing, she was the one who covered the expenses. She bought groceries, for her and her boyfriend and sometimes for his children from a prior marriage when the children were with them for the weekend. She didn't want to control every detail of their excursions; she was willing to compromise, but noticed that her boyfriend would fight her on decisions even when fighting wasn't necessary. "We're having power struggles. It's like—if I'm going to make the money, and make a lot of the decisions—it's not that you can't make them with me. But don't fight me on them. Everything's a battle." He was—she thought—turning ordinary decisions into something bigger. "I'm the woman in this relationship," he would sometimes say. He was comparing himself to her, and coming up short. "He did tell me—I never realized being with a really smart, educated woman was going to be this challenging. He said, 'It really takes a bigger man than I realized.'"

Women Will Have to Adjust to a More Distant Kind of Mothering

When I asked Ginette how she felt about the fact that her husband was the one who got to see their daughter walk for the first time, she said she was happy. She had witnessed her older daughter reach those milestones, and was glad he could have the same pleasure. "He's been working at potty training—he's been sitting and singing potty songs," she said. "He's really good with her. I thought it was kind of special. They had a lot of good times—they would have their little things. It's so funny to hear him say, 'It's her naptime' or 'She hasn't eaten yet.' He knows the whole routine. She was crying for him last night. We usually lay with her until she falls asleep—and she kept saying, 'Daddy, Daddy, Daddy, lay down with me.' I'm like, hon, you can't wake Daddy up."

Ginette didn't feel the need to be a so-called gatekeeper, a term coined to describe women's tendency to want to control the home front. She had ceded that authority to her husband. This, for women, is a big step. In the coming years, more women will adjust to being the more distant parent, and for some, it won't be easy. It's hard being a full-time working mother when your partner is full-time as well; it can be harder being a full-time working mother when your partner is staying home. Women, like men, will feel guilty, worrying they have abdicated a central responsibility. Women will wonder how their absence impacts their children, and will have a hard time finding answers. If a female breadwinner does find herself issuing orders to her husband over the speaker phone in her office, this may well be the reason why. She feels absent, apart, helpless to correct it, less involved in the household than she would like.

Yet at the same time, women will feel quietly overjoyed to see their children enjoying intimate relationships with fathers. In Michigan I also interviewed Kris Betts, a former stay-at-home mother whose husband directed sales for a well-established company that fell victim to the downturn. He was getting a career started as an independent consultant. In response, Kris went back to work in her old field of social services. When we were chatting over the phone she was upbeat and cheerful, but when I asked if her husband's relationship with their sons had changed as a result of his being home, she said, "No, not so much. Um," and then there was silence. At first I thought we had lost the cell phone connection. After a few moments I realized she was crying. "Sorry," she said. "That hit a little bit of a nerve." She was about to enter a meeting and had to go; she rang off, politely, and left me wondering what had caused the tears.

I met Kris Betts several months later. She is a good-natured woman, affable and down-to-earth, with dark brown hair and eyes the color of aquamarine. We met at a diner across the street from where she worked. She had one hour to talk; she had to be back for a 2 P.M. meeting. She was supporting her family on a quarter of what her husband used to make, clipping coupons and planning meals with the precision of a military quartermaster, turning meatloaf one night into tacos the next. But the upside was that her husband "had a fantastic summer" with their two boys, and now that they were in elementary school he was doing a great job of getting them on and off the bus, packing lunches, volunteering in the classroom. "We had parent-teacher conferences for my oldest," she continued. "His teacher called him a saint. She said he's a saint! It's not like he's a terror at home, but it was weird to see."

And then I asked her, tentatively, why she cried when I asked about her husband's relationship with his sons. And with that, it happened again.

Her face got red and flushed, and her eyes welled up, a physical reaction that was visceral and involuntary. "He had worked so hard, for so long," she explained. He had been in charge of sales for the United States, Mexico, and Canada, which took him away from home and meant "the phone's always on, Saturdays and Sundays, phone calls at night." This was the first time her boys were able to spend swaths of uninterrupted time with their father. It was a complicated moment. She wasn't crying out of sadness, or happiness. She was crying out of feeling. She seemed to be struggling to articulate the painful pleasure of knowing the three of them were together, though she was not with them. This, it seemed to me, is a classic breadwinner's emotion. It is an emotion very familiar to men: knowing that with your work, and your absence, you are buying for your family members the opportunity to be together and to thrive.

"At the end of the school year they came home with their art projects," she said, recovering her humor. "I'm going through them, and I'm devastated. All the art projects did not have mom in them. It was all the two boys and dad. I'm like—'Where am I?'"

"It's a joke in the household," she said, "how I was dissed in the art projects."

Breadwomen at the end of the day also must learn how to reenter the household ecosystem. Just as men have done, women must figure out how to insert themselves into a routine that has been unfolding without them. One foreign correspondent I spoke with reflected that when she is away on travels, her husband sometimes invokes her as the authoritarian. They have an adolescent son, and to discipline him, her husband will use the wait-till-your-mother-comes-home scenario. This puts her in the uncomfortable position of having to play the household heavy the minute she steps over the threshold. Her experience suggests that women's earnings can bring about a full transformation, imbuing women—like it or not—with the same command men used to exert when they left the house. And even as she knew that she was able to hold her dream job thanks to her husband's work-at-home status, this woman was annoyed when people made a big deal about it, pointing out: You could never do what you do without him. She was not convinced people had ever praised wives so richly for making possible their husbands' careers.

Women Will Be Jealous, but Not for the Reason You Think

Very few women I spoke to worried that stay-at-home husbands would have affairs with stay-at-home mothers. Female breadwinners did feel jealous, but it wasn't jealousy of hot moms or sultry neighbors with too much time on their manicured hands. Mostly, when women breadwinners talk about jealousy, it has to do with the fact that their husband is the one who knows all the other parents and teachers—their husband is the one attached to the childrearing community. Woman after woman described being unnerved when she went to back-to-school night and found that the teachers addressed her husband by his first name, and had no idea who she was.

"If we went to a school event, he could name [all the fellow parents and their children]—I hated that," said one executive, Jennifer Tyler, who has at various times been the co- and sole breadwinner. Jennifer has an engineering degree from Dartmouth. She works as a plant manager for Steelcase, and when she got an offer to work in England, her family moved with her. Her husband was good-natured about it: in the U.K. he found some other expatriate dads and joined a social club called STUDS, an acronym for Spouses Trailing Under Duress, Successfully. When she got transferred to Atlanta, Georgia, schools were reluctant to include a father in volunteer activities, and only when no mothers stepped forward was he allowed to be the room mom. But he never took his frustrations out on her. And when they returned to Michigan, he was welcomed into the classroom. At birthday parties, it would take kids and parents a while to figure out that she was his wife.

Michigan breadwinner Susan Hawkins described the same scenario. "Every year without exception, I have that renewed jealousy pang when we go to parent-teacher conferences or curriculum night, and here is Danny saying hello to every other parent and frankly reintroducing me to most of the other moms. I was never jealous of the women. I was jealous of the fact that I was Mrs. Hawkins and he was Danny. The teachers knew him, the principals knew him, and I'm the one who comes along for the ride."

"You Have to Do Something. Get a Hobby at Least."

It seems fair to say that there is a double standard lingering in our culture. Many men remain willing to tolerate a woman's desire to stay home, or work part-time, even as children become older. Men accept that women can have a thriving, valuable life that has nothing to do with gainful employment. Women are not always so ready to think this of men. They may be grateful for husbands who are stay-at-home fathers and slow-track workers, but eventually some of these men will have empty nest crises, if for no other reason than that their perceived idleness will drive their wives crazy. In the coming decades, stay-at-home fathers will spend 18 years wiping noses and fixing lunches, and look up to find a wife inviting them to a come-to-Jesus conversation. They will be pointed back into the workplace. Or school. Somewhere.

"The rest of your life, you're not going to do anything?" is how Margaret Gardiner, a stockbroker who lives in California, put it to her husband. When their children were small, her husband, a computer programmer, became the stay-at-home parent. Laid-back and gregarious, he got along wonderfully in playgroups and volunteer groups with other mothers. "He was kind of a novelty," she said, "so nonthreatening that everybody loved him."

But when their kids graduated from high school and it seemed to her that he showed little interest in going back to work, Margaret found this intolerable. "We hardly ever argue," she says, but when she would come home to see he had been hanging out, basically all day, she "seriously hounded him." He went back to graduate school, which was fine with her. It wasn't that she wanted him to be making money—she wanted to him to be moving forward. If there's anything that every woman I interviewed can't stand, it's a partner who seems to be standing still. "At least he's engaged," she said. "It makes him more interesting. He talks to people besides me; he's more fun to talk to. If he had said: 'Forget it, I'm retired,' we would have had a big problem. I just resented that—what, you expect me to go to work every day, but you don't? You have to do something. Get a hobby at least."

And Some Women Will Divorce

For some women, the upending of marital expectations will prove too drastic to accept. The belief that a man should be working and providing and moving forward and self-improving will prove impossible to overcome, and in some cases women will be shocked by the vehemence of their own feelings.

One of these was Alicia Simpson, the psychiatrist in her late forties, who graduated from Howard University in Washington, D.C., and returned to her midwestern hometown to do her residency. There she met her husband, a college graduate who had a white-collar job with the auto industry. Their salaries were roughly equal—about $30,000. But once she finished her residency and started practicing as a doctor, her salary tripled.

When they started a family—they have two sons—they wanted one parent to stay home. Just as Gary Becker predicted, their decision making was based on earning potential. Because of the salary disparity that had already opened up between them, it made sense for her husband to be the stay-at-home spouse. He struggled with his role initially, she said, but she felt she was psychologically prepared to be the primary earner. As the boys grew, their views shifted; her husband became more comfortable while she began to worry he was losing focus. When the boys entered elementary school, she expected her husband to ramp back up and reenter the workforce.

He didn't, or not exactly. He took a job as a part-time teacher's aide, Alicia related, making about $20,000. By that time, she was making six times what he did. She was maintaining the household, paying the bills. When they decided to put the boys in private school, she took on extra work to make the tuition payments. As time went on, she said, her feelings toward her husband subtly altered. He was a great dad; a nice guy; he kept the house straight; housework wasn't the problem. The problem was that "I found myself respecting him less as a man."

This surprised her. She had always been a feminist. She always believed women should earn and work and strive. What she was coming to realize was that she thought men should, too. "I learned that despite all of the feminist drive that I'd had through the years, I thought a man should also, even if the woman is a breadwinner, carry his weight with the couple," Alicia told me, a little wonderingly. "I felt he was not doing that, and the tension started to mount." She did feel guilty that he had lost out on professional opportunities by staying home, so she let the situation go on longer than she felt she should have. She paid the bills and resented doing it. "I'm working my butt off, where is your contribution?" she found herself thinking. "I'm toting the load here." She felt that he had become overreliant on her; that her competence "fostered this sort of helpless state."

He sensed her withdrawing, and reacted, she said, with anger. "It sort of dwindled down to two people coexisting in the same home." She moved out of the master bedroom and into the guest room. Fifteen years into her marriage, she realized: "I don't feel anything for this guy anymore. I've just come to the end of my rope." Once she had the honest talk with herself, she said, "I kind of released it, and I felt good."

Alicia said she was surprised that she turned out to be more traditional than she would have ever expected. I pointed out that she wasn't exactly traditional—she didn't expect her husband to support her. She agreed, but confessed that part of her would enjoy having a partner who earns more than she does. "I hate to say this—I want to sit back and be taken care of," she admitted. "I'm tired. I joke about it, but I really will not enter into another relationship unless he is financially stable. The whole point of life is living and learning. It's got to be more than a nice guy."

Alicia also found it striking that she and her sister, Tracy, found themselves in the same situation. I had dinner with Alicia and Tracy, who were born less than a year apart. Tracy, also a Howard graduate, is a banking compliance officer. Her husband does financial advising, she said, but his income is unpredictable. Tracy had always expected she would be the supplemental earner, but instead, she said, "I've always been the steady paycheck." She felt trapped. They have one child, a boy, and she would like to stay home with him. "I don't know how long I'd like it," she said, but she would love to know what it's like to have a completely clean house, hot meals every night, "all the laundry done *and* put away." Sometimes her husband talks about becoming an entrepreneur—the buzzword around their hard-hit industrial city is entrepreneurship—but she feels this is unrealistic. "Do you think my aspiration was to be an auditor or a compliance officer?" she will sometimes ask her husband. "Do you really think that? No! I can think of a thousand things that I would really want to do, but this is what earns the bread."

"Don't get me wrong; I enjoy what I do," Tracy added. She had bobbed hair and a gray jacket, a blue shirt with a ruffled collar, and pearl earrings. "But there were times when I hated it. I was a branch manager—hated it, hated it. When I opened my eyes every morning, I was like: God, do I have to do it? And now I enjoy what I'm doing. But if I had my way, I'd be a veterinarian." At one point, she said, she and her husband were on the verge of divorce, but she talked herself into staying in her marriage. She willed herself to look at her husband's strengths, rather than his deficiencies. "I made a decision that I'm going to stay in. Because I take into account the other things—my husband's a great dad and I need him there."

Alicia, unlike Tracy, decided to get a divorce. It wasn't that she felt trapped professionally; she liked her work and had no problem working. But she couldn't recapture her feelings. And it showed. When her mother was still alive, she told Alicia she was talking to her husband in a way that was contemptuous and unacceptable. "She said, you can't talk to him like that—don't talk to him like that in public. And I didn't realize it. I was really angry at him. And ever since then, I don't do it. I have bitten my lip until you almost see blood dripping." But, she said, "I knew my anger was going to catch up sooner or later."

Over dinner, Alicia and Tracy tried to figure out why life had turned out the way it had, and reminisced about how their father and grandfather had been committed to their responsibilities as breadwinners, and how their father would take extra jobs to make ends meet. As they talked about it, though, they recalled that when he was in his fifties, their father was terminated and there was a period when their mother, a school janitor, was carrying the family on her earnings. "She became the breadwinner," Alicia realized, as they were talking.

"It had an effect on their marriage," Tracy reflected.

"Sure it did," said Alicia.

"Things weren't going too well," Tracy remembered.

"She slept in a different room," said Alicia. "After all those years."

"She became the one responsible for all the bills," said Tracy.

"She got a little edge to her," said Alicia.

They reckoned that their mother was the breadwinner for about five years, washing floors and scrubbing toilets. "I've cleaned up some places that you wouldn't even want to go into," she used to tell her daughters. But she did what she had to do, borrowing money from her own mother, who also worked as a custodian, to put the girls through college. Alicia and Tracy attended private college on the earnings of two African American women working as janitors. Thanks to their mother and grandmother, their job prospects were exponentially better than the women who came before them. The upshot was that they ended up better-educated than both of their husbands. It was a mixed sort of reward.

When I asked Alicia what her husband's attitude was toward her earnings, she said she had asked herself the same question. "What did he have to tell himself to make this be okay? Entering into a marriage where he knew he would never be the breadwinner? I don't know."

"I'll tell you what he said," said Tracy "He thought it was attractive."

"You think so?" Alicia said.

"He thought it was sexy and attractive that his wife made more than him," said Tracy. "He told me that."

"Really? Really? Interesting! Well, I'm learning something here," said Alicia. They both agreed that Alicia's husband is a terrific guy, but, Alicia said, "It takes more." She also felt that her sons needed to see their father as a working, contributing person.

And the thing is—now they are. Alicia said that her husband

has gone back to school to get his master's and become a full-fledged teacher. He responded to their impending marital breakup by taking steps to improve his prospects. This is exactly what wives have historically done. Stay-at-home mothers, economists have shown, tend to enter the workforce, or prepare to do so, when they anticipate their marriage may be ending. Alicia was happy to see he is moving forward. And she didn't think it would have happened if she had allowed their marriage to continue. Nor did it change her feelings about him. "The damage was done. I just have zero interest in this guy."

Seven
Stigma and Female Earning

Couples, Happy Within, Will Be Sabotaged from Without

In the coming years, many women will feel pleased being the family's high earner. Their husbands will like it, too. The arrangement will work well for the men and women who enter into it, but it will bother third parties. Women's economic dominance will be made to seem problematic by people whose business it really isn't. Remarks will be made at family gatherings. In-laws will signal they are worried. Friends will idly wonder, aloud, when the husband plans to get a job or how often the wife sees her own children. There will be nothing wrong with the union, yet men will be made to feel unsuccessful, women that they have failed in the traditional quest for a prestigious and well-credentialed husband. Couples adapting well to rich and changing times will be made to feel wrong and maladjusted. Society inevitably regards itself as a third party in marital arrangements, and couples who defy convention will feel the sting. They may find it easy to dismiss remarks and commentary from the wider culture, but disapproval will be difficult to ignore when it's close at hand. It's one thing to be stigmatized by strangers; it's another thing to be stigmatized by people who love you and who matter.

"I'm the good-for-nothing freeloader," is how one father, Terry, put it, describing his in-laws' reaction to his stay-at-home-dad status. "I don't make money—who the fuck is this guy anyway. The leech," is his summary of how he is regarded. Terry and his wife, Laura, have achieved a balance that works beautifully for both of them. Laura is a professor who teaches and publishes widely. She works a lot, and loves what she does, but also spends plenty of time with their teen-aged daughters. Terry feels privileged to be the at-home parent, which strikes him as more worthwhile than much of what passes for produc-tive employment in the nation's capital. "I think Washington in partic-ular is filled with completely bullshit jobs, where you sit in a think tank and you blow out hot air that nobody pays any attention to," said Terry the day I interviewed them together. He works in international policy and traveled a lot early in his career. He still recalls a conversation he had as a young father, taking an elevator ride with an older man, a political consultant who started talking unexpectedly about how his children resented him for spending so much time on the road during political campaigns. Terry resolved not to live that way. Several years ago he made the decision to forgo full-time salaried work in favor of part-time consulting, a schedule that allows him to be there when his daughters get home from high school and be a peripheral presence as they do homework or chat with friends. He has enjoyed every minute of it; when they were little, he loved volunteering in their preschool. "I feel like I'm doing things that I like to do, and forever men have not been allowed to do. We always talk about male privilege and there certainly is such a thing, but it has denied men the ability to do things. I'm in a generation where we can." He is extremely proud of Laura, who can pursue her career knowing her daughters are receiving the loose but vigilant after-school supervision teenagers need.

But their choices do not sit well with Laura's parents, who are also very proud of her, but don't seem to appreciate that his support is one key thing that helps her excel in her career. There have been strains with her family since the start of their life together: Laura is Jewish,

Terry is not, and her father opposed their marriage to begin with. Now, Terry's failure to play the provider has diminished him further in the eyes of his in-laws. He deals with this through a degree of psychic estrangement—by disregarding the "deep opposition" he encounters, telling himself it doesn't matter. "I guess because it's long-standing, it has to be irrelevant. They might think this or that about whether I'm working—who gives a shit. It's as if some random person on the street said it." Listening sympathetically, Laura mildly confirmed that her parents "have suggested it might be time [for Terry] to get a job." She hears similar remarks from her sister. It has made her "very selective" in what she tells her family. When they make comments, she deflects them.

For couples who are following their own instincts and forging their own values, the stigmatizing opposition of family members and well-meaning outsiders will make the situation harder than it needs to be. This was an even more acute problem for a couple I interviewed in South Texas, the paralegal Jessica Gasca and her husband, Juan Espinoza. Of the two, Jessica is the one who needs to be in the workforce. She suffered from postpartum depression and does better, emotionally, in an office setting. They have one child together and two from Jessica's first marriage. Juan regards all the children as his own, and treats them with equal tenderness. Skeptical of local day care—he heard rumors of a child left for hours in a high chair—Juan quit a job as a car salesman so he could watch them. When their school schedule permits, he takes customer service positions with local call centers, but inevitably ends up quitting when a child becomes sick and he has to stay home—dogged by the same lack of paid sick leave that affects mothers in low-paying jobs. From time to time, he has managed to earn a bit of spending money in what is perhaps the most stereotypically female occupation: selling Avon.

The day I met with them in their ground-floor garden apartment, Juan was eager to be interviewed. He felt misunderstood and unappreciated and wanted to talk about why. Tall, with a light beard, short hair, and a brown T-shirt with a red skull on it, he spoke about how disrespected he felt by Jessica's family, despite—or rather because of—his efforts to ensure the children are well cared for. In their household, he said, Jessica behaves like an old-fashioned breadwinning father; she tends to be more distant from the children, and when she gets home from work unwinds by going on Facebook. Juan is the one making flash cards and playing games with the kids. "They see me as the father," agreed Jessica. "Whenever they need something—a glass of water—they call him. Something wrong at school, they call him. Everything that a mother does over the years, the mother role, he's got it. I take care of the bills, I take care of the finance, I work to make sure there's food on the table."

All this caregiving had come at a cost for Juan, as it has for housewives. He loves the children, but feels stuck and claustrophobic. "Sometimes I fantasize about, like, leaving her, because I want to feel masculine again," he acknowledged. "Before her, I was single, had my own apartment, had my own car, my own job, paid my bills and everything. Sometimes it's so stressful being the mom—the feminine one. I want to be masculine, I want to go listen to rock music and lift at the gym." This was hard on their marriage, but it had weathered the discontent. The apartment was spotless, the children well behaved. While we chatted, they peered out occasionally from a bedroom where they were watching Disney movies, scurrying after a stray kitten the family had adopted.

Hardest of all, for both of them, was that Jessica's mother did not have a kind word to say about Juan. "Every time I go there, she gives me this huge lecture about my husband," said Jessica. They said that other members of the family tell their children: Don't grow up like Uncle Juan; he's such a loser. "They call me this unemployed, lazy guy," Juan said. Yet according to Jessica, most of her sisters also are breadwinners. Jessica thinks this is because she and her sisters took seriously their mother's urging to get an education. Her mother is vocally unhappy with the consequences. When I interviewed them, Christmas was a week away. Juan was dreading it. "I don't like going over because I get humiliated," he said. Jessica tells him to "act fake" and be cheerful, but he has a hard time managing it. "It gets under your skin sometimes. It does affect our relationship—the wear and tear."

Masculinity Under Assault

While couples may no longer feel they need to "neutralize" their "gender deviance," Juan's and Terry's predicaments show that men married to higher-earning women will continue, on occasion, to have their masculinity questioned. Not always by their wives, who often will be grateful, but by family members and the culture at large. Their stories support the idea that masculinity is a public construct—that manhood is not innate but something men must prove, over and over again, to a skeptical public; a status that must be earned but also groomed and cultivated. This argument has been set forth by any number of studies on masculinity, a body of literature that has been growing since Mirra Komarovsky interviewed laid-off workers during the Depression. Cumulatively, the argument running through much of the literature goes like this: Rather than a secure biological fact, masculinity is a fragile public performance, something that must be asserted, again and again, not only by boys on the brink of manhood but by grown men, day in and day out, who feel compelled to work long hours, excel athletically, compete, go to war, bring home a paycheck, etc., to prove their masculine status. Cultures fashion explicit manhood tests—anything from killing a lion to learning to build a fire with the help of a Boy Scout leader. To take just one recent example, some psychologists tested this thesis by assigning a group of men to braid hair and another group to braid rope. Afterward, men were given the choice of working a puzzle or punching a bag. The hair braiders more frequently chose to punch the bag, and from this the authors speculated that they wanted to reassert their masculinity after engaging in the perilously feminine task of hair braiding. They argued that manhood is a precarious state that is vulnerable to outside opinion, and that it can be lost through social transgressions—like the ones that Terry and Juan Espinoza are committing by choosing to stay home.

In fact, reading the literature, which by now includes work by sociologists, psychologists, anthropologists, and journalists, you'd also be forgiven for thinking that masculinity has never enjoyed a period where it was secure and thriving. People have always worried about the manliness of men. As early as the 1950s, *Look* magazine announced "The Decline of the American Male" with an issue so widely read it was reprinted as a book. Over the course of history—the literature suggests—masculinity has met with one shock after another. Industrialism assaulted the masculinity of the self-employed artisan and sturdy yeoman farmer; the decline of industrialism assaulted the masculinity of the wage-earning worker; and now the combined forces of feminism and globalism and economic crisis have done men in for good. A year or so into the Great Recession, any number of newspaper and magazine pieces eulogized masculinity in a global economy where industrial employment is waning and female overachievers ascendant. Men, it was declared, had created the financial mess; women would fix it. *Foreign Policy* published a piece on the death of macho, and *The Atlantic* ran a rich and provocative cover story on "the end of men." The 2011–2012 TV season reacted to the malaise with a raft of shows about modern men trying to come to terms with their manhood—shows with names like *Man Up!* and *Last Man Standing*. Some are paranoid, sexist fantasies of life in a world of bossy women; some are genuinely funny. In an episode of *New Girl* with Zooey Deschanel, one of her male roommates works in an office of women who make him dress up as "Sexy Santa." In another, a roommate is traumatized for days after she glimpses his penis and laughs.

While the economic shift is hard on men, at a certain point you have to wonder whether the hand-wringing exacerbates the malaise and adds to the stigma. When enough cultural sources tell you you're depressed and failing, pretty soon you'll start to think you're depressed and failing.

Whither Femininity?

Often, too, the conclusion seems to be reached that while masculinity has been shaken by women's ascendance, femininity has been unaffected. The authors of the hair-braiding study venture that femininity is innate and biological, something women don't have to worry about proving. One day a girl begins to menstruate, and voilà, she becomes a woman. Femininity, this line of thinking continues, is something that can be lost only through menopause or biological disaster. Women don't have to take any kind of test. We don't have to worry about whether girls attain femininity, because without even wanting to, girls will.

But in truth, femininity is very much a social construct, and women who are high-earning do worry about being stigmatized as mannish and unfeminine. What is femininity anyway? Even now, it's behavior that is pleasing and cheerful and deferential. It's acting nice in the office. It's being submissive and dependent. It's not being a shrew or a scold. Most women have had the experience walking down the street of being shouted at by a man in a passing car who would like you to "Smile!" Femininity—like masculinity—is located in a set of accepted behaviors, and society has ways to ensure women display them. Women worry, as a result, about the signals their money sends. Any number of women I interviewed acknowledged that they downplay their earnings so as not to be seen as uppity or too independent or non-needy or bragging or having that most unfeminine of qualities: an ego.

The challenge is particularly difficult for single women, who worry about how to present their financial independence to men they are interested in going out with. When creating profiles for online dating sites, women I interviewed never cite their salary level, and some won't even say what they do for a living. "I'm not going to tell you that I'm a doctor until I've known you a little bit," said Brenda Tyler, a physician who works at a big-city hospital in a Great Lakes state. In her online dating profile, Brenda, who is in her late forties, omits both her salary and her profession. And even when dating, she will delay as long as possible even revealing that she is a doctor. That's because once she does, "They put me in a box. They only know the MD." Inevitably, she says, men protest that her job doesn't bother them, and then "down the road it bothers them." I met with Brenda at an upscale seafood restaurant; lovely, warm, and impeccable, she paid for valet parking and handed a plush winter coat to the attendant, then talked about how even these small markers of success are off-putting to the men she meets. "I feel like I'm being punished for being successful. If I was barefoot and pregnant, I probably would have a husband."

Even as a medical student, Brenda felt her accomplishments were a strike against her. As an intern, she seriously dated another intern and expected they would marry. Then she learned that he was cheating on her with a pharmaceutical sales representative. Since then, it has not gotten easier: a guy she met in the gym pursued her, then broke

off their relationship, explaining they had too many intellectual conversations. She found this baffling and, in its own way, funny. He was
invariably the one who started them. "I could just as well talk about
other things," she marveled.

For Brenda, who comes from a high-achieving family of West In-
dian immigrants, religion is a complicating factor. She is a member of
a Christian denomination that subscribes to a pretty specific model of
femininity, in which the man is the head of the family and wives are
subject to his leadership. This is a philosophy espoused by a number
of conservative denominations, particularly fundamentalist and evangelical ones, which ground the argument in biblical passages including
Paul's Epistle to the Ephesians, which instructs wives to "submit" to
their husbands even as the Church submits to Christ. This is a durable if increasingly vexed directive; in medieval England, the historian
Barbara Harris has pointed out, priests and religious tracts "lectured
women endlessly about their duty to submit to their spouses." Contemporary theologians do sometimes point out that Ephesians directs
both spouses to submit to each other, but one still tends to hear a
lot more about female "submission" than its male counterpart. For her
part, Brenda Tyler doesn't object to the idea of man as woman's leader
in a much milder form. She thinks a household needs leadership, and
that ideally the leader should be the man—assisted by a woman who
is loyal and free to speak her mind. She tends to focus on a passage
which, to her mind, sketches out a definition of womanhood that permits a wife to be strong. While we were talking, she pulled out her
Kindle, opened her digital edition of the Old Testament, and began to
read from Proverbs 31:10–16:

> *Who can find a virtuous woman? For her price is far above rubies.*
> *The heart of her husband doth safely trust in her, so that he shall have*
>   *no need of spoil.*
> *She will do him good and not evil all the days of her life.*
> *She seeketh wool, and flax, and worketh willingly with her hands.*
> *She is like the merchants' ships; she bringeth her food from afar.*
> *She riseth also while it is yet night, and giveth meat to her household,*
>   *and a portion to her maidens.*

*She considereth a field, and buyeth it; with the fruit of her hands she
planteth a vineyard.*

To her, this description permits wives to be shrewd and resource-
ful. "I feel that I *am* a Proverbs 31 woman," Brenda said, looking up
from her Kindle. "If you got sick and couldn't work, I could run that
household. I don't *need* to do it—I would love to have decisions taken
from me every once in a while. It's not that I need a husband—it's
more that I think I can bring a lot to the table, and we can help each
other and grow." It is hard for her to understand why men don't seem to
want the kind of woman she strives to be. Within the Church, it is her
impression that the recession renewed the "provider" and "household
leader" conversation with greater urgency, as worship leaders sought to
reconcile joblessness with men's biblical mission. But it's her view that
men don't want women with power and resiliency. "They want the easy
route, someone who's not going to argue." Male friends tell her she's
right. They agree that "it takes more work to deal with a woman like
me than it is to deal with someone who might not be as outgoing and
educated and make as much. They don't care if they have to support
her, because they don't have to work as hard mentally and emotionally."

Whether or not she is right in these hard-won generalizations,
there's no question that hers is no rare, isolated struggle. Churches
may have good reason to preach the ideal of wifely submission; as the
sociologist W. Bradford Wilcox points out, religions that don't emphasize family life put themselves in greater danger of dying out. In
the United States, he has found, religiosity is a key predictor of gender
role attitudes. People in conservative or evangelical religious groups
are much more likely to endorse traditional roles, and "that's one group
where this broader [economic] shift is particularly challenging."

So increasingly, churches that preach the "submission" doctrine will
be faced with the very real challenge presented by women's economic
rise. In a 2011 blog post to a Christian website, a young wife noted the
"decreasing presence" of college-educated men in her congregation.
"When I look at the small circle of my closest and oldest Christian
friends, I realize that nearly all of us have higher degrees than our

husbands," she wrote, noting the ideological confusion couples endure as they try to reconcile biblical edicts about submission with the reality of who is better positioned for the workplace. She wrote that one well-educated friend struggled to resign herself to a life of home schooling her children, having been told this was her duty as a wife and mother; but when her husband proved unable to support the household, she went to work as a teacher, freeing him to be a stay-at-home husband and "worship leader."

This blogger wrote about how she, too, married down. A college professor, she is the higher-earning partner in her marriage. "I wonder if my husband and I would have succeeded on this path if not for the conservative, independent Baptist pastor who married us and discipled us early in our marriage," she wrote. "The pastor believed firmly in the biblical teaching that the husband is the head of the marriage. Yet he also taught, contrary to some ministries, that if the husband, in his biblical role as head, determines that his wife's gifts and calling make her the more suitable breadwinner of the family, then it is simply a matter of responsible stewardship for her to be just that."

This seems to be one loophole that congregations will fall back on: the wife is outearning her husband because her husband instructs her to outearn him. In 2006, when Minnesota Republican Michele Bachmann was running for Congress, she explained that she was a "submissive" wife who pursued a career as a tax lawyer not because she wanted to—she hates taxes, she insisted—but because her husband recommended it. In 2011, seeking her party's nomination for president, she was asked about this and explained somewhat more blandly that she has "respect" for her husband. While her religious beliefs have been treated with respect by the media, it seems clear that submission to one's husband—or wife, for that matter—is a problematic stance for a would-be free world leader. And within households, such an idea can foster dissonance, exacerbate stigma, and do more harm than good to family life. I talked to one young woman who grew up in an evangelical Christian household and who struggled for years to convince her parents—her mother especially—that she was entitled to pursue a career. "Christian culture tends to be hypermasculinized," she said, pointing out that in her Christian high school the top students were all female, but nobody found this threatening, because it was assumed they would make well-educated mothers. The tension arose when she wanted to travel abroad and go to law school. Her parents opposed these choices, and when she defied them, "My mom said that she felt like I had died, [and] she took down all the pictures of me in the house."

"All I Had to Do Was Walk Out to My Car and Things Would Change"

But it's not just women in religious communities who feel stigmatized by their earnings. I was struck by how many women I spoke with instinctively hid their achievements and income, especially when dating. Reporting in South Texas, I interviewed Magdalena Hinojosa, a senior associate vice president at the University of Texas–Pan American. I had set up the interview hoping to get her expert views about why Hispanic women are emerging as more successful students than men. Hinojosa was glad to talk; she said that part of the disparity does spring from the fact that young men see themselves as providers. They usually need to get jobs, which reduces the time they have to study. And even when they are supporting parents and extended families—as so many men in the region are—their income reduces the grant money they can qualify for.

But when I told her more about the scope of this book, she closed her office door so she could talk about her own past experiences dating. Like Brenda Tyler, Maggie Hinojosa is really beautiful, elegant and chiseled, groomed and accessorized, with a French manicure and an olive green suit that happened to match the pale green walls of her office. But she said that for many men her job made her seem unfeminine. One man called her on her work phone, got voicemail identifying her as "Dr.," and told her that using the honorific made her sound like she had a "big ego." She came to realize, just as Brenda Tyler did, that "you have to hide who you are, at the beginning, until that person is comfortable with you."

So, like Brenda Tyler, she developed ways of making men comfortable. When men would ask her what she did, she would say, carefully, "I work at the university." When they asked if she was a professor, she would say, "No, I work in the admissions office," subtly encouraging the idea that she was a midlevel administrator. "I learned to not bring out that I had a doctorate," added Hinojosa. And even when a date was going well, "all I had to do was walk out to my car and things could change." Men would see that she drove a zippy little BMW and comment on how expensive her car must be, even though it isn't any pricier than the enormous trucks and SUVs you see everywhere in the region. "I got to the point where I would be careful about even leaving at the same time and letting somebody walk me out to my car."

"I Said I Was a Hair Stylist": Women Will Lie

Other women will flat-out lie. Sami, a software engineer working in the Washington, D.C., area, finds that men in the nation's capital—a city of political science majors and policy types—can be intimidated by her field of expertise. So she began saying she is a music teacher. Similarly, an attorney who practices in Texas recalled that she happened to be in San Antonio one summer after she graduated from law school. At night she and colleagues would go out to bars, and men would ask what they did, and inevitably telling the truth would result in boring, contentious exchanges. Men would be "a little bit intimidated," she said. They would become confrontational. "They would ask: What are your views? Does this mean you never want to have children?" At one point she got so fed up that she told one guy: "It doesn't matter what I do—I'm not here to take an exam with you."

In response, she says, "They called us 'complicated.'"

After several nights of being labeled complicated, she and her colleagues changed their occupations to something simpler. They became cosmetologists. "We went out and I said I was a hair stylist and my friend would do nails." The change was palpable.

"It was so silly," she said. "We had so much fun. They were no longer asking what did I do. That whole night we had so much fun."

Women Will Keep Strategies in Their Back Pocket to Assuage Men's Egos

Even young women in cosmopolitan urban environments soft-pedal their income and find ways to save face. One of the women I interviewed in Atlanta is the entrepreneur who makes sure to carry lots of petty cash when she goes on dates so that she can pay for drinks and tickets and entrance fees, and not have it seem quite so evident she is doing so. "I'll go on first or second dates with guys, you go somewhere and you have to pay to park, and I'm like, 'Well, I have a ten-dollar bill,' or 'Oh, I have singles for the valet,' or 'Oh, let's leave the tip in cash,'" she explained. "It doesn't come across as I'm paying for it—it's like, I happen to have bills. And so I always have bills. Of all sizes. I'll say, 'I know the wait staff likes tips in cash, and I've got the perfect amount of cash.'" Her strategy amounts to sleight-of-hand. "I never say when I pay for something that I make more money," she says. "I never try to put it that flatly. I usually say, like, you got dinner last time, or oh, I'll just get the drinks, even though drinks cost more than dinner." This woman currently has a boyfriend who does not own a car. When they are going on an outing, she deliberately hands him her car keys. "I like it more when he drives," she said. "I like being a passenger."

While making these observations, the entrepreneur was sitting at a restaurant table with a group of friends, who began sharing other strategies they had developed. An investment banker talked about how, when she spent several nights in her boyfriend's apartment, she would restock his pantry. If he caught her, she would tell him she had to go shopping anyway. "I was like, sweetie, I was grocery shopping for myself, and I want to have the right food at your place, the food that I like. But I got all the stuff that he likes, too."

As they talked, though, there were hints that men weren't necessarily troubled by their affluence; the women in some ways seemed more uncomfortable than the men whose egos they were protecting. The investment banker recalled being at a bar with colleagues, and some male medical students suggested the women stand them a round of drinks. "You make about twice what we make, and that's *before* your bonuses," one of the men said. "We were like—oh, that's not going to work," said the banker gaily.

"I guess the guys sometimes don't get it so fair," mused an engineer who works as a consultant. "We still typically expect certain things of guys. When you're first dating a guy, say you made twice as much as he does—you're still going to expect him to pay for dinner." But once in a serious relationship, she said, "I would pay."

The consultant also seemed to feel stigma around having a boyfriend whose career didn't seem to be on the same level as hers. This was the woman who was dating a manager at a Waffle House. "I don't feel embarrassed," she protested. Her lack of embarrassment was a theme she returned to, until it became clear that if she didn't actually feel embarrassed, she felt something very close to it. "People will say to me: 'What does your boyfriend do?' I say, 'He's a manager at Waffle House.' It's not a stellar job—but they do take only college graduates. People look at you and go—and *you* do what? What's she doing with this guy? That's what I imagine them thinking."

At the same time, the Atlanta women were proud of their degrees and their income. Most had worked to put themselves through college; several spoke of having grown up poor. "My grandmother was just so happy when I graduated college—it was her living through me," said the consultant, whose father worked in construction and who already was making more than her dad ever had. "I just grew up with nothing." But they were still figuring out how to wear their success, particularly in relationships with men who were having trouble finding their own way forward. The consultant wasn't sure how to handle the fact that her career was thriving even as her boyfriend's was stalled. After getting a larger-than-expected raise, she called her boyfriend, then afterward worried that maybe she shouldn't have. "I don't want to say too much about my success, because I don't want to hurt his feelings or put him down," she confessed. "I was at work and I was just really excited, and I called him. You know, and after the fact, I felt bad. Maybe I shouldn't have said anything. But when I got home and we went to dinner, he was like: 'I'm so proud of you!' He's really supportive and I don't think it affected him. But still, to me, I was worried."

Her boyfriend had no problem with her achievement. He loved her for who she was: a power-lifting, self-made engineer from a blue-collar background with a great job and a promising future. The whole reason he took the Waffle House job was so the two of them could be together. He could have job-hunted outside Atlanta, but she told him she didn't think a long-distance relationship would work. "I feel like I have to take some of the blame for his job description, so I do end up defending it," she said. She feels guilty—"all the time"—about restricting his job choices. "But if he stays there, he can move up really quickly and make a lot of money. He could make more money than I do." And he repeatedly reassures her, saying he would be much more unhappy if he had taken a job far away from her.

The entire relationship surprised her. Before him, she had a boyfriend who liked to impugn her femininity. The old boyfriend would tell her that while she might be considered good-looking at her science-oriented alma mater, she wasn't nearly as hot as the girls at his big state university—who, he implied, put a lot more work into physical appearance. This new boyfriend doesn't put her down. "I never intended on dating this guy at all. I don't know, all of a sudden something just clicked," she reflected. The women at the table asked if she might marry him. More and more she had been thinking: a guy who loves her, who supports her ambitions, who congratulates her when she gets a raise, who is willing to relocate for her? Who talks about settling down with her? Yeah, that could work. That could be good. Expect more women to come to this realization.

Eight
Sex and the
Self-Sufficient Girl

Sex as Resource: Darwin's Return

There is a popular theory which holds that women don't like sex as much as men do. The theory has taken bit of a drubbing in recent years, but it's still with us; in fact, it's enjoying a renaissance. The theory is based on a number of studies, including one published in 1989 in which student researchers approached undergraduates of the opposite gender on the campus of Florida State University and invited them to have sex. "I have been noticing you around campus," is how the researcher would phrase the proposition. "I find you to be very attractive. Would you go to bed with me tonight?" To this startling invitation to sleep with a stranger, men for the most part said yes and women said no. From this, any number of experts concluded that women just aren't into sex the way men are—rather than reaching a more plausible conclusion, which is that women learn early in life that a stranger approaching you with sex on his mind and a stalkerish interest in your movements is not somebody you should deal with or even speak to, and is likely to be weird and scary even if he looks normal, and what he may have in mind is to rape you and kill you, so best to say: Thanks, but no thanks. (Actually, what the women tended to say was: "What is wrong with you? Leave me alone.") Just because a woman doesn't want to have casual sex with an unnerving stranger doesn't mean she doesn't want to have casual sex with the cute guy sitting next to her in organic chemistry class. Or fond, frequent sex with her husband.

Nevertheless, women's indifference to sex remains an oddly persistent concept. So does the coldhearted Darwinian notion that when women do have sex, they are having sex not because they have fallen in love, or even because they have fallen in lust, but because they want something concrete in return. "Sex is a female resource," asserted psychologists Roy Baumeister and Kathleen Vohs in a 2004 paper, arguing that sex is something women offer, not something women necessarily want, and that what they want can be any number of things—dinner, gifts, "a long series of compliments"—including, especially, commitment. And because this is why women have sex—because they are always trading our services for things like food and shelter, some proponents of this theory further hold that all the good things women are experiencing—education, success, prosperity—are bad for women sexually because they create a situation where there are all these terrific women and relatively fewer terrific men. Given an abundant supply of sexual partners, men can have sex with as many women as they want, with little pressure to commit. Never mind that men are anxious, uneducated, underperforming, freaked out, unkempt, depressed, half-assed, piss-poor; contrary to what you might instinctively suspect, this iteration of the theory argues, unconvincingly, that these very qualities somehow give men the upper hand. Seen this way, a driving force behind so-called hookup culture is women having sex as a way of competing for the dwindling number of men who are on their level. They are having sex in the hope that some half-decent guy, somewhere, will be willing to marry them.

"If women were more fully in charge of how their relationships transpired," writes one proponent, the sociologist Mark Regnerus, coauthor of the book *Premarital Sex in America,* "we'd be seeing, on average, more impressive wooing efforts, longer relationships, fewer premarital sexual partners, shorter cohabitations, and more marrying."

Hmm. To accept this argument, there are some dubious corollaries you also must buy into. Chief among them is the part about women not liking sex. Now, it may be true that women don't think about sex with the obsessive frequency men do—or it may not; new studies have challenged even this cherished stereotype—but at a certain point everything is relative. In general, it seems safe to say that when women have sex, they are having it because they enjoy it. The other dubious corollary is the trading part. The theory is in fact puzzling: if sex, for women, were about nothing more than securing commitment, at present there would be very little sex going on, because there are relatively few men worth committing to. There would be a small pool of men who get to have sex with a different woman every few minutes, and a much larger pool consigned to lonely evenings watching pornography on their laptops, if they happen to own one.

A more persuasive argument could be made that women's economic ascendancy gives women the upper hand. In fact, contrary to the women-don't-like-casual-sex argument, I would argue that women are becoming the gender that desires sex more than men do. Women's sexual energy and self-confidence have been unleashed along with women's earning power. Having independent resources frees women to be more assertive and adventurous, which of course was exactly what all those 19th-century marriage experts feared. Women are less likely to rely on sex as a strategic way to get resources, because women have more of the resources they need.

To be sure, the overabundance of women at colleges and universities makes dating—and sex—more challenging to obtain. No question. When you're a female undergraduate at a college that's 60 percent women and 40 percent men, the odds are not in your favor. "All my closest girlfriends were single," said one alumna of Boston University, which is about 60 percent female. "I didn't date much," said a recent graduate of UCLA, where the gender proportions are similar. And in fact, perhaps because of this disproportion, evidence suggests that rampant hookup culture is not as prevalent as it's said to be: a report using data from the National Survey of Family Growth found that in 2006–2008, almost 29 percent of women ages 15 to 24, and 27 percent of men, had had "no sexual contact with another person," ever, up from 22 percent for both sexes in 2002. The study suggests that college students are having less sex than people think they are. Of course, most do have at least one uncommitted sexual encounter at some point. And among those students and young singles who were having sex, my interviews suggested that women were having sex because they wanted it, and men often were having it with the hope to commit. As one MIT graduate put it: "If you have a random hookup with this guy you know from class, you start dating him and he's often more into the relationship than you are."

Not every woman I interviewed was having sex all the time, but quite a few were having quite a bit. The reasons were because they enjoyed it; because it was available; and because—far from being anxious to commit to one man—they wanted to have sex with as many men as they could, to see who was best at it. The women were using their resources to have more sex and better sex. The overwhelming majority wanted to *delay* commitment. And they could. They didn't have to get married right away, because they didn't need a provider. And because they were supporting themselves, they could experiment. One woman actually referred to this as "test-driving a lot of cars before you buy one."

Women want to have sex for sex's sake, and men—I'd argue—are a little taken aback.

"I Couldn't Go into a Restaurant Without Him Gawking and Flirting"

If there are sexual problems that arise from women's financial ascendancy, my interviews suggest that they may be more likely to emerge in existing relationships, when women find themselves outperforming partners in a way that puts men off or makes the women uncomfortable. Contrary to the idea that men are the ones who want sex, and think about sex, and have to have sex all the time, quite a few breadwomen confided that they were eager to have sex with their husbands and partners, but found to their dismay and confusion that their partners had become unwilling to have sex with them. This is one of the most painful problems female breadwinners face in their personal lives. Sometimes, men became uninterested after suffering job losses and setbacks that made them depressed and self-doubting; sometimes the men felt jealous and competitive. Just as women are said to do, men in some cases withheld sex strategically as way of exerting what power they felt they still had. The problem for these women was not a surfeit of men who were willing to have sex with but not commit to them; the problem was men who had *already committed* and now didn't want to have sex. For a woman, it is very hard to hear all the time about how sex-crazy and always ready men are, and to find that this is not at all the case in her own bedroom with her own partner.

This was the case for a woman named Felicity, a high-level executive at a major IT provider, where, thanks to salary and stock options, she amassed a substantial nest egg by her late thirties. Felicity didn't want children, but she did want a mate and thought she had found the perfect one in a gregarious salesman who patiently wooed her. He made $75,000 a year; she made three or four times what he did; he was a recovering alcoholic; none of this was a problem for her. She loved him. They married. Golf was a joint passion. She paid for trips abroad to play the links in Europe. But even as her husband enjoyed the lifestyle her money could buy, he grew to resent it. He started working less and playing golf more, and when she came home stressed from her workday, he wasn't supportive. She won a big contract and got a nice bonus and he wasn't congratulatory. "He thought that was going to take me away from him even more. He got angry and distant when I was telling him about our win. It was a multimillion-dollar contract, but he wasn't happy for me. He shut down."

Worse, Felicity's husband took to staying up at night watching TV instead of coming to bed with her, yet behaved with exaggerated charm toward other women. Felicity was no longer attractive to him, but apparently every other woman in the world was. "We couldn't go into a restaurant without him gawking or flirting." So in a way it was no surprise when she found the cache of pornography on his computer. She ended up going into therapy over his addiction to online porn. "The therapist said he's doing that because he's insecure—it makes him feel more manly. I am filling the traditional male role of the primary breadwinner, so he's going to pornography, or flirting excessively with women—you know, searching the Internet, Facebook, too."

I had a similar conversation with Jessica, a law student whose boyfriend celebrated—at first—when she scored higher than he did on the LSATs. He seemed less enthusiastic when she got into a more prestigious law school than he did, and made law review when he didn't. As she continued surpassing him, he had a harder time handling it. "He was wincing as I got good news. Me beating him on getting onto the law journal was the thing that really hurt. He just had this 'ouch' look on his face. He was kind of cold and detached and didn't want to talk about it," said Jessica. After her law review triumph, her boyfriend went on a trip to South Africa, and there appeared on his Facebook page a photo of him kissing a woman he met there. He later took a trip to Moscow, and when he came back there were messages from another woman, whose photos showed her gauzy and sunlit in a field of flowers. "I was really surprised that he was having these pseudo-emotional flings," said Jessica, who eventually ended the relationship. Her boyfriend wanted to move in together—he wanted to commit to her—but she had this uneasy feeling that even if part of him was attracted to a woman who was lawyerly and challenging, another part wasn't. "He sought out these girls who massaged his ego."

For some men—I would argue—it may be more appealing to have sex with a stranger on the street than with a woman you are close to who seems to be surpassing you. And in fact, a new study suggests this is the case, contributing to the idea that men may be the ones sexually disadvantaged by the new state of affairs. Lamar Pierce, the business professor at Washington University in St. Louis who is interested in the psychic fallout of salary comparison, teamed up with a Danish researcher, Michael Dahl of Aalborg University, to explore how such comparison affects intimate partners. In Denmark, the researchers were granted access to an anonymous social security database that can link a person's salary to a list of medications prescribed to that person. Searching the records of married couples, they found that men whose wives earned more than they did were more likely to take medication for erectile dysfunction.

Like many raw findings, this data could be interpreted in a number of ways. It could be that the men earning less than their wives had an underlying health problem to begin with. To control for this—to make sure there was a causal relationship between a man's relative earnings and his sexual potency—the authors refined their search, looking only at marriages where men earned slightly less than their wives, and at men who earned slightly more. That's because populations to either side of a dividing line tend to have similar characteristics. They found the disparity still held true. Even men who earned slightly less appeared to have impotence issues, compared to men who earned slightly more. (Of course, it could also be that the men found their wife's earnings so arousing that they wanted to have sex all the time, and sought an extra boost, but . . . well, let's just table that idea.) Talking about the study in an interview, Pierce surmised that the men were comparing their salary numbers to those of their wives—an "unexpected shock"—and this was affecting them physiologically. His intuition is supported by the choice of words that the blogger Aaron Gouveia, writing on the Good Men Project website, used when describing his elation at landing a job that enabled him to outearn his wife. "I felt like walking into the kitchen, unzipping my pants and unfurling my manhood on the kitchen table next to my offer letter." It's affirmed by another blog post, this one by writer Gail Konop Baker, who wrote on *The Huffington Post* about how many women she knows are reveling in their success, emotionally and sexually, but find that men are put off. The "first man I dated after separating from my husband while initially thrilled that I wanted sex as much if not more than he did, wanted less as the relationship progressed," she wrote. "Soon my daily drive outpaced his."

Sex research is now both voluminous and, like so much research, contradictory; when I contacted researchers doing work in the field of women's sexual responses, few felt they could give a good answer about how sexual response is affected when women, not men, are the providers. But to the degree that the correlation between sex and female breadwinning has been explored, some researchers and clinicians have uncovered trouble. Some couples have such a powerful physical chemistry that it's impervious to who is doing the earning. But in other cases, men "are intimidated sexually by the fact that the woman makes more than he does or has a more important job. They get to feel insecure, and as soon as they feel insecure, they go one of two ways—they either become dominant, or they can't perform," said Judy Kuriansky, a clinical psychologist who teaches at Columbia University and specializes in sexual issues. "It's not always that they have sexual problems in terms of erections, though that happens. Men also may try to become more assertive in bed and more dominant, or request sex more or want more quickies or want rougher sex because that makes them feel they are more of a man." There are a number of ways in which male insecurity can manifest itself, she says, "none of them good."

Mira Kirshenbaum, clinical director of the Chestnut Hill Institute, seconded this view, pointing out that self-esteem is one of the most "explosive" variables in marriage. If a man's self-esteem is damaged by his partner's achievements, he may begin to feel his needs are secondary or overlooked, and there could well be a sexual impact.

The new science around testosterone also may hold relevance: a body of literature is emerging that suggests men's testosterone levels fluctuate depending on their living circumstances. Men, for example, experience a drop in testosterone when caring for young children. I had a conversation about the possible impacts of female breadwinning with a psychiatrist, T. Byram Karasu of the Albert Einstein College of Medicine, who holds weekly group therapy sessions with male executives. Karasu has found that alpha men through their relentless one-upmanship drive down one another's testosterone levels, and it was his view that an alpha woman could have the same impact. To be sure, he said, there are alpha-alpha couples whose life consists of competing and clashing and having great makeup sex—you may notice them arguing in restaurants—but for the most part, he said, alpha women have a dampening effect on men in close proximity. Men, he said, may reclaim their manhood by finding a beta woman to have an affair with. His analysis does offer a way to think about the experiences of Felicity and Jessica, as well as political scandals in which public men like John Edwards, Bill Clinton, Eliot Spitzer, Mark Sanford, Arnold Schwarzenegger, and others marry strong women—alpha women, I guess—yet find themselves drawn to affairs with housekeepers, interns, fawning campaign videographers, and prostitutes.

Then again, men have been having affairs with so-called beta women for considerably longer than women have been outearning them. And just because a woman is outearning her husband doesn't mean she is an alpha woman. Moreover, as Mira Kirshenbaum points out, mismatched aggression levels have always been a risk factor in relationships. Alpha women have always existed, and in prior generations these women were forced to channel their energy into their husband's careers, a dynamic that created its own problems. "It's a serious mistake to think that in the old days, when men and women necessarily lived in separate spheres, there was no competition," cautions Kirshenbaum. Back in the feminine mystique era, women who were naturally competitive expended their energy and effort pushing their husband's career, and "this often resulted in enormous conflict, as many husbands deeply resented their wives" pushing them for reasons of their own.

An alternative theory holds that earnings disparities are an issue that couples find it hard to talk about, and that communication difficulties lead to a lack of intimacy and, along with that, a lack of sex. Kirshenbaum points out when small, destabilizing changes set in, couples often don't know how to put them into words. If the woman is outearning her husband, and if he starts to feel he's less important, he may be reluctant to say so, or not know how. Sensing his chagrin, the woman may feel she has to downplay her own accomplishments. She may stop confiding—stop talking about the things that are important, stop downloading the events of her day, stop mentioning the great contract she won, or the big challenge she faces in an upcoming meeting. She may start to feel she can't say anything of importance, really, at all. Pretty soon the couple has stopped talking about the things that matter most, and the space between them gets wider. Tiny changes in the relationship have a cumulative impact, as a result of incremental alterations they set in motion. It's a kind of systems theory of relationships. A small-scale resentment, when it's not aired, can lead to growing estrangement; one partner pulls away, becomes just a little colder, just a little more hostile, the other partner does the same, and eventually there is a yawning gulf where there used to be warm attraction. In situations like this, Kirshenbaum said, "even a small earning or success differential to the advantage of the woman [can] lead initially to conflict and before long to distance." This can lead to affairs, on the part of either the man or the woman, as one or both seek a partner who is not alienated. Seen this way, when sexual problems do arise it's not the earnings themselves, or fluctuations in testosterone, or the woman's alpha status at the heart of the discontent. It's the failure to communicate, and the "bitterness and rancor that grow out of competition-generated fights."

That communication is a crucial aspect of sexual intimacy is affirmed by a 2011 study by Michelle Hindin, a Johns Hopkins professor who works in public health. Hindin and colleagues looked at women in a variety of African countries to determine the amount of sex they were having and how it related to their standing in the household. This is of course a different context than the one Western women live in: for women in many parts of Africa, where HIV rates are high and men may have many sexual partners, it's as important to be able to say "no" as it is to say "yes." She found that in marriages where women made most of the household decisions, they were less likely to have had recent sex. This is not entirely a bad thing: it means they were empowered and able to say no. But when I talked to Hindin about the study, she pointed out that the women with the most active sex lives were those who had egalitarian relationships, where decision making was shared. These tended to be marriages with open lines of communication. Her study suggested that when women grow dominant to the point of being domineering, when it seems to one or both partners that her earnings entitle her to all the status and decision-making power, when men give up on a certain level, then sex is bound to deteriorate.

"You're Not a Whore if You're Not Getting Paid for It": Women Will Become More Sexually Secure

But the good news for women is something Kirshenbaum also is seeing in her practice: more and more, men are attracted to high-achieving women. And staying attracted. Men, she says, "are increasingly turned on by women who have interesting, dynamic careers and are turned off by women who just stay home and have little to talk about at the end of the day." The good news is that sexual tastes are changing, which is not surprising if masculinity and femininity are social constructs. More and more, women's earnings and the vitality they reflect are markers of sexual desirability. On campuses, men's scarcity may enable some to play the field, but women's independence is a powerful countervailing force. Of the younger women I interviewed who were having lots of hookups—especially once they got out of college, and had a larger pool of men available—many were very clear that the purpose was maximum exploration. "I generally tend to have sex fairly early in my relationships," said one 24-year-old woman who estimated she had had forty sexual partners. "I feel like I will have very thoroughly investigated my options when I do settle down."

These sentiments were borne out by the women at the brunch table in Atlanta. Though they took pains not to embarrass men in public by conspicuously paying for everything, in their intimate relationships these women felt their independence made it much more possible for them to have the kind of sex they wanted. They talked about this for hours, sitting on a sunny Saturday at a tavern called Marlow's, smartphones arrayed on the table before them much as women in a prior generation might have fanned out bridge hands. "I think it gives us more confidence," said the entrepreneur, who in her early twenties was making close to $90,000. Even before she was earning that kind of money, she felt her ambition endowed her with sexual assertiveness and a willingness to speak up about her needs. Back in her undergraduate days, she recalled, she went to a routine ob-gyn visit during which the doctor—also female—asked if she was having sex. She said she was not having intercourse, but was having lots of foreplay. Her doctor told her that was ideal, both for health and sexual satisfaction, and recommended she stick with just foreplay as long as she could get away with it. "She was so adamant," the entrepreneur related. "I was like, you're right! So yeah! Even after college, I was still just: that was all they were going to get. And they knew it, and they were just happy, and it was awesome. I was really amazed that I went so long without actually having sex when I was getting naked on a regular basis."

The entrepreneur reminisced happily, remembering that when she was in college she would tell friends: "Oh, I hooked up last night, it was amazing, and I kicked him out—I was like, 'Okay, I'm done.' And my friends were like: Wow, you do that? I was like, yeah, I was done with him!" In college she owned a couple of vibrators, and when word got around, she started getting random emails from classmates. "They'd be like, 'I need to go . . . *shopping*. Will you go with me?'" On one excursion, she escorted a friend to a sex toy store and discovered an adjunct professor working there. He suggested she take his class. "And my friend was like: 'Isn't it embarrassing to have him know who you are?' And I'm like: 'No!' And we bought it and put the batteries in, and I was like, 'So this is how it works,' and my friend was like, 'Is this how fast it normally goes?' and I was like, 'This is very normal. It's nothing to be embarrassed about.'"

"I think women typically treat their sexual lives differently because of their success," reflected another woman at the table—a willowy engineer. "It's more okay to do things and be more like a man, because you're more in a man's world."

The investment banker, sitting at the opposite end, agreed. The banker recalled a conversation she had in college with a culturally conservative roommate who couldn't imagine having more than four or five sexual partners. The banker, who had already broken double digits—she refers to this as joining the "big girls club"—tried to get that roommate to reconsider. "I was like, honey, it's a different generation. It's a new millennium. You're not a whore if you're not getting paid for it."

"I'm Kind of Repulsed by Him with His Shirt Off"

The banker also provided intriguing evidence that women are responding to their wealth and independence by getting pickier about the appearance of the men they have sex with. The old wealth-beauty trade-off may be reversing: increasingly men may be the ones offering beauty—and sexual services—in return for the economic security women offer.

And woe to the men who don't hold up their end of the bargain. The banker was dating a student in a professional degree program; a native of South America, he had come to the States to study. Since arriving, he had gained weight. The banker knew this because she had checked the waist size of the jeans he brought with him, and compared it to the waist size of the jeans he wears now. "He was a 30—now he's 35," she related, with dissatisfaction. "He has literally *skinny fat*; his arms and legs are skinnier than mine, but he has a little potbelly." She returned to the topic several times; it had become an obsession. "I poke at his belly and say: 'Sweetie, we have to work on this.' I'm, like, 'If you keep this up, you're going to have hypertension and diabetes by the time you are fifty.'"

"You're going to be changing his diaper," agreed the entrepreneur languidly.

The banker, dark-haired, wearing a pale pink sheath, loopy silver necklaces, and matching earrings, sighed in agreement and tackled a steak salad. "I'm such a fitness freak. I'm training for a half-marathon. He keeps saying he'll go on a run with me." She noted that her boy-friend cooked big breakfasts for her in the mornings when she was getting ready for work, which she thought awfully nice of him but insufficient to make up for the soft belly defect. "I'm already debating breaking up with him, just because I am not that physically attracted to him," she said. "To tell you the truth, I'm kind of repulsed by him with his shirt off."

At the same time, the women were unwilling to upgrade their own beauty when requested to do so. Every woman at the table was well groomed and nice-looking. They worked out, they highlighted their hair, they dressed in shorts and silk shirts and cute dresses. But they also were united in the feeling that, as the entrepreneur put it, "this is as good as it gets." If a lover requested modifications, they felt free to decline. A friend of theirs had recently broken up with a boyfriend after he requested that she wear more makeup. The banker recalled a time in college when she was going out with a med student who told her she was pretty but would be prettier if she lost 15 pounds. "I was just like—are you serious? Are you serious? Do you know how many guys I could get if I went to [a local bar] with my cutest dress on? You're lucky to be dating me!" recalled the banker with gleeful outrage, reenacting her response. " 'You might be in med school right now, but

I, too, will be making a lot of money one day! I, too, will be really successful one day. I don't need you!'" She got worked up just thinking about it. "He was on track to be a neurosurgeon, and I was like, 'You're going to make a million dollars a year, but you know what? I apply myself and I might be able to do that, too!'"

The other women knew just the kind of man she was talking about: the man who feels he's entitled to change you and wants to make you better-looking than you already are; the man who wants to turn you into his trophy, so that your looks will make him look better. Forget that guy. "I have a rule," said the entrepreneur. "If they met me and were attracted to me and wanted to date me, with me being a certain way, they're not allowed to change the rules later. That's my rule of thumb. If someone ever says to me, 'Lose weight,' I'm like 'Okay, if I've gained 10 pounds since we met, it's like fair enough, you plan some dates that are athletic.' But if I'm the same size as when you met me, then forget it."

"I'm very confident," said the engineer. "If somebody insults my body, I'm like, sorry: I love it."

"There are tons of girls who are skinnier than me, taller than me, and have bigger boobs than me," reflected the banker. "But they are not as smart."

"And that's their full-time job," added the entrepreneur. "Their job is to look good and find a man, and they react when a man says they're getting too much jelly."

The women felt their earnings were a sexual asset. The investment banker recalled that she had recently met a guy in a bar who told her he was an accountant. When she revealed her own job title, he admitted he was head of finance for the Middle East division of a major development bank. "He didn't want to tell me right off the bat what he did," she related, with amusement. "He thought I was a hot girl in a bar looking for a rich guy. He was surprised. I was like: 'Yeah, I'm a hot girl in a bar, but actually I have my own career. I don't care that you have so much money, because I'm going to make money on my own.'"

Contrary to the women-trade-sex-for-commitment school of thinking, none of the women at the table was eager to get married.

They wanted to live with a guy first, not because they were being forced to settle for cohabitation by reluctant boyfriends, but because they were intent on finding a guy who would chip in his share of domestic duties. The women at the table didn't judge men on earnings. They judged men on willingness to take out the trash. Their attitudes correlated with another line of sexual research, which holds that men who help with housework are the men having more sex. This research has found that women feel more warm and affectionate when men pay attention to what needs to be done around the house, and when women feel warmer and more affectionate, couples have livelier and better sex lives. Rather than being exhausted by housework, couples are invigorated by doing things together. This argument has intuitive resonance. "It's doing the dishes," said one very happy breadwinning wife I spoke with. "It makes you feel that bond and closeness."

So maybe women do trade sex for something, and if they do, the Atlanta conversation suggested it's not commitment—it's labor. Every woman at the table agreed that it's important to test-drive a man not only on his sexual competence but also on his willingness to sort whites from brights and carry his dishes from the table. The entrepreneur made this point forcefully. When she was younger, she said, she used to think she would get married and wait a couple of years to have children. But she has reconsidered. Now she thinks it would make more sense to move in with a guy, live with him for a couple of years, then get married and have a kid right away. Cohabitation seemed to her an important way to weed out jerks who expect to drop their wet towels in a sodden heap on the floor and have somebody else put them in the hamper.

In fact, while she is happy to pay for dinner, the entrepreneur said she really wants a boyfriend to remember who did laundry last. "I keep tabs on cleaning and cooking," she said. "I like it that they don't notice about the payment, but it bugs me sometimes when they don't notice that I'm the one doing all the laundry if they leave their stuff at my place." She recalled how her older sister moved in with a guy who seemed promising, and "he was just a dud. She would give him simple tasks: 'You made this big mess, you clean up the sink,' and he never did. She was like: 'He's not going to change.' And she broke up with him.

They broke their lease. He took the computer. She took the furniture. It was a 20-minute conversation instead of a $20,000 divorce."

So consider this possibility: in the future, high-earning women will have the kind of sex they want, and they will look the way they want to look—not the way their boyfriends want them to look. If men want to date these women, it's the men who will have to watch what they eat and how much they weigh and what they look like.

And men had better not expect a woman's constant ministrations because women will demand space and time for themselves, and insist that their men show emotional autonomy. "We're at a point of historical flux—historically unprecedented for our population," points out evolutionary biologist Justin Garcia. "Women value autonomy more than ever before. They want their own bank account; they want to be able to go out with their girlfriends."

The women at the Atlanta brunch table agreed. "If they are clingy, I can't handle it," ventured the engineer. "If we've only been dating for three weeks and you can't even have your time with your friends . . ." Her voice trailed off. She had a number of criteria for what did and did not make a man attractive, but clinginess was the worst attribute a guy could display. "If after two dates he starts calling me baby," she said, "it's over."

The banker concurred. Which reminded her of another problem with the design-student boyfriend. After they had been dating just a week, he wanted her to sit next to him on the couch and Skype his dad with him. "He was like, 'I want you to meet my dad.' I'm like: '*Seriously?*'"

"You don't have to stick in a relationship," said the consultant. "I would rather not be in a relationship that I'm not happy with. If that entails me ending up an old maid, then it will. But I'm not going to suffer and put up with things that I am not happy with."

They also scoffed at the idea that women have sex as a way to secure commitment. The engineer described having a one-night stand with a male friend, and how a lot of their mutual friends felt awkward about it because they figured she must be attached to him and might have felt hurt. "I'm like—look, this is what happened. We didn't date.

It's not like we're exes. There was no emotional attachment there. We had sex and hooked up and that was it."

"A lot of people don't think girls are okay with that," mused the consultant.

"They just assume that when it's over, you can't handle it," said the engineer.

"That you're crushed when it's over," said the investment banker.

They laughed.

Part Three

THE PROMISED LAND

Nine
Desirable Women

The granite face of Stone Mountain rises unexpectedly from the flat landscape near Atlanta. An easy hike is all that's needed to get to the summit, so it's a popular destination for day trippers looking to get out of the city. Up Stone Mountain this day—a mild afternoon in late winter—a young woman, Jennifer, is walking with her boyfriend, Edward. The two have been dating for a year. Jennifer earns twice as much as Edward does. Her apartment is bigger and nicer than his, with a better view of downtown Atlanta. They are affectionate with each other, and considerate. The slope of the mountain is not extreme, but the surface can be slippery, and at times Jennifer leans on Edward because she is afraid of heights. At one point he slips and takes her down with him. Edward is carrying the backpack with the food in it; Jennifer carries the pack with the water. She is the one who paid the entry fee and purchased lunch ingredients; he is the one who made the sandwiches and packed them tidily in plastic containers. In her early twenties, Jennifer contracts with a major corporation to do brand management. Edward does network support for a cellular provider. The corporation Jennifer contracts with is known for an iconic product, while his cell phone company is known for dropped calls. At parties, her job elicits squeals and his tends to prompt a cascade of complaints.

Edward bears the contrast with equanimity. Jennifer's income is not a problem for him. To the contrary—it's an asset. "In our relationship, I am very happy to think that I have a partner who is ambitious and successful," says Edward, a thoughtful, precise person who would rather date an achiever like Jennifer than a woman who expects him to pay for everything or pursue a career he doesn't enjoy, just so he can provide for her. "I wouldn't want a partner that expects off the bat that I'm going to support them, and that if there's a hiccup in my career, the relationship is shot," he says. When he was in graduate school, where he studied engineering, Edward would take note of women's reactions when he told them he was a student. "I wanted to see how they would react if I said I wasn't employed—if they didn't see that there was going to be a material reward," he said. "There have been plenty of girls I've taken out, and I think things are going okay on a date, and I get somewhat serious, but if I don't say that I'm going to be a lawyer—if there's not some way that I can convey that I have money, there is a subtle change. I've had women not call me back."

In contrast, when Jennifer met Edward, she thought his studies were a sign of industriousness and intelligence. She thinks ambition and hard work are important in a partner, but she is not so concerned about earning potential. Over the years she has had more than enough hot air blown her way by men bragging about how ably they will support her, and has developed a healthy skepticism about their claims. As they hike, Jennifer and Edward talk about career goals as well as family life—testing each other to see whether they might be compatible in the long run. Neither wants an all-consuming work life, but Jennifer is willing to put in a more substantial workday than Edward is. Right now he can work from anywhere, fixing network problems remotely from his laptop, and he doesn't have a set schedule for coming into the office. That freedom would be hard to relinquish in any job he takes in the future. "I would definitely sacrifice a little bit of salary in order to get flexibility," he says. This offhand statement is striking, coming from a man. Being willing to sacrifice salary to get flexibility is the mindset women up to now have been notorious for—it's a chief means by which employers get away with shortchanging female employees. If men start to think this way—if men begin to accept lower salaries in return for time with their families—that will be one more factor depressing men's wages and elevating women's. Edward argues that there are diminishing returns to working long hours, and past a certain point you don't get much done. There is one old-school guy in his office who works 10-hour days, and sometimes gives Edward a hard time for coming in at 10 or 11. But Edward has noticed that old-school guy spends a lot of time on non–work-related computer tasks—reading, gaming—and might as well be gone anyway.

There are other ways in which the attitudes of Edward and Jennifer suggest a role reversal in views about work and family. When Jennifer was in college at the University of North Carolina at Chapel Hill, which, she said, is so heavily female that women pass tampons freely over the desks, not even bothering to hide them, she took a women's studies class where she was assigned to write a paper outlining the next step for women's equality. "Affordable day care" was the topic she chose. Jennifer expects to work full-time from now until she is 65, and would like to have at least one child. "My ideal scenario: I would have a job that ends at five, and we would have a nice day care," says Jennifer. "I'd almost be better with day care than a nanny."

Edward listens skeptically. "I'm big on parental involvement," he counters. His mother stayed home when he was a child, and taught him math, and as a result he was so advanced he never had to study until he was in high school. He grew up in the kind of old-fashioned household where his mother put her own education to use by educating her children. A generation or two ago, he might have been able to require Jennifer to stay home to ensure that any child of theirs enjoyed the same benefit. But if a stay-at-home parent is what he wants his children to have, Edward may have to be that parent. He sees that. He gets it. And he doesn't rule it out. "I would consider being a stay-at-home dad," he says.

Men Will Marry Up

This conversation suggests how the future is going to look different in a world of female earners. Here is one prediction: there will be more and more men like Edward who correctly perceive that marrying a successful woman will relieve them of sole breadwinning duty and give them more time for leisure and children. Far from having sex with women and discarding them, men will compete for high-earning partners, just as women used to do, and they will offer their domestic services in return—packing the sandwiches, volunteering for child care—just as women used to. There is strong evidence that men are sizing up women's earning potential just as women formerly eyed the future earnings of men. A study published in 2001 by University of Texas at Austin psychologist David Buss and three colleagues asked men and women to name the traits they considered most important in a marital partner, and compared these responses to those of previous generations. Among men, the authors found that in five decades there has been a huge jump in the importance men attribute to women's earnings, and a sharp drop in the value they place on women's domestic skills. Overall, the study found both sexes are increasingly similar in the qualities they deem important; good looks have risen in importance, for men but also for women. This suggests that the wealth-beauty trade-off is getting more complicated—that men are becoming more interested in wealth, and women in beauty. Demographer Christine Schwartz agreed in a paper that "men are increasingly looking for partners who will 'pull their own weight' economically in marriage."

Jennifer wasn't the only woman I interviewed whose partner welcomed her success and the material reward it augured. "We've had discussions about it—and he sees me as the person that will end up making more," said Amanda Macdonald of Winnipeg, Canada, who was fresh out of undergraduate business school and dating a man who was working in construction and planning to become certified in a trade. "I have always seen myself as working—I've been very focused." Amanda was making about $44,000 in Canadian dollars, and her boyfriend was making about $3,000 less. Given that she is college-educated and he is not, they both anticipated that her salary would continue to surpass his, by wider and wider margins. "He's definitely okay with that," said Amanda. She is, too. "If you want to marry me, I'm not going to be a stay-at-home mom," she has told him. "If anything, I would love for you to be a stay-at-home dad." She said it lightly but she wasn't joking. She didn't feel she would be happy staying home and wanted to ensure she wouldn't take a wage hit upon childbearing. She has mentioned the stay-at-home dad option several times, and "It's definitely something he'd be open to." Thinking about it, she added: "That would be much more pleasing to me—to come home at the end of the day and have supper made."

Now it's true that what many modern men may want is a woman who can provide on exactly the same level, rather than a wife who makes more. When it comes to matching, men are in an enviable position: there are so many college-educated women that it's theoretically possible for every college-educated man to find a spouse who matches him in education, even as this is not possible for every woman. But men also have another option: marry a woman whose credentials exceed his, and encourage her and push her. Expect to see more men placing their bets on high-earning women. People are adaptable, and men aren't stupid. In fact, you could argue that men are now presented with an opportunity that has never been open to them, not at this level of historical magnitude.

A Historic Opportunity

It's possible men have been willing to marry up all along. Until now, it's been hard to assess this, because men have had few opportunities to do so, at least not in large numbers. But Ran Abramitzky, an economist at Stanford University, found a way to test how quickly men can adjust to a new opportunity, working with two colleagues, among them a French economist whose extended family included several great-aunts and uncles who came of age during World War I. Out of four aunts, the only one who married did so before the war. The other three remained single. Of these, one explained that all the marriage proposals she received were from men who came from socioeconomic backgrounds humbler than hers was, so she did not accept them. But there weren't better offers forthcoming. The war's carnage gave men who survived it the opportunity to marry better—and men hastened to do so.

Intrigued by the aunt's recollections, Abramitzky and his colleagues looked at census records for regions of France that suffered heavy casualties during the Great War. The conflict killed more than a million of the country's soldiers and officers. Before the war, almost everybody in France married, and men often married down. Marriage rates plummeted at the war's outset, but in the four years after the war ended, more than 2 million marriages took place. By then, there was a major gender imbalance in favor of men. Looking at single people 30 years old or younger, the economists found men in regions with a greater gender imbalance were making much better marriages than men in regions that had been hit less hard, marrying women of higher social classes than they otherwise could have. Men were able to vault out of their social station and land in a life that gave them more resources and better prospects. From this, they concluded that men—like women—may be happy to marry up if they can; historically, this has just not been an option.

Alas, because of the limitations of their data, Abramitzky and his colleagues were not able to bring to life the details of these courtships, nor the aftermath. They could never know how the marriages evolved. Were the marriages happy? Did the women hold their money over the men's heads and berate them as low-class? Did the men remind the women they were lucky to have husbands? One wishes a Flaubert or Jane Austen had emerged from the ranks of the postwar citizenry and written a novel of manners set in the war-decimated villages of France, in which a lonely aristocratic woman meets a working-class veteran in a market and plucks him out of the arms of some devastated merchant girl. "We will never know how the wife and husband behaved to each other," acknowledges Abramitzky. One way for an economist to get at this would be to track the children of these unions, but World War II truncated too many of the lives of the next generation.

The surprise, to Abramitzky, is "how flexible this marriage market was." His study suggests it could be that men and women both would like to marry up—and fate determines which sex gets to do this. If this is true, it pretty much drives a stake in the Darwinian argument that women are hardwired to seek providers. His research suggests that everybody, pretty much, is hardwired to seek a provider, and that men are delighted to pursue women capable of making their lives more comfortable. However, the experience of his colleague's maiden aunt reminds us who the losers are in this equation: women in the middle and lower parts of the socioeconomic spectrum will look at the men who are left, sniff in disappointment, and walk away. In the United States, this is a real danger. Sociologist Bradford Wilcox worries that educated women "may be marrying the cream of the working-class crop," which may be good for them, "but worse for the female working class." If these patterns persist, he points out, we could see the "same retreat from marriage" among the working class that we have seen among the poor.

Boxed In as the Higher Earner

Here is the other consequence: as more and more young men accept that their girlfriends have better prospects, and endeavor to help them, women will be obliged to deal with their doubts and ask themselves how they feel about being a longtime primary earner. In Atlanta, I had breakfast with Lindsey Goodman, an outdoorsy 27-year-old with dark blond hair, green eyes, and purple-tinted sunglasses pushed to the top of her head. Goodman got her undergraduate degree in applied physics from State University of New York–Binghamton. There were lots of women in her classes—she recalls that as many as half the students in her major were female. When we spoke, she was working on a Ph.D. in materials science from Georgia Tech, a grueling regime that has been the defining experience of her life. At one point she had had a boyfriend in the same program who competed with her incessantly. If she'd had a hard day in the lab, "He'd be like, 'Oh, you think *your* day was bad? Mine consisted of pressing powder and breathing noxious fumes!'" She and her friends developed a term for this dynamic: "one-upper syndrome." His work was proprietary and so he couldn't write or publish papers, and he would get jealous when she spoke at conferences or published her work.

After they broke up, Lindsey developed a relationship that was much more supportive. She got to know her current boyfriend during rock climbing excursions, a pastime that has become a major shared interest. At the time we spoke, he also was working on a doctorate, though she was working, it appeared, a little harder. "At the end of the day, he's the one who says, 'I can't work anymore.' I say, 'I'm still focusing pretty well,'" said Lindsey. She took breaks at his urging, which she felt was a good thing: he relaxed her and loosened her up. Rather than competing, they were finding ways to build niches—areas of specialization and expertise. "He has written more papers than I have—he knows a lot more about certain subjects than I do. It's not like he is the less hardworking or not as smart—he's as smart as me."

A year from graduation, her job prospects looked excellent. She had interned with Shell, but was thinking about moving away from the oil and gas industry toward a career in failure analysis, which is figuring out what caused a crash or industrial accident or product failure. She had had discussions with a consulting firm called Exponent.

Up to then, she always assumed a husband's career would proceed at the same pace hers did. "I figured we'd earn about equal." But recent conversations suggested her boyfriend saw her prospects as superior. "He's said to me—with me not saying anything—'Wow, I guess you're going to earn a lot more than I will,'" she related. "I was like, 'Do you think so?' He said, 'If you're going to work for Exponent and do failure analysis, you're going to earn a lot more. You're going to make a lot more money than me.'" He was thinking it might make sense to put her career first. "He's said to me, more than three or four times: 'If you get a job and have to move to California, I'll just find something out there.' He's actually willing to compromise for me." He had even thought of dropping out of the Ph.D. program, because his adviser was so discouraging. He thought since Lindsey was going to stick it out to the end, maybe he should just get a master's. She was encouraging him to persist. "He's in a place where he's like, he's just—I don't know—losing motivation. He'll find it again. I'm trying to be motivating."

They had talked about how much time they would have to spend apart if she took the job with Exponent. He thought he'd be okay with it—and this is an important concession. Up to now, one of the pressures making it hard for women to thrive in demanding positions is men's lingering expectation that a woman should be available to a man when he wants her. When she asked him if they would be okay if they knew, going in, that they'd be apart a lot, he said, "I hope so."

Finding Common Ground

As more women do marry men with less education and income, they will need to find a new way to make these relationships feel equal. Given that women do want a partner "on my level," couples will have to find a means of achieving equilibrium. One factor that will help is a shared interest outside the realm of work. It's significant that Lindsey Goodman and her boyfriend both enjoy rock climbing and being outdoors and also trained for a half-marathon together. These kinds of pursuits are where many couples will find their balance. A theory set forth by economist Betsey Stevenson lends support to this idea. Stevenson argues that times have changed, and now that domestic workloads have shrunk, men and women are no longer looking for complementary marriages where one spouse earns and the other stays home. Instead of "producing" efficient households, Stevenson argues that what modern couples want to produce is shared enjoyment. She calls this "consumption complementarities." Couples want to produce time in which they can do things together. They want to travel; attend movies; go hiking. If this is true—if "matching" more and more means matching on leisure and interests—this will be the means by which marriages will work when the wife is higher-earning and better-educated. Expect to see more and more women partnering with men who share their passions and pleasures.

This, too, is already proving true in a number of couples I interviewed. Amy Antonellis is a law student in Vermont who when we spoke was engaged to an auto mechanic, and very much looking forward to their upcoming wedding in a Vermont country inn. Amy, who is from Massachusetts, grew up in a working-class family where her mother stayed home and her father was the breadwinner, working two jobs as a janitor and maintenance worker. She knew she would not be a homemaker like her mother, and needed to "get as many skills as possible for making myself marketable." She assumed she would be working in the context of a dual-earner marriage. "It wasn't that I wasn't going to have an income—I assumed that whoever I was going to be with would make more money." But that's not how things turned out. She met her fiancé, Dave, in high school. Both came from working-class families; both absorbed the work ethic that goes along with it. "He's just very industrious," she said. "He is very much like me—he's a hard worker. Very much like my father." Her fiancé tried four-year college, found it wasn't to his taste, emerged with a two-year associate's degree, and began working as a carpenter. "He's very hands-on," she says. "Very spatial."

For her fiancé, the skilled trades offered the path to a stable job; for Amy, there were no similar options. If she wanted to move up in life, she had to go to a four-year college. In conversations with her fiancé, Amy "made it abundantly clear that I was going to do things with my education." Once she decided to go to law school, she told him that if he wanted their relationship to continue, he would have to follow her to Vermont. He did. "He has never questioned anything I've wanted to do. He's never tried to hold me back. He is nothing but supportive. That means the world to me."

And so her fiancé did what fiancées used to do: he took a job that could sustain the couple while his spouse accrued debt as well as earning potential. For him, moving for the sake of Amy's career involved real sacrifice. When we spoke, he was working as an auto mechanic in Vermont, where wages are lower than they are in Massachusetts, but the upside is that "he's getting a lot of experience. Vermonters are much more trusting, and it's a smaller shop, and they let him do anything—rebuilding, getting experience that shops in another state would appreciate." He also shares all their domestic duties.

"Dave's a very adaptive person," she said. "He's got a very down-to-earth quality. People like him and want to talk to him. Once they see what a hard worker he is, he has never had trouble finding employment."

And the fact that he isn't a law student is an asset. The last thing Amy would want is a partner who matched her by being in the same field. "I can come home and I can shut my profession off. I can come home and be comfortable. I'll be like, gosh, let's talk about anything but the law. I keep that very separate. When you're in a situation of advanced study, people can easily become obsessed with what they're doing—classmates dating each other, it's very competitive."

But the shared interest is crucial. They both love the outdoors, and spend a lot of time hiking. Having a third domain in which they are doing the same thing and on an equal footing keeps them close. More and more, women will marry down and men will marry up; what they will share in common will be interests that exist apart from the world of earning and education.

Women Will Raise Men Up

And marrying "down" doesn't have to be a permanent phenomenon. People grow; they change; they change one another. That's the essence of any good relationship: mutual encouragement. In some cases, women who want an equal partner will devise another solution. They will marry men who did not go to college and make them enroll. Driven by the conviction that the best partner is an educated partner, women will take the dating pool they've been given and tweak it to make it better. They will exhort and encourage and fill out the forms for the registrar. They will employ moral suasion. In an interview, economist Betsey Stevenson ventured that the rate at which men are not going to college is "untenable," and pointed toward exactly this solution: if women want to marry a college graduate, they may have to fashion him themselves.

This is where social comparison can work in a couple's favor, and in society's favor as well. In fact, social comparison may even solve the imbalance problem. As the field has continued to explore the impact of comparison on intimate partners, psychologists have found that it's not always a source of competition or resentment. To the contrary: comparison within relationships can be a powerful incentive to do better, because there is another coping mechanism partners can display, beyond undermining or leaving. Faced with a wife who is outperforming them, some men will cope by asking more of themselves and trying harder. When people are in close and supportive marriages, they will react to a spouse's higher achievements by improving their own, concluded a 2008 study whose authors interviewed scores of couples. And when a spouse isn't doing as well as they are at something, loving spouses will attempt to change their partner to bring about a closer match "between ideals and perceptions."

In this study, psychologists interviewed spouses about the circumstances under which they compare themselves. One husband acknowledged that his wife's higher salary had become a personal benchmark. "I compared my income vs. her income. I did this to use as a gauge, a guide of the potential I can achieve in earning income. Not in a jealous way but more as an inspiration." The authors add that in good marriages, both men and women tend to idealize their partner and see the best in them—and people also help their spouse grow into that ideal. Women who idealize their husbands can help them become that idealized version; men who respect and admire their wives will seek to be the best partner they can be. Marriage, at its best, is a machine for mutual self-improvement.

And so, expect this: rather than emasculating men and driving down their testosterone and wiping the floor with them, many high-achieving women will inspire the men they live with to do better and be better. These women, by striving, will make men strive, too. Lindsey Goodman kept urging her boyfriend to look past an unsupportive Ph.D. adviser; she thought that if she took a job first, that would give him time to sort himself out and find his way forward.

Over and over—unexpectedly—this was the story I heard from women living in South Texas. You don't find a lot of diversity in the marriage market there, but women by and large don't want to relocate; their families are there, and they feel deeply rooted. Women who are outperforming men academically often respond by marrying men who didn't graduate from college—and then pushing them to do so. Among these was Desirée Mendez, the high-achieving congressional staffer who is happily married to her high school sweetheart, Jasson Caltzontzint. Jasson was raised without much family support, practical or emotional, for his schooling. In high school, a teacher pointed out that Desirée was the best thing that had ever happened to him, something Jasson wholeheartedly agrees with. They started college together, but Jasson found his course work intimidating. In order to pay his tuition he had to take a job; in order to get to the job he had to buy a truck; in order to make the payments on the truck, he had to drop some classes. "I didn't qualify for grants or loans because I had a job, and I didn't want to burden my parents," he says, so he took a hiatus, and before he knew it he was working forty hours a week for the city of Edinburg.

In the same period of time, Desirée got both her undergraduate degree and her master's. She set about coaxing Jasson into returning to college full-time. "It's really important that you finish," she told him. In his early thirties, Jasson did. She encouraged him by citing her own example: "I said, 'I struggled with statistics—who likes it? The teacher!'" Her empathy and belief in him made all the difference. "I couldn't have done it without her," Jasson told me. "She would drop me off, pick me up, help me with some of my homework." He adds that when he went back to college, he noticed a change in the composition of students. "There were more young women" in the classrooms, and in the job market as well. "In a short period of time, I could see how everything was reversed. You have women wanting to seek positions with Border Patrol, with the government, FBI, Customs, it's pretty surprising. And lately we're starting to see Hispanic females join the state police. It's not uncommon to see a female state trooper in our area. Before, that was taboo. Now you'll see them regularly."

When I talked to them, Jasson was still getting his career under way. He was at an insurance claims adjuster training session out of town on the weekend when I interviewed Desirée in person. She is a charismatic, easygoing woman with a ready laugh, lipsticked and wearing thick turquoise jewelry. It was easy to see why Jasson didn't like being away from her. "He'll call home and say, you know, 'I'm surrounded by white people,'" Desirée said, amused. "He said, 'I don't know if I can do this, I'm away from home, I don't have your cooking, this isn't fun.' I said you know what—just a little longer. I said: 'Pull your professional self together!'"

One of the many things she loves about Jasson, she said, is his childlike quality; he has a great sense of humor, which lightens her up. Early in their relationship—back in high school—he invented an imaginary character who embodies the white guy Desirée will eventually leave him for. Jasson thought of the most Anglo, the whitest name he could, and invokes him as a third person in their marriage. Sometimes the white guy's name is Chris McAllister; sometimes it's Chance Wilson. Either way, "he's blond, blue-eyed, and on the polo team," says Jasson, and he always gets a laugh of out Desirée. It's a shared marital joke. But it's also a phenomenon he sees a lot: when women in the area join the military or attend college out of state, Jasson notes that they come back married to some version of Chance Wilson.

When I asked Jasson if he did fear that Desirée would leave him, he invoked the memory of his late mother, who, he says, suffered in a marriage that she couldn't afford to leave, and said he would never force Desirée to stay in a marriage if she didn't want to. At the same time, he was working hard to make sure this is a marriage she would never want to leave. Desirée, in addition to her job in the local congressman's office, was thinking of starting a Ph.D. program in leadership. "I'm totally in support of that," said Jasson. "I'm just going to have to step it up. So she can fulfill that dream, I would probably have to do more of the housework. If she does go [back to school] and we have a child, I'm going to have to do all the child care. There's no way around it. I'm looking at it as an investment for the family. Once you get into the doctoral program, it's a heavy load. I don't want to burden her—hey, you're writing this paper, cook for me."

More and more, women are becoming the ones who sacrifice their income for the benefit of their dependents; more and more, men are becoming the ones who sacrifice leisure time and professional advancement to further the prospects of their wives. Even as Jasson expects to work, he figures Desirée will have the more high-powered career. At the time we spoke, he said, she was making $47,000 and he was making about $44,000, but she was the one with the government job and retirement benefits. He was happy to be her cheerleader, her head cook and bottle washer, her domestic support system; to be the primary parent, if they have children, and to keep the household running. He was happy to give her the encouragement she had always given him. When I asked Desirée if she would consider running for political office someday herself, she didn't rule it out. Jasson would be the ideal political spouse: funny, willing, supportive, and in love with her.

"I am putting all my chips on her," he said.

The Adoring Gaze

Psychologists talk about "reflection": basking in the glow of the achievements of someone you are connected to. Women traditionally have basked in the glow of their husbands' jobs and community standing, a truth embodied in the classic posture of the political wife: behind her husband, gazing at him adoringly. What the above anecdotes suggest is that men can experience the same reflected glory. When I interviewed a bestselling author about how her success affected her marriage, she laughed and said of her husband: "He thinks it's happening to him."

"I don't think he resents me," said another woman I talked to. A teacher for the gifted, she had married a man who suffered from learning disabilities that led him to become disengaged from high school. After a tumultuous youth and some brushes with the law, he found his way as an electrician and viewed marrying her as his best achievement. "He has always [been] proud of what I've accomplished, and that he managed to marry somebody who's got so much going for her," this teacher said. She continued: "There's all kinds of things I don't worry about. I don't worry that he's going to leave me or cheat on me. In a way, that's a very stable scenario." This, too, was a telling comment; it confirms that men are now the ones with more to lose from marital dissolution.

Ten
The New World of Nonmarriage Choices

"I'll Keep the Dog and Get Rid of You"

In the summer of 2011, the nation's best and most experienced statisticians gathered on the campus of the National Institutes of Health in Bethesda, Maryland. They came from every counting agency imaginable: from the U.S. Census Bureau, the National Center for Health Statistics, the National Center for Family and Marriage Research, the Bureau of Labor Statistics, from colleges and universities. They had gathered to try and address one central question: Now that so many more American households are inhabited by people who are unmarried, how should these households be counted and described? What new living arrangements are people coming up with, quietly, and how should the government characterize them, if at all? And why is marriage falling out of fashion in the United States and elsewhere? This country, like much of Europe, has seen a striking decline in marriage rates: just over half of American adults are married. Births to single mothers have risen, from 5 percent of births in 1960 to 41 percent of all births in 2008. Cohabitation rates have doubled since 1990. Men and women (and men and men and women and women) are forming relationships but not legally committing to them, at least not in the ways people once did. For the better part of two days, statisticians and demographers discussed the complex arrangements that constitute the modern household: married, single, cohabiting, in love but not cohabiting, cohabiting but not in love, cohabiting as roommates, cohabiting and having sex, having sex but living in different countries, married but not living in the same city. Europe has seen a growing movement called LAT—living apart together—in which people consider themselves partnered but do not live in the same house or even the same region. There are signs that the same arrangement is catching on here. The creaky government bureaucracy tries to cope with these changes, because it matters when assigning Social Security payments and coming up with tax policies. The conference attendees agonized over the wording of census questions and asked things like: If people are living in the same home, but not having sex, can we consider them partnered? No? What about married people who are not having sex? What does partnered even mean anymore?

There is no question that women's rising resources are part of what's behind the splintering of trends in human living arrangements. Marriage, at least for the near future, will be the chosen living state of a smaller group of people. Most Americans say they want to get married, but fewer are. Some are just waiting longer. Others are easing their way into arrangements that bear some resemblance to marriage but do not involve quite the degree of formality. The London *Times* was right. Some women who can afford to eschew marriage will eschew it. If women must choose between being single and being in a bad marriage, women will choose being single. The independence effect is real and it is a good thing, all in all. "It was so much easier to dump him since I didn't depend on him financially," said a mechanical engineer named Sophie, whose boyfriend was threatened by her higher earning and took it out on her by driving her car while he was drunk, and when she asked him not to, verbally abusing her. She kicked him out, took her energy and resources, and began devoting them to community projects. She talked with some old friends who agreed that they don't need to be married to be complete. They used to think they did. They don't think that any longer.

And remember Felicity? The high-earning IT executive whose husband wouldn't come to bed with her, and spent hours watching porn, and got mad when she had a big win at work? Well, what happened to that marriage is this: Felicity wanted to get a dog, and her husband didn't want her to, he thought the dog would absorb too much of her time and affection, and the argument went on, and she got the dog, and he got mad about it, and then one day she had a brainstorm: *I'll keep the dog and get rid of you.* And that's what she did. The dog is extremely supportive of her achievements.

Both of these women, Felicity and Sophie, are uncertain whether they will ever partner again, and if so, under what circumstances and in what form. The statistics tell us this: the more academic resources women command, the slower they are to remarry after divorce. Those who remarry fastest after divorce are men with higher education, and women with lower education, according to economist Betsey Stevenson. For women like Felicity and Sophie, with skills and resources—and skepticism—it makes more sense to wait around to see what, or who, materializes.

For some women, bad experiences with competitive and ungrateful partners will make them unwilling to commit to remarriage. Ever. "The most I could ever see doing is cohabiting," said the ex-soldier I interviewed who at one point found herself married to a man who refused to move for her career—a man who expected her to buy him a television so he could play videogames while she worked to support him and ran up their joint credit card account to the point where he wrecked his credit, and hers.

What will households look like, then? When women do manage to dump that freeloading or competitive partner, and when they choose to spend time living on their own, how will the future unfold? Here was one of the more intriguing patterns that emerged from conversations with women breadwinners: women will divorce men who are underperforming, and then cohabit with them. The trajectory goes something like this: woman marries husband; woman out-performs husband; husband stops trying; woman loses respect for husband; woman divorces husband; ex-husband gets his act together and improves his prospects; woman moves back in with him, this time unmarried. This was the compromise solution that Alicia Simpson, the psychiatrist, was contemplating. Even as she had lost her wifely feelings for her ex-husband, she liked him and continued to value his strong relationship with their sons. When I interviewed her, she was considering having him live with her—maybe in a separate apartment. "It's like, minus the personal relationship, we get along just fine. It's the weirdest thing," she said. In this case, they would not be romantically partnered; they would be co-parenting in the same residence. This suggests that one impulse behind the trend in cohabitation is women's unwillingness—at all socioeconomic levels—to yoke themselves to men who seem to be unstable providers. Alicia was thinking she might buy a new house, big enough for all of them. Envisioning a life where they were living under the same roof and he was helping with chores just like always, she joked, "That way, I still wouldn't have to take out the garbage."

The same thing happened with another woman I interviewed, a university professor whose husband, a police officer, had seemed to her to be stagnating. He was supportive of her career, but she felt he grew too dependent. "He got very comfortable with that—he looked to me to be the breadwinner," she related. As they thought about things like new cars and private school for their child, he would look to her like: How are we going to pay for this? What are you going to do to make this happen? Much like Alicia, this woman grew weary of that dynamic and sought a divorce. Much like Alicia's husband, her ex pursued additional schooling after they divorced. They moved back in together, but did not remarry. "I figured the things I was unhappy about in the scheme of things were probably pretty small, and we fixed the other things," she said.

For less affluent Americans, there is even more skepticism about marrying a weak provider. Somewhat paradoxically, working- and lower-middle-class Americans tend to express a strong belief that you should not get married unless and until you are capable of supporting a household. When men can't contribute, women won't marry them. End of story. This is the cohort among whom marriage is declining most dramatically. It includes a construction worker I interviewed one day over the phone when she was painting the walls in a public housing project. Her ex-husband had shot her in the head, and she divorced him. Now, all the men she met wanted her to pay their way. None of the men she knew seemed to have any money. She taught herself construction work, and works rehabbing houses. She used to work as a nanny, but finds the wages in men's work much higher. When I asked her about the pool of men available to her, she said: "It's scary. It's a scary pool."

"Sometimes We Get Weird Looks, as Though We're Lesbians"

Other women will turn to one another, but not necessarily in a sexual way. Women will stay single and do it happily; they will go out with other women and they will value the time they spend together. Women will revert to the kind of intensive female friendships that were widely accepted in the 18th and 19th centuries, when women might write testaments of love without having their sexual preferences examined. Sometimes this will mean staying in: "It's not unusual for us to stay home on a Saturday night and watch a movie, eat some ice cream," said Ashlie Brown, who when I interviewed her was living in Atlanta, and organized a portion of her social life around her female friends. "I think [our] prevailing theory is that it will just fall into our lap when it happens, and it's sort of not worth your time to go out and look for it."

Other times it will mean going out, in big groups. "When I go out to restaurants, all I see are women," said Annette Alvarado, the schoolteacher in South Texas. In the same region, a lawyer named JoAnne Garcia and her female friends get together all the time, on what amount to big group dates. JoAnne, who went to law school at the University of Texas at Austin and now works at a firm in the McAllen area, is a single mother; her family helps with child care and so do her friends, many of whom she has known since childhood. One weekend, I had brunch with JoAnne and a number of the women she socializes with: fellow lawyer Nereida Lopez; Dana Campos, a Tufts graduate working on her master's at UT Austin; Elizabeth Tovar, a first-grade teacher; Cassondra Dominguez, who had just graduated from UTPA; and Patricia Dominguez, Cassie's older sister, who was working in rehabilitative services. The women agreed that men in the area had little interest in them. "We've kind of thrown up our hands and said 'Oh well,' we'll enjoy each other's company," said JoAnne, an exuberant woman with luscious black hair, nails painted bright red, and retro thick-framed glasses. She said the men in her region are either intimidated by their salaries or they are high-earning and prefer a woman who is not an equal. "I haven't found many middle-ground men."

JoAnne and Nereida are very involved in a local committee of young lawyers, but they've noticed that male lawyers don't date them. They prefer to socialize with each other anyway, because if work intervenes and one of them has to run, the other doesn't get offended. The women are struck by the number of women in their region who are single. They appear before a lot of women judges, and can't think offhand of one who is married. The local saying goes that for a woman lawyer, becoming a judge is a guaranteed divorce. "They are very highly prized women in their professions, really good lawyers, really good community leaders, and I've never known any of them to be married," remarked JoAnne.

In an ironic way, having this many dynamic, unattached women has a salutary effect on the region; without men taking up their time, the women channel their expertise and energy into community projects. One woman at the table, Dana, founded a nonprofit that is attempting to turn around the local dropout rate by recruiting college students to work on art projects with high schoolers. Dana put JoAnne on the board of directors. Raising money, she noticed that a lot of donors were female doctors and attorneys, and after a meeting, Dana says, "We always joke—are they married? Do they have a ring? We had a meeting with a really successful head of a bank down here, and she was telling us how to make it sustainable, how to make a business plan, and after the meeting we were saying: She's not married."

The night before, the whole group had gone out to celebrate Cassie's graduation. They ended up dancing together, because that's what they do now: they go out and they dance. "Everybody there was with a partner, and it was just all of us by ourselves. It was fun," said JoAnne, laughing. "We go out and don't have expectations about meeting anyone. We don't even look at anybody."

"They won't come up and talk to us—every time we go out, people don't come up and talk to us, and if they do, it's because they are very inebriated," she continued. "A couple of weeks ago, my dad was like— 'You need to be very careful when you go out in town. Somebody got shot there. It's getting dangerous. If they look questionable, do not talk to them. Don't talk to anybody. If they're spending money too easily, you know something's going on.' And I said, 'Dad, you don't have to worry. Nobody ever talks to us!' He was, like, 'Really? And you all just go out girls? And just go out by yourself?' And I was like: 'We do it all the time.' He's like, 'Good.'"

"We love to dance," she finished, "and I guess maybe they recognize us as those dancing girls and they won't come up and talk to us."

"They're intimidated," said Nereida.

"Sometimes we get weird looks, as though we're lesbians," mused JoAnne. "Remember when we went to the nail salon, we were getting a pedicure, there was a gentleman doing our nails—[he and his coworkers] were like so, what are you doing tonight? And we said: We are going out. They said: With your boyfriends? We said no, with each other. And they were like: Just you two? And they kept looking at each other and we said, we always go out together! We like one another!"

Women Will Own the Houses

In the future, after a lively evening with friends, women will return to houses they own. While waiting for a relationship to materialize— or not—they will purchase homes, settle in, build equity, wait. They will form close and enduring relationships with properties they have and hold and love and cherish. They will commit to mortgages; invest in their future; easily qualify for bank loans at a time in their lives when they have fat incomes and few or no dependents. Women will be deemed—correctly—excellent credit risks. If and when women homeowners do marry or cohabit, they will expect men to adjust to these surroundings.

That future is already visible. "Single women [are] already buying twice as many homes as single men, a ratio almost certain to increase given fundamental trends in income dynamics," Reach Advisors president James Chung wrote in *Urban Land* magazine in 2010, echoing some of the themes that emerged in his firm's analysis of women out-earning men in cities. Ever since the late 1940s, he pointed out in an interview, builders have regarded baby boomer families as their target audience, providing them in childhood with modest Levittown-type developments, and later, as that demographic matured and got wealthier, vacation homes and McMansions. Now, he pointed out, builders need to adjust their forecasts. Single women even rival married couples with children as a home-buying market.

"Now that I think about it, a lot of the men I know rent," said Meredith Hopps, an Atlanta engineer, hearing this. "Yeah, a lot of the men. That's weird. I didn't think about it before. Even men in their thirties, they rent."

Hopps was sitting on a bar stool at Octane, a coffee lounge in a newly gentrified part of Atlanta known as West Midtown. A personable, self-assured 25-year-old, Hopps recently purchased a condo in that area. After graduating from Georgia Tech, she was working in the aerospace industry and pursuing a master's. She was doing well and had every reason to expect this will continue. Industry chatter suggests there will be massive retirements in the aerospace field, the upshot of which, she speculated, is that there will be "a lot of very young executives." It goes without saying that these companies will want women.

To her, there were lots of reasons to buy. She has no plans to move away from Georgia; her parents live north of Atlanta, and she wants to stay close to them. Back when she was renting, she had a string of bad roommates, and reasoned that buying would give her more control over whom she lived with. She was renting out one of her bedrooms, so she had income from her home as well as her job. The federal government's incentive program for first-time buyers came for her at the right time. "I'm not waiting around for a relationship to have something that I can call my own," she said. She was dating, in theory, but found the pool immature and unsatisfactory: men who send emails in response to her online dating profile often see fit to make beer jokes, and she gets tired of pointing out that beer is made with hops, not hopps.

Annette Alvarado, the 29-year-old teacher in South Texas, bought a brand-new three-bedroom, two-and-a half-bath house in a development outside McAllen. She looked around, saw a shortage of men at her earning and maturity level, and responded by calling a real estate agent rather than a matchmaking service.

"This is the garage; this is the half-bath," said Alvarado one Saturday evening, giving a tour of her new home. The collapse of the housing market and ensuing fall in home prices enabled her to buy more than she thought she could—in this case, 1,700 square feet. She couldn't find anything smaller. Developers in her region have not yet gotten the message; aiming their new constructions at families, what they got was an unmarried fourth-grade teacher who felt entitled to be choosy. "I told my Realtor I want a brand-new home. I didn't want a used home—I didn't want to worry," she said. In the garage was another acquisition she was proud of: a 2006 Mustang, Vista Blue, complete with pony pack. Her very own muscle car. It was the second vehicle she had purchased. She gave the first one, a truck, to her parents.

She has a fifteen-year mortgage, and pays a little over $900 a month. She walked me past the first-floor powder room, the pantry and laundry room, the kitchen with tile floors and faux granite counters, the living room, the patio, and the fenced backyard. Upstairs were three bedrooms and a sitting room, all furnished. There was a sleigh bed in her bedroom and a computer station in a guest room. It was not clear to her what a man could add to the setup. She stood for a minute, looking at two flat-screen televisions she had not yet unpacked, in part because she did not know how to hang them. Maybe a man could help her with that. "I wouldn't know how to put in those mounting things," she said. Then again, her dad could do it. Or she could hire a handyman. She already has a lawn service to mow her grass.

There was a downside, though, to her comfortable, well-maintained home: it scared men away. Not long after moving in, she went on a date with a guy, several years older, who came to pick her up. "That's a nice house," he said admiringly as they were driving away. When he asked if she lived with her family, Annette told him she bought it herself.

"The first thing he asked me was: 'How did you do that?'" she related. "I'm like, 'What do you mean how did I do that? I graduated from college and saved my money and invested it.' He did not say anything. He was just, like, speechless. And I was like, 'And how about you? Do you live in an apartment?' He was like, 'No, I live with my mom and my grandmom.' I'm like, 'Okay.' And we would talk and stuff, and then like in a week or so, he just stopped calling." In that sense, she thinks, her house is a strike against her. "My guy friends would tell me: It's because you have a home. They compare themselves to you and feel like you have more than they do."

Yet the men who see it as attractive are also problematic. After buying her place, she heard from an ex-high-school boyfriend who works construction. "He just wanted to date me because I had a home and I'm financially set. He wanted to rely on me. My mom told me: Be careful."

Ultimately, though, Annette thinks her house will inoculate her against the situation a number of her girlfriends find themselves in, dealing with possessive partners who react to the new economic order by insisting that their wives not work. She loves teaching, never wants to give it up, and feels less vulnerable in a property that has her name on the title. "If my husband says: I want you to stay home, I'll be like: No. I do see myself marrying with kids, but I'm not quitting." If she does marry, her husband will have to move in and live by her rules. So expect this: more than having a room of their own, women will have an entire house, and the men in their lives will have to confront, and adjust to, that incontrovertible truth.

Other Voices, Other Grooms: Women Will Travel Beyond Racial and Ethnic Boundaries

Here's another thing women will do: they will behave like gay men. Women will consider all sorts of not-on-my-level arrangements. Of all the people who partner permanently—straight married people, straight cohabiting people, lesbian partners—gay men are the most willing to travel outside their comfort zone and partner with someone outside their age or race or degree set. Women will start thinking the way gay men think. Some have been predicting this for a long time. Back in 1964, the sociologist Milton Gordon argued that the notion of "race" was becoming a meaningless, vestigial concept, and predicted that as countries like the United States became forward-thinking and modernized, categories like race would fall away, and qualities like education would become more important to people seeking partners. This did not happen quickly. The flowering of identity movements in the 1970s and 1980s encouraged racial solidarity. Over the years, people have shown themselves slow to abandon same-race pairing.

But Gordon's prediction is coming true, and it will continue to be truer. There does come a tipping point, and educational disparity is one of them. Among Hispanics, college-educated women are more likely to marry outside their ethnicity than their less-educated peers, hence Jasson Caltzontzint's pointed jokes about Chance Wilson and Chris McAllister. Hispanic women I interviewed invariably said it's more important to find a partner who is college-educated than it is to partner with somebody who shares their ethnic background. "I have a group of Mexican friends here in New York, and we all date foreigners," meaning non-Mexicans, acknowledged Sandra, 26, who was born in Chicago and raised in Mexico. She attended university there, then moved to New York to get a master's at the Interactive Telecommunications Program at NYU. She and her friends have a word for themselves: they are *malinches*, a term they use to describe women who like foreign men. It derives from the story of an indigenous woman, her behavior now the stuff of mythology, who some say helped bring about the conquest of Mexico by consorting with the Spanish conquistadores. Sandra says she would love to date a man who shares her culture—"I would like to have somebody who spoke my same language"—but has found this difficult. In her experience, Hispanic men tend to be traditional and to disapprove of her citified habits; or they are intimidated and "really admire you too much."

In the coming decades, racial and ethnic intermarriage will increase as women seek partners who share their education and worldview. At Stanford University, sociologist Elizabeth McClintock did a study of hookups among undergraduates, and found that Asian women are more willing than Asian men to enter into interracial liaisons. It is not clear whether this is because Asian women are seeking to partner outside their own culture, or whether they are "eroticized" by white men and actively pursued. Among African American men and women, the converse holds true: black men are willing to hook up interracially, while black women "are very committed to the idea of having a same-race partner, and find it problematic to have an intra-race partner," McClintock said. "The black women are really excluded; they're being left single." The reasons for this are complicated; as McClintock pointed out, sometimes black women felt rejected by nonblack men and attempted to circumvent this by avoiding the situation. Interracial relationships between white men and black women have a painful history in this country, starting with the long period when female slaves were forcibly subjected to the sexual attention of white masters. But by now, any number of respected black academics—Donna Franklin, Ralph Richard Banks—have argued that it's time for African American women to expand their options by dating men of other races.

And in fact, things are changing among black Americans. In 2011, Zhenchao Qian and Daniel Lichter published research showing that intermarriage between black and white Americans has increased markedly since 1980, and education is a major reason why. "It used to be that race trumped everything, including education, when it came to marriage between blacks and whites," said Qian as the study was announced. "But that is changing. For the first time, we found that highly educated blacks and whites were more likely to intermarry. That is very significant and is another sign that racial boundaries are blurring."

In conversations I had with African American women, a number voiced willingness to date outside their race. "I haven't dated a Caucasian guy in a long time—I'm open, but I never get asked out," said Brenda Tyler, the single, big-city physician. "People will say to me: Did you ever consider dating outside your race? I've dated Hispanic men, that's never been an issue, but very few men outside my race ask me out." On an online dating site, however, Tyler had been contacted by a man who turned out to be Caucasian. She had gone out with him and was feeling guardedly optimistic. She liked that he was proactive; rather than expecting her to make all the plans and decisions, he had of his own accord gotten tickets to basketball and hockey games. "He plans ahead," enthused Tyler. She was finding that he was "on the quiet side," but with a good sense of humor. Her friends told her he looked like Kiefer Sutherland. She thought he looked more like Hugh Laurie. Whatever. "I'm open to it," she said. "We're very similar. We have a good time. He was very considerate. So I'm open to it."

Reach Advisors president James Chung predicts that women will experiment in all kinds of directions. Some will veer in the direction of a less-educated but wildly attractive trophy husband; others, determined to date a fellow college graduate, may be willing to consider a man who is not as good-looking as they might like. "Some people I said I would never date—I am willing to take a second look," conceded Nikia Williams, the electrical engineer in Detroit. Williams is African American, and directs the singles group at her local church. "I truly want to be married," she said in an interview. Lately, she was finding that Facebook offered unexpected possibilities. She had not intended to use it for dating, but found herself getting messages from men saying they liked her postings and wanted to get to know her better. One contacted her through Facebook, then came to visit. "He seemed like a pretty decent guy. Just off of looks, if he was walking down the street I would not have kept looking." Connecting with men online, she said, "gives people a chance to get to know them, and not just go off looks."

Traveling in Search of Mates "On My Level," Women Will Keep Airlines Aloft

In 1620, a ship of brides arrived in Jamestown, Virginia, laden with maids of "gentle birth" who had crossed the Atlantic seeking husbands. Their transport was paid by the Virginia Company, which had established the colony and wanted it to grow and prosper. The women's contract stipulated that they were to marry free men—not servants—who would be able to repay the company for their passage. The women were seeking men on their social level, and were willing to undertake a dangerous voyage and uncertain future to find them. Humans have always been adaptable; we always have been migratory; and we always have been willing to migrate to mate.

In the future, something similar will happen. Women who remain determined to find a partner "on their level" will travel to seek this elusive species. Women with resources—especially women in big cities with airport hubs—will rescue the travel industry, keeping airlines aloft in the pursuit of long-term companions. Or even short-term ones. Women will take advantage of frequent-flier miles, cheap out-of-season airfares, and digital follow-up. Around the country—around the world—a restless, ceaseless movement will intensify, in which women use air travel as a means of enlarging their mating pool and finding men who are their equals.

There is a writ-small version of this going on among undergraduates at colleges with a high percentage of women. In the Washington, D.C., area, where many universities are now majority female, women travel from campus to campus—from American University to George Washington to Georgetown—seeking new men or more men or simply different men from the ones they are accustomed to. "Me and my friends joke about how, well then, we'll just go to GW to look for guys," said Hana Le, an undergraduate at American University, who said freshmen women panicked when the campus paper published a piece on the preponderance of women at AU. Apparently this came as news to them; maybe it had not been mentioned in the college catalogue they looked at. "People definitely were wanting to go to parties at GW."

Other women will take more extreme measures. Among them is Betsy Soler, the Florida International University student who in the fall of 2010 was finishing up her senior year and also earning $70,000 a year managing the school's social media community. "My father constantly told me how hard work will take you far," said Soler, whose parents are from Puerto Rico. She was raised in the New York area, where her father worked his way from busboy to chef; her mother went to fashion school and worked as a pattern designer for high-end houses. Soler completed her high school requirements by the time she was sixteen. Her parents invested in her future by relocating to Florida, where she was able to enter community college on scholarship, then proceed to FIU. At 20, Soler had a presence on Facebook and Twitter, as well as Tumblr, LinkedIn, and YouTube. She joined an undergraduate public relations society because it seemed like a good place to network. "I've gotten a really early start on my career," said Soler, who aspires to be a marketing director. "I'm in a really good position."

When I first talked to her, Soler had been without a steady boyfriend for a year and half. FIU is about 55 percent female, and her major—mass communications—is dominated by women. Ideally, she wanted to find a partner who aims as high as she does. "Somebody who is driven by success—it just means a lot to me. And I don't feel like I'm asking a lot." Yet her campus didn't yield many prospects, and in greater Miami the pool of residents seemed to consist either of men working lower-end service jobs, or rich men—businessmen, athletes, guys with family money—who want a trophy girlfriend. She tried the life of a trophy, going on a couple of dates with an NFL player, and it didn't suit her. That her community was yielding a dearth of partners is not surprising; for all its image as a mecca for bronzed businessmen and bikini-class companions, Miami is near the top of the list of major U.S. cities where young single women outearn young men. Soler described this as a "lack of market." She was beginning to wonder if she would ever find a partner, and if so, what his role would be in her life. She knew some women who were considering pregnancy by sperm donation. "I don't think I would like to go that route," said Soler, but "it's something that I've thought about."

Unwilling to give up, she pinpointed a solution: Miami International Airport, with cheap flights and easy connections. Or the airport in Ft. Lauderdale, which has faster security screening and is often cheaper. Come winter's end, she was learning, lots of high-achieving Miami women evolve into a migratory species, flying north with the white pelicans and piping plovers. "We're going to other cities to date. We all have long-distance relationships," she said. "Among my friends, my colleagues, it's almost like a fact of life—going into other markets. We kind of see it as a joke, me and my girlfriends. Some of them work in government affairs; they go to Tallahassee and Washington. We'll also go to Seattle." She was thinking about taking a couple of friends on a dating trip to San Francisco.

But the biggest draw is Manhattan, where, she said, "you have more successful people. And more men." Actually, this is not true: women who live in New York feel a pretty acute man shortage. But it seemed to Soler that the men in Manhattan are different from the men she meets in Miami—tech-savvy and ambitious, and not put off by a woman who aims as high as they do. At the time when we talked, her favorite hangout spot was midtown's Ace Hotel, which she described as homey but upscale, with lots of locals. She liked the scene at the Breslin Bar there, and the lobby with its deep couches, full of cool startup people socializing with their laptops open. "You wouldn't be surprised if you run into Fred Wilson, the famous venture capitalist, or the Facebook founder, Mark Zuckerberg," she told me, knowledgeably. People from Foursquare are "there all the time. This is like the tech watering hole."

Once back home, if they happened to have met an interesting single man, she and her friends would follow a subtle post-meeting etiquette. "You keep in touch either through Facebook or text messages—not phone calls. You're building that relationship without being desperate, and phone calls, unless you're in the same city, seem desperate. You accept that they might be dating somebody else. You develop it through text, Facebook, maybe a little Twitter, then afterward maybe you can take another trip, say hey, let's meet again." The purpose is romance but also networking. "If you're dating these guys that are really successful, half the time they can get you a job. The guys I used to talk to—they're like, yeah, if you need a job, they'll start asking around, and kind of provide for you. Get you a little bit situated." Her choice of language—"kind of provide for you"—is telling. She and her friends are looking for providers—but providing has evolved to mean providing the contacts that can help a young woman realize her own breadwinning aspirations.

The women in Atlanta had hit upon the same solution: itravel. "I have a bunch of friends in New York, and visit them periodically, and one day I randomly ran into this guy who started talking to me. I saw him later that weekend, then I went to visit him and he came to visit me," said one Atlanta woman. "There's a lot of flying—to go on, like first, second, third dates, which is something that never, ever would have happened to my parents." When I talked to her again, she was getting ready to visit a guy in Boston; she had met him at a bar in the W Hotel in Atlanta.

Eleven
The View
from Abroad

Learning to Say "I Love You" in a Different Language

In a banquet room of Yoshu Charo, a popular Chinese restaurant in the Japanese port city of Yokohama, three dozen Japanese men and women are learning to make traditional Chinese dim sum. Participants in today's cooking lesson have made the day trip from Tokyo and other nearby cities, and find themselves seated boy-girl, boy-girl, at three large tables. They have been given numbered badges to wear, alcohol to disinfect their hands, and fresh towels for easy cleanup. Plates have been distributed, and mounds of dough, and aprons. Self-consciously, with a bit of nervous chatter, the men and women practice flattening dough by pushing it gently downward with one hand, using the other to move the plate in a circular fashion. That accomplished, they pass their uncooked buns to a restaurant employee who takes them to be steamed, and set about learning the crimping technique for pot stickers. Next, participants—here as part of a group dating event—wait for the final mini-lesson of the day, which turns out to be a starter course in the Chinese language.

For this, the men and women are given sheets of paper on which are printed common Chinese words and phrases. Their instructor, a vivacious woman engaged by Partner Agent, the Japanese dating agency that is sponsoring today's outing, starts by teaching the assembled participants to say *ni-hao*, the standard Chinese greeting. She moves down the list, teaching them how to say "delicious" and "farewell," how to ask for "water," how to call for "Coca-Cola," how to say "venerable person." She tells them how to say "baseball" and shows them how to count from 1 to 20. The group repeats each word or phrase in unison. "Now you're all ready to go shopping in China!" she congratulates them. She concludes by teaching them to say, "I love you." This time, she wants every man and woman to turn to the adjacent person and say the words directly. "I love you," the men and women murmur obediently.

As they do this, every single person looks down, as if seized by a common impulse, and speaks to the table.

There is just so much radical cultural change a person can take in one sitting.

It is the dog days of August, and Japan, a country extremely susceptible to fads, has been overtaken by a craze called konkatsu, which translates as "marriage hunting." Around the nation, agencies have begun offering dim-sum-making excursions and jogging expeditions and baseball outings to men and women who are eager to get married but uncertain how to go about it. Konkatsu is part of an array of efforts—some organized by the Japanese government, others commandeered by private agencies—to bring men and women together for fun events of limited duration, with the hope that this will nudge people down the path toward love, life together, and procreation. That last aspect is important. In Japan, marriage rates have declined precipitously and so has childbearing, to the point where the nation's population is shrinking.

And Japan is by no means alone. Other Asian countries are seeing what is being called a "flight from marriage," and with it a flight from stable reproduction. Part of this, clearly, is the result of women's rising education and earnings, which have come amid rapid economic expansion, in societies that are still highly traditional when it comes to domestic life and gender roles. Around the world, women's economic power is having a tectonic impact, permanently changing the way humans meet, form unions, and raise families—or don't.

Expect this: the same trends transforming the United States will transform the world. These trends are actually further along in some European countries, and they will continue to unleash radical new social dynamics throughout Europe, Asia, South America, Africa. Demographers predict that by the year 2050—at which point there will be 140 college-educated women in the United States for every 100 similarly educated men—women will outrank men academically in most parts of the world. By the middle of the 21st century, women in Japan will be the most educated human beings on the planet. "In a country like Japan, we are predicting that 80 percent of women will have a university degree by the year 2050, compared to 60 percent of men," says Albert Esteve, a Spanish demographer. Esteve and two colleagues have created a mesmerizing dynamic chart that predicts how trends in education will play out globally. The presentation begins with a scatter plot depicting the situation in more than 100 nations in 1970, when men were more educated than women in most places. On the chart, blue dots represent countries where men are more educated than women, and red dots represent countries where women are more educated than men. As images replace one another and successive slides march decade by decade toward a projected future, almost all the dots turn red and move to the right, pointing toward a world of dazzlingly well-educated women and less-well-educated men. By 2050, South Korean women will rival those of Japan for best-educated status, and among the diverse list of countries with a surfeit of supereducated women also will be Singapore, France, Chile, Ireland, Belgium, Canada, the Philippines, and Norway. Whether this is a utopia or a dystopia depends on how you look at it, and, to a certain extent, whether you are male or female.

One thing that's inevitable: marriage patterns will alter as movements taking place in the United States play out in other countries. "The fact that women are getting more and more education is going to change something we thought would never change," Esteve told me in a conversation over Skype, speaking from his office in Barcelona, together with his colleague, Iñaki Permanyer. "Women will start to marry down. Otherwise they will have to remain single." In the spring of 2011, Esteve and Permanyer delivered a talk to a convention of world demographers in Washington, D.C., titled "The End of Hypergamy." In it they showed that the ancient female tendency to marry up—that's what hypergamy means—is steadily disappearing, and will continue to do so in many countries as women's education ramps up.

As a result, a variety of reactions is becoming manifest. In some countries, men and women are proving flexible, as women begin to marry men with less education than they have. Marrying down, for women, is already more common than marrying up not only in the United States but in France, Greece, Hungary, Italy, Portugal, Spain, Israel, Jordan, Mongolia, Brazil, Colombia, Cuba, Panama, and Puerto Rico. Elsewhere, in parts of Europe, marriage is being replaced by cohabitation. In Sweden, more than half of all births are to unmarried women—most of them in cohabiting unions—as is the case for 66 percent of births in Iceland. Unlike in the United States, births to unmarried mothers in these European countries are not seen as a social problem; they simply represent a new way of having families and raising children. And in many countries, women are marrying later; their resources are affording them the luxury of taking their time.

But in a number of more developed Asian countries, the situation is approaching crisis levels. In some ways, Asia represents the dystopian vision of what the world will look like if attitudes fail to adapt to the new reality of women's earnings. In these countries, a portion of the population appears to be abandoning marriage *and* childbearing, in large part because women's empowerment is so at odds with a culture that remains attached to the idea of women as dependent. Japan for generations has been among the world's leading exemplars of the Beckerian specialization model: men worked insanely long hours in offices and corporations, women stayed home to raise children and tend the house unaided. This arrangement is rapidly going the way of the tea ceremony. Nearly a third of Japanese women in their early thirties have not married, and half of those likely never will. Similarly,

in Taiwan, 37 percent of women ages 30 to 34 are single, as are 21 percent of women ages 35 to 39. In Hong Kong, more than one-fourth
of women ages 30 to 34 are unmarried. In China, the growing ranks
of educated unmarried females are referred to as *sheng nu*, or "left-
over women." Unlike in Europe, many Asian countries retain a taboo
against unmarried childbearing. When women cease to marry, they
cease to reproduce. In East Asia, fertility has fallen from 5.3 children
per woman in the late 1960s to 1.6 now, well below the rate of 2.1 at
which a population replaces itself. In these countries, the rise of women
is leading to the decline of families, as people cling to the idea that it's
women who should marry up and men who should marry down, even
as this is becoming unworkable. In South Korea, *The Economist* noted,
young men lament that women are on a "marriage strike."

If women are, it's easy to see why. Working women are a driving
force behind the so-called Asian miracle. The economic rise of countries like China and South Korea has been accomplished with the substantial input of female workers. In East Asia, two-thirds of women
now have jobs, and in South Korea, the employment rate of women
in their twenties has *overtaken* that of men in their age group. Just
over 59 percent of young women in South Korea are working, compared to 58.5 percent of young men. In Japan, single women under
30 now make more, on average, than Japanese men their age do. And
yet even as they surpass men in earnings and workforce participation,
women have enormous difficulty achieving anything like work-family
balance. Part-time jobs are rare. Even when working full-time, women
are expected to do the bulk of the housework, which includes not only
child care, cooking, and home maintenance but care of elderly relatives
and in-laws. In Japan, a woman experiences a staggering surge in her
domestic workload when she marries. Working wives in Japan spend
some 30 hours per week on housework, compared to three hours a
week for husbands. This is why, in Japan, there is a word for "husband"
that translates loosely as "big bag of trash."

The result, some argue, is that women feel leery of what now seems
an unfair and disadvantageous contract—a contract they can afford to
forgo. A number of studies have concluded that well-educated Asian
women are devising their own version of exchange theory. Instead

of using their money to get men who are more inclined to help out around the house, women—recognizing the futility of that—are buying their way out of marriage altogether. They are using their resources to purchase their freedom. A 2003 survey of women in Beijing found that half of women with salaries commensurate with a university education are unmarried. Half of these cited financial independence as the reason why. "Why should I have to settle down to a life of preparing tofu soup, like my mother?" asked one.

But media accounts that put the onus entirely on women are misleading. It's not that high-earning women have walked away from marriage with cold hearts and no regrets. In Japan, most women—like most men—tell researchers that they would like to marry. Japanese women by many accounts are *more* inclined toward marriage than men are, or at least more proactive. During the summer of 2009, when the konkatsu movement was at a fever pitch and I was in the country reporting and interviewing, organizers were inundated with female participants. Executives at Japan's marriage and dating agencies reported that around 2005, women began to outnumber men among people signing up for memberships. "In the past, we had more men, but recently the ratio has been reversed—now we have more women," said Atsushi Nishiguchi, the manager of the marketing department for O-net, a Tokyo marriage agency.

Moreover, Nishiguchi said, their female members tend to be exactly this demographic of empowered women. "Our newly joined female portfolio—they are highly educated and have a high career. In many cases they have a higher salary than the men who are registered in our pool."

No, the problem is not that Asian women don't want to marry—it's that women still prefer to marry men at their level, or higher, yet these men persist in not wanting to marry them. The problem, said Nishiguchi, is that while male executives may wine and dine the female colleagues they meet in the office, at home they want wives who are economically inferior. Getting out of his chair, Nishiguchi went to a whiteboard and drew a series of horizontal lines, representing Japanese men and women of different salary levels. At every salary level—high-earning, middle-earning, whatever—men prefer women who earn less than they do. The truth, he said, is that in Japan—unlike in the United States—women's earnings do not yet make them desirable partners; attitudes remain so entrenched, even as economic fortunes have reversed so rapidly, that women's success renders them untouchable. "It's a fact of life. The market value of women as they become older, even if their salary level becomes higher, comes down in terms of marriageability. Men want someone who is younger and not so high salary."

"Please Don't Talk One-sidedly"

While this is a big problem for men and women, and for the reproductive future of nations, it's great for the commercial dating industry. In Asian countries, the clash in marital expectations has led to the extreme commodification of dating and marriage, as entrepreneurs have emerged to capitalize on the mismatch, align expectations, and create new opportunities for encounters. In Japan, some of these are traditional marriage agencies like O-net, whose employees have begun actively coaching members on how to communicate and what to expect.

Up until now, Japanese men have been spared the necessity of learning how to court or even really talk to a date. For generations, the country adhered to a custom called *omiai*, in which men and women were introduced informally by a friend or relative or community matchmaker, liberating men from the need to develop real, actual dating skills. In the 1970s and 1980s, when *omiai* was waning, it was replaced by an informal system whereby bosses would often introduce men and women in the workplace—fully expecting the woman to quit when she married—and men could assume that earnings alone would make them desirable. For men, being able to fulfill the provider role was the central asset they needed. Now that women can provide for themselves, the challenge for O-net is to teach Japanese men how to approach women like intelligent beings. Or even just approach women at all. "Some men haven't had much experience sitting face-to-face alone with a lady," said O-net "relationship advisor" Yukari Hirakawa. To help them, she persuades them to do some role playing. "I pretend that I am the lady, and starting right from the beginning, to say: 'How do you do? Nice to meet you!'" said Hirakawa, who was pretty and animated, with a striped suit, sparkly watch and hair clip, and shoulder-length hair slightly curled up at the edges. Even this gentle icebreaker, she said, makes men nervous, and they often react with panicked logorrhea. "They can talk one-sidedly for half an hour or an hour," said Hirakawa. "I say, 'Please don't do that.' They don't know the type of topics that are well received by women. I say: 'Please don't talk one-sidedly for a long time; the ladies get bored repeatedly listening to the same thing.' I tell them to listen to the lady, much more than talking."

The agency also endeavored to teach men what is an appropriate restaurant to take a woman: not too cheap, not too fancy. They developed an illustrated pamphlet that attempts to bring a lighthearted approach to etiquette, citing humorous anecdotes of past dating disasters. One illustration depicts a man at a restaurant table, blathering away while his date looks at him despairingly. Other cautionary examples include a man who shows up for a date dressed in a track suit, and another who insists on splitting the dinner bill down to the last yen, which is worth about a penny. O-net gives men tips on grooming and self-presentation, advising them to show up clean. "We usually advise to men: please don't wear clothes from five years ago," added Hirakawa. "You can go to a store like Uniqlo which is selling reasonably priced clothes, and buy them not at an expensive cost."

As for women: all Hirakawa can do, really, is try to manage expectations. Though many of their high-earning women members would like to marry equally high-earning men, these are precisely the men who don't need to sign up with marriage agencies, so the trick is to persuade women to feel satisfied with the middling pool of men who do. This is not an easy sell. There are those who argue that the real impediment to marriage in Japan is materialistic single women determined to hold out until they land what one sociologist calls a "gentleman of resources." Toko Shirakawa, a Japanese journalist, ventured in an interview that it's women who are clinging hardest to the old-fashioned notion of the man as provider and that there remains a "comic mismatch" between women's expectations and the reality of men's earnings. The sociologist Masahiro Yamada went further, claiming that women in Japan are reacting to their own success by attempting to bail out of it, engaging in a "feeding frenzy to go after a small percentage of men with high income." To the extent that this may be true, the practical explanation is that women in Japan, like men, are obliged to work such excessive hours that the only way they can have a family is if they marry a man capable of supporting them.

But the experience of O-net is that women can be talked out of this mind-set. "I tell them, 'Please be patient. And open and generous,'" said Hirakawa. "Don't start deducting points and doing negative points on him."

Meat-Eating Women

The upshot has been even more frenetically organized activity: events that go beyond looking at online profiles, speed dating, and attending mixers. Entrepreneurs are thinking up every conceivable circumstance for getting people together, preferably in settings where men and women could do something other than sit there trying to think of something to say to one another. One of these imaginative businessmen was Yosuke Shionagi, a self-described "love essayist" who, when I interviewed him, had his hand in all sorts of endeavors. Among other things, he was writing a romance advice column; maintaining a website devoted to matters of the heart; organizing singles parties; running a konkatsu enterprise; and doing all he could to create a "love culture" that would make Japan a place where "everyone can spend their daily life with a smile on their face." Shionagi, the day I met with him, was sitting behind a desk in the conference room of a modern apartment building in a newly developed neighborhood near Tokyo Bay. He had curly hair that went down to the nape of his neck, and was wearing pointy-toed cowboy boots, pin-striped faded jeans, a white button-down collar shirt with embroidered flowers on it, and a gray-black straw fedora tipped up at the brim, cowboy-style. He was drinking a cold oolong tea that, he claimed, had the ability to absorb human fat. Piled on the desk were scrapbooks stuffed with photos of couples. He said that women in Japan are avidly interested in marriage; what's different now, he said, is that women are much more assertive in seeking it out. Once upon a time, it was shaming for a Japanese woman to take anything but a passive role with regard to her marital future. Now, "the women are actually enjoying the konkatsu activities or events, while men, deep down in their hearts, want to get married, but they cannot show that." He reflected that women have become far more socially adept, whereas "men have become much more tame and quiet." In fact, it was his impression that men and women in Japan had traded personalities.

The reason, not to put too fine a point on it, is money. In Japan, the infamous "lost decade"—the wrenching economic crisis of the 1990s—drastically eroded the standing of the Japanese salary man. Up until that point, a Japanese man assumed that as long as he worked hard and loyally, he could expect lifetime employment and steady raises. Now, young men find themselves working at short-term jobs organized by temp agencies, if they are working at all. The ensuing crisis of confidence has been acute and well documented by a foreign media that loves to write about Japanese eccentricities and sexual fetishes: it far eclipses any so-called emasculation of the Western male. As a result of the upending of the old employment system, Japan has seen the rise of various traumatized cohorts including "shut-in men," who won't even leave the house; and a related species, herbivorous or "grass-eating men," who opt out of competitive business culture as well as competitive romantic culture. Not surprisingly, sex is down, too: 61 percent of unmarried Japanese men report not having a girlfriend, and 45 percent say they don't care.

This is a big change since the 1980s, said Shionagi, who recalled that bars and clubs during that period of economic expansion were full of what he called meat-eating men. "It was a very explosive type of atmosphere, a feeling in the air. Everyone was looking for girls. If you bumped into another man, it was like you could almost expect a fight. There was that kind of tense feeling—men were so eager, more outgoing. Nowadays many of the men have turned so quiet and tame, even if they bumped into each other, if their shoulders touched someone's, they would say quietly: 'Sorry!' The reason they have become so quiet largely has to do with the economy. If you don't have enough money in your pockets, you don't feel like going out to parties or asking a girl out for a drink."

Now, he said, women are the meat eaters. Their rising level of achievement has made them outgoing and confident, and Shionagi was doing his best to cater to their appetites. Among his offerings were talks promoting something he calls "sudden marriage," a super-efficient courtship aimed at the busy executive, which were attended entirely by women. In these sessions, Shionagi gives women advice on how to get men in a "love mode": he urges them to be bold and call up men they know and ask them to set up parties where they can meet still more men. He also advises women to enlist their own mothers. He himself got married, he confided, when his now mother-in-law suggested it. He asked for her permission to live with her daughter, and she replied, "If you are going to live together, why not get married?" It is an approach he recommends, because a question like that is difficult to rebut.

Importing Pliant Brides

For now, though, what's widely occurring in developed Asian countries like Japan, as well as South Korea, Taiwan, and Singapore, is what demographers call a "marriage squeeze," and it's affecting two cohorts. A marriage squeeze is a situation where a group of people find themselves disadvantaged in the marriage market. It can be created by any number of disruptive events, including wars that kill off a number of young men; the emigration of male workers to jobs in other countries; or sex-selective abortion to eliminate females. Any of these upheavals can result in a pool of people, male or female, who face a void where there should be mates. In developed Asian countries, the disruption is created by women's education among other things, such as industrialization and rapid urbanization, and the cohorts affected are women at the top of the educational and economic ladder, and men at the bottom. The men at the bottom are often rural workers, low-wage, working in agriculture or industry. The problem is sort of like musical chairs. As women move up academically in relation to men, they have fewer options for marrying up; meanwhile, uneducated men at the bottom have fewer options for marrying down.

In some countries, the plight of so-called rural bachelors is receiving more and more attention. Hyunok Lee, a South Korean sociologist who received her Ph.D. from Cornell University, argues that in Korea government and media seem more concerned about the needs of the men at the bottom than the plight of women at the top. Whenever a rural bachelor commits suicide because he cannot find a bride— something that did begin happening in the late 1980s, and became a national issue—the papers are all over it. And she does have sympathy for the bachelors. She interviewed many of them as part of her academic fieldwork, and found that they often are men who in their twenties might have been regarded as decent providers, but they delayed marriage until they were better situated, and now find there are no women who want to marry them. At the same time, Korea remains a patriarchal country in which it's paramount for a man to perpetuate his lineage, and government creates initiatives to help these men. For men, she argues, "there is a specific industry to support their needs."

The industry is commercialized cross-border marriage, a growing enterprise that goes beyond dating and konkatsu and is also becoming popular among urban working-class men. Agencies are springing up that arrange marriages between men in developed Asian countries and poorer women brought in from less-developed ones. It's a regional version of the global "foreign bride" industry, in which women from a variety of cultures are marketed as excellent wives, generally because, being poor, they will be tractable and subservient, or even just available. In the Asian version, women ethnically close to the male target group are brought from one country to another. For example, women from rural Vietnam might be brought into Taiwan, South Korea, or Japan to make up for the dearth of homegrown mates. Sometimes, agencies promise they will be virgins, and that a new bride will be supplied if the first one runs away. When Hyonuk Lee gives talks about cross-border marriage, she concedes that there has always been international marriage—remember the ship of brides to Jamestown—but there's a lot more now than there once was. "It's growing globally, yet the growth in the Asian region is conspicuous," she says, and has to do with massive urbanization in Asian countries, and the clash between new economic realities and older social values.

As for the educated single female—since nobody is importing

grooms for them, they have another option: leave. Hyunok Lee is in her early thirties. When we spoke, she had just completed her doctorate, and was on her way to Singapore to continue studying trends in Asian marriages. Not long before that, she and classmates from her prestigious Korean university held a Facebook reunion, and she noticed that "most of the women are in the States or some other country. It says something about this generation, that women have a drive to leave." Women, she said, are subjected to a regular barrage of why-don't-you-get-married commentary; when this gets too much to handle on the home front, women will go far away so that they no longer have to listen or produce a socially acceptable answer. For Asian countries struggling to devise new social attitudes, it's not just that they may lose their next generation of children; they may lose the very women they have educated so well.

"Women Are Looking to the Future, and Men Are Looking to the Past"

In the coming decades, expect to see this: even more globalized mating movement, a restless shifting of populations as men who feel disoriented by the changing economic climate seek out pliant brides with "traditional" values, and educated women seek a place—any place— they will feel welcome. Occasionally, it will be the men who are moving. In 2010, the *New York Times* published a piece about a region in Thailand known for the Western men who relocate there to enjoy the low cost of living and the sweet attention of indigenous women. "Thai women are a lot like women in America were fifty years ago," before feminism made them "strong-headed and opinionated," Joseph Davis, of Fresno, California, twice divorced and now married to a Thai woman, told the paper. The problem with American women, he said, is that they "know they are equal, so the situation is not as relaxed and peaceful as it is between an American and a Thai lady." In one area, an avenue where Western men gather is known as "Foreign Son-in-Law Street." The American men are paying a higher price than they realize to maintain the old marriage bargain. "When you get married in Thailand, you are marrying the whole family," pointed out a local expert, explaining that husbands are expected to support not only their wives but an array of in-laws. "Often the lady expects that, but the man doesn't understand."

In Europe, something similar if more subtle is happening. Globalization and the creation of the European Union have led to a marriage market that crosses borders and cultures, spontaneously rather than in an organized commercial manner. Spain in recent years has seen an increase in immigration from Latin America, point out demographers Albert Esteve and Iñaki Permanyer. As a result, Spanish men are marrying immigrant Latin American women, who have more traditional domestic views than Spanish women. And Spanish women are marrying men from the northern countries of the European Union, where men are more open-minded. Everybody wants what they don't have at home, and they are taking steps to find it. "There's clear selection there," Esteve reflected. "In Spain it's very clear. Men are looking for women that no longer exist, while women are looking for men that have yet to exist." Cross-border marriage is one improvised way to bridge the time gap.

Gradually, though, men's attitudes are changing, and as they do, the demographers believe Europe's own fertility crisis will begin to reverse itself. For decades, people worried that women in many European countries weren't having enough children for the population to replace itself. There is some sign this is turning around. "Demographers theorize that fertility will rise as soon as men get ready to cooperate a little bit on the family business—complete the gender revolution," Esteve commented. "We have observed this feminization of the labor force, but now we still have to see the masculinization of the home front. The household tasks, children, and everything."

The Significance of Being 39 and Unmarried

As the Yokohama konkatsu lesson draws to a close, the steamed buns and pot stickers are brought back from the kitchen, delicious and cooked, along with fried rice and a puddinglike dessert in tall glasses. Men and women get to relax and eat together; as they rise to check out the dessert, they are encouraged to sit back down in a new place, next to whatever member of the opposite sex has come to seem intriguing. Emissaries from Partner Agent circulate, encouraging interaction. People are told to write down the badge numbers of people they would like to spend more time with. Men are urged to "get out there and speak to ladies," and ladies are urged to "radiate to attract the men." Mixing and mingling, participants are able to observe who rises to get seconds, who eats neatly or messily, who has a sense of humor, who doesn't, who bosses everybody around in organizing plates and dishes, who put together an unlikely outfit for a weekend excursion, and draw their own conclusions.

As they do so, it becomes clear that what gets lost in academic discussions of dating markets and so-called marriage strikes are the deep and actual emotions of men and women. As they pick up their belongings and prepare to depart, today's participants share the wistful hope that the outing will have some tangible outcome. A man in a plaid shirt says this is the fifth or sixth konkatsu event he has attended. He is 39, works for an IT firm, and would like to be married by 40. "I know no one who has gotten married from something like this," he admits. He goes out weekly for drinks with coworkers, hoping to meet a potential wife. But he thinks konkatsu events are more promising, if for no other reason than they are attended by people bent on the same mission he is. "There's something about being in a roomful of people all serious about having a married relationship." Asked whether his parents are putting pressure on him, he smiles, in a harried sort of way, and says, "You wouldn't believe it."

Another 39-year-old man, who works as a translator, invokes his parents. It's not so much that they are pressuring him. It's that his mother and father have set a fine example for what a happy family feels like, and he would very much like to enjoy the same contentment. Yet it all seems to have become so complicated.

Twelve

Our Female Future

"A Lot of Masculinity Is Just Bravado"

Fortunately, there's another vision of the future, and it's old-fashioned and strikingly new. In some ways, it marks a return to the Beckerian model in which spouses find ways to complement one another, but it's not a retreat. This future will see some couples reject the notion that everything must be perfectly egalitarian and 50-50. Because let's admit it: sometimes, perfectly egalitarian and 50-50 is an impossible way to live. Something has to give, particularly for couples with children, and particularly for women to succeed at the highest levels. In this version, women will be valued for their earnings and achievements; they will thrive in their occupations, ably supported by men who understand just what they have won in the bargain: emotional lives that are richer and life trajectories that are more varied than men's once were. The state of marriage will evolve to accommodate female breadwinners, and more men and women may even re-embrace marriage as they become accustomed to new responsibilities and come to value different things in spouses. In families such as the Hawkinses, where most adult siblings have eased their way into woman-supported setups, it's possible to see the full array of reasons why this happens—and why it works.

The Hawkins siblings, now in their forties, for the most part are still living in the Midwest, far from the bicoastal debate over whether men are still winning or whether women are starting to win or whether everybody now is basically tied. As such, the three brothers-in-law who find themselves happily married to breadwinning wives—Danny Hawkins, Damon Ajlouny, and Hank McNally—receive with amusement the idea that this represents a flaw in their makeup or failure in their fortunes or an assault on their masculinity or that it is in any way something they should feel concerned about. What, exactly, is a problem about having the time to coach your daughter's basketball team and turn your children into prodigy golfers, about being the go-to guy all the PTA moms are secretly in love with, about taking a call from your wife, who is in China, and informing her that you are sitting at the kitchen table playing poker with your daughters? What is problematic about getting to be present when your eleventh grader discovers who she is and what she wants to be in life—when she blossoms, just as she did when she was a toddler, into a new person? "I've thought about that a little bit," offers Danny Hawkins. And after thinking about it, all he can say is this: "In some ways, you know, a lot of masculinity is just bravado."

There. We've said it! Masculinity is just bravado. And easily dispensed with. The whole conversation!

Expect this: in a world of female breadwinners, there will be very happy couples, and very fulfilled men, and wives who, thanks to the support they get at home, are able to take their careers to important new levels. At the end of their workday, these wives will come home to find the house clean and dinner cooked, and they will relax and enjoy the company of their family over a game of Uno and a bracing drink of their favorite alcoholic beverage. And the women will appreciate this. They will not take it for granted. Couples will make pragmatic decisions about who should work and who should stay home, about who should be the primary earner and who should be the secondary one, based on what works best for each family. And here are some of the good things that will result: women will feel rightly proud of their ability to put food on the table and send children to college. Studies show this already—they just attract less attention than do the studies suggesting a future of loveless single people. So you might not know this: in 2003, a group of social scientists interviewed female breadwinners and were unable to find a single negative consequence. Women "suffered no penalties we could discern when they earned more than their husbands," wrote the authors, who also found that men continue to hold themselves responsible for breadwinning, and because nobody expects this of women—not yet—women tend to get a lot more high-fives. Just as people overpraise men who cook dinner and diaper the babies, women earners in this study got lots of you-go-girls. Another found that many women enjoy the authority their breadwinning gives them. They recognize it sometimes gives them the upper hand, and they secretly like it.

Men, meanwhile, will feel liberated and enlarged. Those who hate office politics and competitive alpha posturing won't have to put up with it. They will be able to choose whether to work for pay, or not, just as women have in the past. Men in coming years will be judged on something other than their ability to generate income. Husbands who help will be considered wildly desirable. "I look around, and think: You're a catch. I don't know who's got you, but she's lucky!" ventured Christin Roman, a graduate of Florida State and New York University, who was living in Brooklyn and walked each day through McCarren Park, marveling at all the fathers she saw. "It's just amazing to me," she said. "These guys are staying home and taking care of the kids, or maybe they're freelancers or maybe cutting back on hours, and maybe Mom is going off and working full-time—but for some reason, these guys in the middle of the day are pushing strollers." Making her way through the park, she would often think about growing up in Florida, where her parents were divorced and her father was a "Disney dad," the local term for divorced fathers who saw their children for weekend trips to Disneyworld but were detached from the family's emotional workings. Here are all these guys forming intimate relationships with their own children. Considering them, she wonders how her own life will unfold. Christin, who has tens of thousands of dollars' worth of student loans, worries about how childbearing could affect her career as a Web designer. She can't afford to opt out. One thing she knows is that she needs a husband willing to push a stroller.

Here are some of the subtle forces that will swell the ranks of men who are not only willing but eager to do so: as long as men are expected to put in killer hours in the workplace, a growing number will say goodbye to all that. A man will look at his own breadwinning father and think: You know, he was a terrific man, but I want to be able to spend more time with my children than he was able to spend with me. And if the workplace makes it impossible for men to have this kind of balance, men will leave. And women who have grown up absorbing their dad's example of hard work and stick-to-it-iveness will take their place. In part, this is because women—I would argue—are often more likely to enjoy flexibility and indulgent bosses.

"It Was Just a Tremendous Relief"

This was what tipped the balance for Susan and Danny Hawkins, who along with Danny's extended family conjure an optimistic image of what a future of women earners will look like—and a nuanced look at what the tradeoffs and rewards are. When they went to the University of Michigan more than twenty years ago, Danny was an economics major and Susan was majoring in industrial engineering. Starting out, they both worked full-time—Susan as a "management engineer" with the Henry Ford Health System, Danny with a company that manages corporate benefits plans. They both got master's degrees while working, and rather than wait until a "good time" to have children, decided to make life more complicated by taking on parenthood right away. After the birth of one daughter, Stephanie, and a second, Jamie, about three years later, they managed to maintain that fragile balance familiar to many parents: the day care, the dropping off, the commuting, the working a full day, the racing back home, the scrambling to assemble dinner, the night classes, the juggling of doctors' appointments and work meetings and the pulling out of planners whenever a child got sick to see who could stay home and who couldn't.

But gradually, a distinction emerged. Susan found herself advanced through the ranks by bosses sympathetic to her life as a working mother, who at various times offered her flexible configurations including a four-day workweek, or whatever, really, she needed. As a result, Susan was able quickly to move up the organizational ladder, something that has made her as a manager sympathetic to parents, male or female, when they ask for flexible schedules.

For Danny, the workplace was not nearly so forgiving. He put in a 60-hour workweek—which, together with a daily commute of about an hour, seemed to him too much time away from his children. His bosses disagreed. They wanted more. Danny told them they couldn't have it. After a number of discussions, Danny's bosses told him he could go down to 40 hours a week—for as long as it took him to find a new job. But when he did decrease his hours, the fact that somebody in the office was going home at five created so much discontent that he was obliged to leave right away. He spent a couple of months job hunting, and realized that he enjoyed being home. Meanwhile, "my life went from being überstressful to manageable," recalls Susan, who was able to increase her work hours and be even more productive. "All of a sudden, someone was making dinner. I didn't have to rush to get to the babysitter in time. It was just a tremendous relief." They started joking: maybe Danny should be a stay-at-home dad. This was in the mid-1990s, when the concept hardly existed. Then it stopped being a joke. It began to seem possible. When Danny got a number of job offers, he decided not to take any of them.

Part of the reason the Beckerian specialization model worked so well for them in reverse is because Danny has little interest in office politics and is happy playing a managerial behind-the-scenes role, keeping the household running smoothly and making it possible for Susan to perform at the top of her game. A secure, independent-minded person who doesn't care what other people think about his choices, Danny, she says, insists on describing himself as "homemaker" when they file their taxes. "Danny had his priorities—his family was first, golf was second, and work was a distant third," says his sister Lori. "He's a good worker—I would hire him in a second; he's got a great work ethic—but he didn't care for the politics and the demands on his time." Another reason it worked so well is because Susan is an early adopter who likes living in the newest cultural spaces. Like her own mother, who was always the first on the block to have a microwave or a snow blower, Susan is the kind of person who wanted an Acura Integra when they came on the market simply because they were interesting and new. She felt the same way about a stay-at-home husband. The latest model of man? For sure, she wanted to try one.

Danny and Susan figured out how to run a household on one income, enacting their box-with-divided-sections budgetary system—with sections for things like food, entertainment, and the mortgage payment—so they would not be tempted to live beyond their means. They made sure to leave a cushion at the end of the month for unexpected expenses. They made all their decisions together. They forwent things like big home renovations. Danny became the COO and CFO of the household, a job he accomplished with aplomb. He pays the bills, does the grocery shopping, keeps that calendar tracking chores and appointments. He actually—this fascinates his own mother—has "laundry day." Several years ago, Susan was made vice president overseeing three departments at Henry Ford, with duties so complex that as she described them to me, I lost track and wondered aloud why they weren't apportioned between three people. She laughed and said I should ask her boss.

When Susan and Danny first came up with their arrangement, their second child was two and a half. They figured that around the time she entered elementary school, Danny would move back into the workforce. Now, that child is in her final year of high school. "We've never looked back," Susan says now. "We've never even had a serious conversation. It's just worked so well."

They talked this through while sitting in Toasted Oak, a restaurant in the Detroit suburbs. It was a Friday night. Susan, who had just finished a full workweek, was wearing gold hoop earrings and a black shirt dress. She has shoulder-length reddish hair and a flair for telling stories. Danny was wearing an open-collared button-down shirt and an air of good humor. For dinner, they shared red wine, a steak, and after much discussion a butterscotch brownie. Susan offered several funny anecdotes about office disputes and her efforts to deal with them fairly, and as she talked it seemed clear that she is the kind of ultra-competent and big-hearted person who was born to administrate and manage, and who views the daily barrage of cubicle drama and office entanglements with seriousness but also, when necessary, humor. Danny listened fondly. It was easy to see why, when I interviewed Susan, one of the first things she said—describing why their situation worked well for them—was: "He is very in love with me, and we have an excellent marriage." This was not something she said lightly. She is aware that it is thanks to Danny that she is able to have both a family and a serious career. She well knows that lots of women are forced to choose one or the other. Recently, she had attended a party organized by a networking group for female Michigan executives; looking around, she realized she was one of the few who had children.

She also acknowledges the downsides, among them the way Danny was the member of the Hawkins family known to and beloved by all the teachers and fellow parents. In the years since Danny opted out of the full-time workforce, stay-at-home-dads have become a vocal advocacy group, and sometimes complain about being excluded from playgroups and parenting organizations by school administrators and territorial mothers. For Danny, the opposite was true. "They were very welcoming, to a point where it was almost embarrassing," remembers Danny, who is easygoing and social, and got used to being called one of the moms. "They were just so appreciative to have a man involved." It helped that he was willing to serve as treasurer, one of the hardest volunteer jobs to fill. Every year, at back-to-school night, Susan experienced those guilty pangs at being the parent people didn't recognize.

It is also the case that Danny's daughters adore him. Sitting down for dinner, Susan joked about the girls' "Electra complex." In contrast, there have been periods where she has undergone her share of mother-daughter tension. She and Jamie watch *Dancing with the Stars* together, and the other night, when Susan asked if she wanted to watch it or whether she had too much homework, the invitation for some reason was maddening, something to do with Susan asking too indirectly. Listening to her description, it sounded to me like garden-variety parent-teen conflict, no more or less than what mothers confront every day, regardless of whether they are working full-time or part-time or staying home. And while Susan works long days during the week, her weekends are free and relaxing, because chores are done.

Her company's CEO—a woman—urges employees to take every last hour of their vacation time.

Another ingredient of their success is that Susan does not view her standing as deriving from her husband. "My abilities and confidence aren't based on what my husband does for a living and how much he earns, and perhaps releases him from pressure to do that—to take a job he doesn't like," she reflects. It also helps that Susan doesn't second-guess Danny's running of their home, doesn't need to tell him what he's doing wrong. Her mother-in-law, Marcelle, described an outing she took with Danny and Susan when the girls were little; they met for dinner at the end of Susan's workday, and one of the girls did something—got sick, spilled her water, Marcelle doesn't remember—but what she does remember is that Danny cleaned it up. It struck her, for a minute, as unusual. Then she reflected that Susan was in her work clothes, and this was just how their household functioned. Susan from the start was willing to let Danny handle mishaps without interfering or believing she could do it better.

At least, she doesn't interfere much. "You do have certain things at home that you micromanage," Danny teased her, over dinner. "Like, where every Christmas decoration goes."

"The stockings," Susan replied airily, knowing immediately what he was talking about. "That's not controlling. That's decorating."

In fact, there's very little for Susan to micromanage, because Danny is the most detail-oriented person imaginable. As a child, his mother says, he kept a statistical analysis of his golf scores, and as an adult is always crunching numbers and figuring out mathematical ways of looking at things. At Christmas, he likes to track their spending and divide it into categories like "family" and "other people" and "work." Problem is, he does it in real-time, sometimes looking at receipts and running the numbers before December 25, which puts him at risk of figuring out what he is getting. The prior year, he sent Susan a spreadsheet and she sent him an email back, saying: "Thank you for taking the joy out of gift giving."

"Actually, you said *sucking* the joy out of it," corrected Danny, conceding that he is very, very organized.

Amidst all this calibration, there was a question beginning to emerge. Now that Stephanie was in college, Danny had been able to relinquish some outside parenting activities. With Jamie still in high school, he still had some school-related volunteer duties, but the time was coming when that, too, would end. He is a competitive and highly able golfer, and has a weekly racquetball game with childhood friends to whom he remains close. He also was working in a part-time position as business manager of their church. But pretty soon he would have more free time, once both girls embarked on their adult lives. What would Danny do then?

"Yeah, what will you do?" asked Susan. "Truth be told, we've never thought about it."

So they thought about it, there at the table. Danny could get another full-time job—but why? "It's not like we need the money," Susan reflected. Thanks to her income and his money management, their house was nearly paid off. And what was so nice is that he could get ahead in his church accounting and take vacations when it worked for her schedule. "Who would make dinner?" she wondered. Danny reflected that he was thinking about taking a substantive, formalized volunteer position with a charity. "That would be really cool," said Susan. They started talking about a gala benefit they were attending the next night. "We love getting dressed up," he said. Then, to her: "Who are we sitting with?"

"Fun people," said Susan, naming the people at their table.

"Good!" said Danny agreeably.

Drink Before Entering

It also made things easier, for Danny and Susan, when members of the Hawkins sibling set made the same decision they did, for much the same reason. As female breadwinning becomes more common, the stigma will diminish and vanish. It has vanished in this family, not that it ever existed. As it did for Danny, the flip just sort of happened for his sister Leslie Ajlouny, a soft-voiced, mild-mannered woman with strawberry-blond hair who is part of the top echelon of leadership at her Detroit-area transportation and logistics company. Leslie's husband, Damon, has both an MBA and a law degree, credentials that contributed to the familial expectations that he would be the primary earner and Leslie would be some version of a suburban mother. But when Damon tasted a corporate environment—taking a job at a big accounting firm, then as a tax attorney—he had a severe allergic reaction. He departed the world of billable hours in favor of becoming self-employed as a real estate broker. They evolved a balance where Leslie became the primary earner and Damon the secondary earner with the flexible, child-friendly schedule. "We said from the very beginning, if anyone wants to swap roles, they can," Leslie recalled. "He's got all these degrees and all this education, I never wanted him to feel bored or not challenged. So we had that agreement: Anytime, one of us can call it." But neither did. They had three children in four years. Leslie took about six weeks maternity leave with each one, and has continued to love her field. Like his brother-in-law Danny, Damon over the years has helped out in their children's gym classes, done cafeteria duty, taken the kids to orthodontist appointments, coached basketball, and turned all three children into high-level golfers. "It's great for the kids, and great for him," says Leslie, who, like her sister-in-law Susan, trusts her husband to run the house and admires how well he does it. Like Danny, Damon is family CFO, paying the bills and reporting to Leslie on their finances. "We talk about it, but he manages all that, pretty much makes all the decisions with the kids. Though if there were something I felt strongly about, I would disagree," says Leslie. "He's really good with money. I wouldn't have the patience, but he goes to Sam's for this, and Costco, and Wal-Mart for that."

The day I interviewed them, Damon and Leslie were relaxing on a Saturday morning in their home in the Detroit suburbs. A picture window in the back of the house framed a piece of Michigan's wild landscape: reeds and cattails, in a strip of marsh where deer and foxes can sometimes be seen, too. Leslie had just been through a grueling 48 hours during which she had attended her company's Christmas office party; spent the night in a downtown hotel so as to get up super-early and head to the airport; flown to Virginia for a business meeting; flown back; arrived late; and fallen immediately to sleep. Now she felt reasonably rested. The house was peaceful; their sons, 16 and 15, were out fetching their daughter from a friend's house. The older son was driving and the younger one was texting Damon, keeping him informed on their progress. Reflecting on how parenting had changed, Damon ventured that one factor behind the increase in stay-at-home fathers is that people are having children later, giving men a chance to mature and become better equipped for hands-on parenting. "I can't imagine—knowing how I was at 21, 22, 23—me at college age, that would scare me, taking care of kids," joked Damon, who is tall and athletic, with a shaved head, gold chain, and a Michigan State shirt. "I wouldn't want me watching them."

Listening to the description of his parenting—coaching, driving, helping at school—it also struck me how much childrearing has changed. There is so much organized activity, and kids are on all these teams, and in that sense, parenting involves less laundry folding and more shepherding of sports gear and is more masculine than it used to be. Then again, Damon folds plenty of laundry, and when Leslie wakes up in the morning, she can hear Damon downstairs unloading the dishwasher. Leslie has a group of female friends she gets together with for dinner; when it's their turn to host, Damon enjoys planning the meal and preparing it. During parties, when husbands congregate at the bar in the basement, Damon tends to stay upstairs with the women, serving drinks.

And Damon doesn't just cook for admiring crowds of partygoers. He also does the maintenance cooking, the unheralded daily job of making meal after meal each weekday. When I asked if his family appreciated his nightly offerings, he said, deadpan, "Yes, they all stand up and do the wave." But people in their social circle make up for it. "Women are always—I feel like they're envious of this great husband," said Leslie. "Neighbors, friends, especially the people I work with—they see that I put in a lot of hours at work, and some of them do, too, and they have to go home and do everything, or don't have the support at home." Men she works with, maybe sensing this and feeling a little threatened, occasionally make comments. "I have had men every once in a while joke: 'Oh, Damon's on the golf course and I'm at work, how does he get such a great life?'"

"Danny and I would hear that once in a while, while we're out there playing in the daytime in years past," agreed Damon, who, like

Danny, seemed impervious to being needled. "Once we were out there around eleven, and somebody said: 'Look at you, Mr. Moms, you've got the wives working so you can come out.'" Damon, who often gets up at 5:30 to work on the computer for several hours before the kids wake up, finds there are so many men at home now during the day he hardly ever hears that anymore. There is another father he coaches with; they text each other so often that Leslie refers to the other dad as "your boyfriend."

One thing that also struck me listening is that both Leslie and Damon are intimately acquainted with the domain in which the other person is moving. As the sexes trade places, they will retain memories of the old order, and this will give them imaginative empathy. Leslie knows how hard it can be to run a household and Damon knows how hard it can be to prevail at work. "Damon knows that if I'm working late, it's not that I want to be at work—if I come home late, he feels bad for me," says Leslie. "He respects what I do." She understands that Damon has sacrificed the prestige offered by an executive career; he understands that she has sacrificed flexibility and time with the children. "You have to work at it—appreciation," said Leslie. "You know what the pros and cons are in each role." She considers Damon to be a provider in the most complete sense of the word. "As a parent, you want to provide what your family needs emotionally as well as financially," she said. "For us, it's about what's best for the family."

Hardest on Leslie was the time away from her children. "I miss dinner a lot," she said. "A lot of the reasons he cooks [is because] they eat before I get home, and I hate that. I hate that part of it." But she is also the one who gets to be the special parent. When Leslie arrives home, the cry goes up that "Mom's home" and the kids come scrambling from all corners of the house for kisses and hugs. "I never get that—DAD!" said Damon. "They see me all the time."

And Damon goes the extra mile, to ease her transition. Sometimes at the end of a tough day, Leslie will send him a one-word text—"red"—and he knows to have a glass of red wine waiting. Then there was the time that her day had been so demanding that she fired off the "red" text and drove home and stumbled in and started telling him about it. After about fifteen minutes Damon laughingly asked if she noticed anything when she came in. Stumbling back outside, she saw that there was a freshly made margarita on the doorstep, and a sign that said "Drink before entering." In answer to the old Freudian question of what women want, I can attest that a fresh margarita on the doorstep, and a spell of sympathetic listening, is quite a satisfactory answer.

The Good Husband

Interviewing various members of the Hawkins family, I couldn't decide which gender had adapted best to the new world order. The men, who were flexible and domestically competent and proud of their wives? Or the women, who sucked it up and embraced their tough days at the office? It was hard to decide. But here is another emerging truth; in couples with breadwinning women, an important criterion for happiness is that women embrace the provider role. Lots of women don't think of themselves as permanent, full-time providers; lots of women cling to the hope that it will be temporary. And sometimes it is; couples often trade back and forth. But sometimes it's not, and women only grudgingly accept this. Sometimes they actively resent it. The most successful relationships are the ones where women adopt the breadwinning role and inhabit it. I admired Susan and Leslie for doing this; even as they acknowledged the guilt they felt being away from their children, they understood the decisions they had made, embraced their lives, and made peace with the trade-offs.

For the same reason, I felt a lot of admiration for another of Danny's sisters, Rhonda McNally, who described her job as not nearly as important as that of Susan—"she's really very powerful and articulate and all-around awesome"—despite the fact that Rhonda's job as a global marketing director increasingly requires travel to Europe, South America, and Asia. Rhonda, self-deprecating, down-to-earth, with tousled brown hair and an easygoing demeanor, met her husband, Hank, back when she was taking college classes and waitressing at a Steak and Ale where Hank worked as a manager. Once Rhonda began her career at Magna International, Hank worked his way through the ranks of his own industry. They married, and not long after their first child was born—they now have three daughters—Hank came to Rhonda and told her he wanted to quit and be the caregiver for their baby.

At that time, Rhonda figures, she was making in the low $20,000s and Hank was closer to $50,000. But she did have better benefits and was advancing. And Rhonda understood Hank's emotional calculus. He had been raised by a single mother who supported them with factory work, and wanted his children to have the kind of intimate relationship with a father that he had not had himself. Rhonda also knew that the restaurant industry requires brutal, irregular hours; working and being a full childrearing partner was already exhausting Hank. She knew that if they felt squeezed, he would pick up bartending or whatever kind of job was necessary. So Rhonda became the full-time worker, and for the better part of a decade Hank was not so much a stay-at-home dad as a "run-around dad," ferrying their girls to lessons and meetings and events. Like Danny and Damon, he was a godsend to the PTA moms, who were overjoyed to have somebody with a background in restaurant management who knew how to stage an event and organize tables. Rhonda would go to PTA meetings and assuage her working mom guilt by volunteering Hank for everything: playground committee, whatever they needed, a practice Hank referred to as "living through me." When I asked if she was jealous that Hank got to be at home for their children's milestones, she said, "Oh yes. I was very jealous, but also very glad." If it couldn't be her seeing the girls walk or hearing their first word, at least it was him. Hank picked up work here and there, and maintained a degree of sanity by staying in close touch with old friends, with whom he takes an annual ski trip. Occasionally, he said, they tease him. "Like I'm home popping bonbons," he said, comfortably.

In some ways, Hank was the person I admired most. When their girls were school-aged, he went back to work full-time as general manager at a high-end café. He loved the work, but when Rhonda got a promotion that required even more extensive travel, Hank knew what was necessary. Rhonda didn't need to tell him. And he didn't hesitate. As much as he liked his job, he resigned. He knew Rhonda was expected to take trips at short notice and needed to feel secure knowing the home front was covered and that the family would function while she was gone. He made a concession—just as she had made a concession years earlier for him. "She's had to make a lot of sacrifices to get where she is," Hank reflected. "It would be wrong of me to say: 'Oh, you're not taking that next step, because I'm ready to do what I want to do.' I didn't think that would be fair. Over the years, she's sacrificed being home with the kids. She's really put forth her effort into her career." His boss was reluctant to let him go, so they devised a schedule where Hank could continue on a part-time basis.

When I asked him if he had gotten any affirmation for favoring Rhonda's career over his, Hank told the story of how he was sitting in the car with his boss, talking over his resignation offer, and his boss asked if he resented the fact that Rhonda had to travel so much. "I said, 'I don't think I complain too much,'" recollected Hank. He turned to Rhonda: "Then I asked you: 'I said, do I complain a lot?'" The next day, he says, his boss told him out of the blue: "You are a good husband."

"I'd have to agree," said Rhonda.

It worked out. Hank has been able to realize a dream and open his own restaurant, an Italian takeout that has become a family endeavor. The girls are old enough to help. One daughter met her boyfriend there. Hank is delighted to have another male around the house. Still, it's an exhausting schedule. When we talked at a local diner on a Sunday morning, Rhonda, just back from China, was getting ready to drive to Canada for a meeting. They sat for longer than we had planned, talking about how their marriage had evolved and what the hardest parts were. Hands-down, for Rhonda, was the travel: with teenaged children, there is always something you miss—a game, a performance, a birthday, though texting enables her to be in communication with them from anywhere. They text her when she is in China to see if they can have a sleepover. When she travels, she never stays an extra day for sightseeing; she gets home as soon as she can. "She carries a lot of guilt," said Hank. "I don't really have any guilt." For him, the only downside was watching her make her way in an industry that is still very male-dominated: while she loves her company and has done extremely well there, Hank points out that marketing, by dint of being a woman's field, tends to have a lower salary base than many sectors in the car industry. "At every pay point the pay level has been less than what a male counterpart can be."

The End of Stigma

Another reason the flip has worked well for the Hawkins siblings is that Danny and Leslie and Rhonda's parents—Gary and Marcelle Hawkins—are pragmatic people who figure that whatever works, works. In this family, stay-at-home dads suffer no stigma. Nor do working wives. Gary, the retired Ford engineer and family patriarch, freely acknowledges—in fact, he tells anybody who will listen—that he regrets not spending more time with his six children. Nobody blames him for it. They understand this was how things were. And they appreciate how Gary exemplifies the American work ethic: by being productive and noncomplaining, he set an example for the entire family. "Her dad is my hero," says Hank. "He's always been solid, he's always been just the strength of the family. Rhonda got a lot of his qualities. I don't think she ever thought twice about working—she's never gone, oh, I should quit and stay home." Rhonda agrees that her dad taught her how to navigate the American workplace. "He always taught us, even as teenagers, that you don't quit a job without finding another one," said Rhonda. "And you don't *not* give two weeks notice. You're responsible for your workplace and for your role in your workplace. You don't burn bridges no matter what. He was a great role model."

Conversations with Gary and Marcelle bore this out. They are equally pleased with all their children: "not a dud in the bunch" is how Marcelle likes to put it. When Gary suffered a perforated ulcer and was hospitalized in Detroit, Marcelle lived with Danny and Susan and drove into work every day with her daughter-in-law. She was glad to get to see Susan in her work environment, and impressed to hear how highly she is regarded. "Everybody knew who she was." She brags about how ably Danny runs a household. She is struck by how her grandchildren all have close relationships with their fathers: "The kids *know* their dads," she said, with wonder. When she was a young mother and Gary was a young engineer, "we had all these little kids," she said, her voice getting high, "and he was working all the overtime he could" and it was hard to savor each new baby. Even so, she never felt her own role was subservient: her job as she understood it was to make a comfortable home for her family, not to wait on Gary. She had no reservations about throwing him a load of laundry when he was watching television and asking him to fold it.

Whatever Works, Will Work

The Hawkins family illustrates another, lesser-noticed truth: even as same-sex couples seek the legal protection and stability of marriage, they offer a model of labor division that straight couples will follow. This is not to suggest that same-sex couples are perfect or that there aren't breadwinning and other tensions. There are—a truth subtly explored in *The Kids Are All Right*, the 2010 movie starring Julianne Moore and Annette Bening, which looked at a lesbian couple in which the stay-at-home partner was struggling with insecurity and empty nest issues, and the working partner had a tendency to condescend. But overall, same-sex couples offer a model in which people play to their strengths, not to their gender. Another of Danny's sisters, Lori Hawkins, is in a committed relationship with a same-sex partner. Together they are raising her partner's teenaged son from a prior marriage. When she was much younger, Lori says she struggled with feeling lesser somehow, because she wasn't married and didn't have children. Much of her self-worth came from her job. "I was very good, accomplished, made a shitload of money," says Lori, who, like Danny, went into finance, but says she wasn't disciplined about spending her income. For that reason, her partner, Sherry, who works for the U.S. Postal Service, is the money manager in their household. When she suffered a bout of unemployment, "My partner was just terrific. She had my back the whole time. God knows how we made it."

Sherry also keeps them on task with regard to housework, but Lori is the one who makes sure everybody gets fed. "If I don't cook, we don't eat," says Lori, who also does the repairs. When Danny was complaining about not having a power tool he needed, she told him, "You should ask your lesbian sister." After more than five years of living together, she and her partner "very much have our roles," and what those roles are have nothing to do with gender and everything to do with what they are good at.

The New Masculinity

The comfortable accommodations of the Hawkins men also suggest this: in the coming years, our understanding of masculinity will change and broaden. If indeed masculinity is social, and public, that means masculinity can acquire a different definition. This is already the case in Scandinavian countries, where fathers enjoy paid paternity leave and women find it wildly sexy when their husband puts the baby in a backpack and goes off cross-country skiing. Men will develop a masculinity that permits at-home achievement as well as extreme manly pursuits. The testosterone men may lose in one venue they will find in another.

For sure, men will continue to become more domesticated. They will become bigger performers in the kitchen, which could cease to be a feminine domain altogether. Slightly more than a century ago, the French philosopher Elisabeth Badinter points out, French intellectuals were horrified by the country's educated women agitating to join their academies and their ranks. "[W]e men will be the ones making the jam and the pickles," exclaimed one of them, panicked. Men's worst fears have come to pass and they couldn't be happier. Men in the coming years will expand their incursion into the kitchen, using the preparation of hot meals as an outlet for competitive instincts—iron chefs on the home front!—and a venue for sexual display. They will deal with the short-term recession and the long-term loss of industrial jobs and the never-ending rise of women workers by going Full Pleistocene, grilling and frying and buying ribs and salt-rubbed steaks and huge slabs of beef.

Kitchens will change. Once upon a time, kitchens were airy and homey places, which is to say feminine, and not all that well equipped. Kitchens had appliances, but the appliances were not massive, and neither were they pricey. Now kitchens are gleaming masculine spaces, all dark cabinets and giant stovetops and granite counters, not unlike abattoirs or hospital operating rooms. Who do you think is driving the market for immersion blenders and indoor grills and Sub-Zero freezers and deep-fat turkey fryers and coffeemakers the size of shuttle launchers? Who do you think has filled the kitchen with twenty sizes of kitchen knife? When your own mother could get by, pretty much, with a paring knife and one that was serrated? Who has filled the kitchen with tools? And what are tools but a throwback to cave days? "The kitchen is the new garage," celebrity chef Marcus Samuelsson, cofounder of Food Republic, a food website for men, points out. Tools, the most primitive of masculine artifacts, will continue to move out of dreary peripheral spaces—the garage and the basement, once men's only domestic territory, along with that recliner in front of the television—and into the center of the house.

Because that's where men are and will continue to be: in the center of the house. Man-caves will become a thing of the past, because the whole house will become a man-cave. Men will make the home a tapestry into which their fantasies can be woven. "Traditional gender roles have been turned upside down," observes Samuelsson, whose website joins a number of others in appealing to the butcher-knife set. Men are buying books like *Man with a Pan* and *Cook to Bang*, understanding that women have boundless sexual craving for a man who knows how to make a decent omelet. Cooking has been legitimized as a contact sport, an approach encouraged by chefs like Gordon Ramsay, who in his reality show *Hell's Kitchen* presents high-end meal preparation as an obscenity-laced boot-camp experience, and therefore acceptable for males. In the past two years, at the Institute of Culinary Education in New York, the percentage of men enrolled has risen from 20 percent to 32 percent. Since 1970, men have tripled the time they spend cooking, while women have cut back dramatically. "The sociological changes are such that [kitchens] are available for guys now," observed my friend Robert Freis, a newspaperman living in our hometown of Roanoke, Virginia. Thanks to the job of his beloved wife, Linda, a health insurance account manager—Roanoke, like many aging rust belt cities, has seen its jobs base transform from a male industry, railroading, to a female one, health care—Robert was able to renovate a house he had inherited.

Robert's goal during the renovations was a beach house atmosphere that would be conducive to entertaining. He ended up with a wine cellar (he prefers to think of it as a beer cellar) and well-furnished kitchen and, of course, a grill. Plus two smokers. The last time I was over there, they were getting ready to host a New Year's party and had a half-keg from a local microbrewery. It was so different from what either of us had known, growing up on meatloaf and Tater Tots. "It's just a lot more fun to be around home than it used to be," Rob reflected. In homage to our Appalachian upbringing, he refers to what he does as "cooking in tongues": showy, externalized, charismatic cooking.

"Cooking—that's my creative outlet," agreed Michael, the Northern Californian, for whom cooking was an important distraction when he was suffering his period of underemployment. "I'm pretty obsessed about taking care of my kitchen. I like finding some interesting ethnic dish and making it four or five times until I have it down."

Men will combine new skills with old ones, fashioning intriguing ways of being men. In conversations with women earners, I was struck by how cooking and hunting both kept cropping up in their descriptions of what their husbands did all day long. Far from a crisis in masculinity, among many couples I talked to there was a marked expansion, a broadening of the category to include pleasing domestic pursuits as well as old-fashioned subsistence activities. Amy Antonellis, the law student, mentioned that after they moved to Vermont, her carpenter husband had embraced the local hunting culture. Stephan Schmitt, the laid-off mechanical engineer, was hunting partly as a pastime, and partly to provision their household; his next goal, he said, was to learn how to butcher a carcass. And when I happened to be chatting with Sonia Goltz, a professor of organizational behavior at Michigan Technological University who is an expert in wage inequality between men and women, she reflected that in her own husband's extended family, clustered in the steel mill regions of northwest Indiana, it became clear at a reunion that "all the men were out of work and all the women were working. The men were having lots of time to go fishing and hunting, and we're feeling really overworked and stressed." More men of the future will be cooking in kitchens where the freezer is stuffed with game they have shot and butchered themselves. The more things change, the more they stay the same.

To today's self-sufficient, economically providing woman, a man who fishes and hunts will have the same elemental sex appeal he has had since the beginning of time.

The Importance of Clubbing

In my conversations with breadwomen, the word "golf" came up a lot when they were talking about their husbands. Golf, like hunting, is a traditionally male pastime that requires stretches of free time. Like hunting, it attracts a variety of participants, including men who are working, men who are retired, men who are unemployed, and it has an equalizing effect that way. Best of all, golfing involves clubs. And what are clubs but a return to—well, you get it. Smart women breadwinners will retain that family golf club membership even when there is financial stress involved. "For him, that's a critical part of his social life and social standing," said Deborah Wahl Meyer, the Michigan executive whose husband moved for her career when she got a job offer from Chrysler. Similarly, the executive Jennifer Tyler reported that when her husband relocated to England for her, they were living in a region with no real expatriate community, but "once he found his golfing partners he was fine." Similarly, in Boise, Idaho, Jill Singer, who works a full-time job as a construction manager, appreciates the restorative qualities that 18 holes offers to her lower-earning husband. "Go play golf all you want, honey," she tells him. "Go be with your men friends, make sure you have a poker night. Drinking is important, golf is important, entertainment is important."

Protection Racket

Other masculine qualities will come to the fore, displacing the emphasis on earning. Anthropologist David Gilmore, in his book *Manhood in the Making*, traveled the world to explore how manhood is asserted in any number of cultures, developed and primitive. After spending time in such disparate places as Tahiti, New Guinea, Spain, and Brazil, he concluded—persuasively—that in all its many guises, masculinity seems to reside in the ability to protect, to procreate, and to provide. In the future, we will see a renaissance of protection, a quality of masculinity that has perhaps been undervalued of late but one that has been undergoing a revival, as men find ways to protect their high-earning wives as they foray into a world of corporate alpha males and political skullduggery. One prominent author whose first major bestseller made her sought after as a public speaker recounted that her husband was delighted by her renown, and often accompanied her to events. Developing his role, he undertook to rescue her from aggressive admirers and tedious conversations with fans who wanted to monopolize her. "Sometimes it was a conversation I was enjoying, and I would say—What did you do that for?" she recollected. But she appreciated the way he watched out for her and they eventually devised a discreet signal she could use when ready to be rescued.

As men adjust to being political spouses, expect them to become their wives' most tenacious bodymen. You can already see this in the personas of Todd Palin, husband of former Alaska governor and one-time Republican vice presidential nominee Sarah Palin, and Marcus Bachmann, known for being protective of his wife, Michele. Bachmann once blocked a fan from taking a photo of her and sometimes physically grasps her to move her through crowds. It is possible to carry this too far, of course: overhandling can be a way of undermining. But a striking number of women I spoke with talked about husbands who held doors and put on their coats for them, an old-fashioned chivalry the women found charming and reassuring.

"I love it that my husband still opens the door and does all that, and will grab suitcases," reflected Deborah Wahl Meyer. "He's bigger and stronger. He does everything—tons of things for me, to make life easier and to make sure everything's there." And: "He spends a lot of time teaching my son the door, the manners, and how to take care of people."

The example set by these early adopters suggests other ways in which couples can successfully adjust to a world where women can enjoy their earnings and men can enjoy lives that are full and varied. Among these:

- Women need to resist the urge to gatekeep. They need to trust their husbands to run the home, and show appreciation when men do.

- Women should talk up their partners' strengths. Remind people what a terrific job your partner does at whatever he's doing. Women shouldn't shore up their husband's egos to the point where they become exhausted or it seems false, and they shouldn't diminish their own achievements. But pointing out what a great photographer or cook your husband is—making sure people know he excels in a realm of endeavor—can only help. Everybody likes to be praised. Everybody likes to be thanked. When he makes you dinner, thank him.

- For couples who struggle sexually, there's nothing wrong with looking for realms in which the man can appear conventionally manly. Hunting, fishing: those are all good. The writer Aaron Traister diarized in *Salon* about how he was feeling bad about his wife's breadwinning—"I became sullen and lethargic"—until he went outside one day and shoveled snow for a number of their neighbors. His young son helped. In some way he could hardly put his finger on, the sheer physical expression of his masculine strength made him feel—masculine. "It was at that moment that it occurred to me how much I like being a man," he wrote. "I'm big and I'm strong and I can shovel snow and install air-conditioners for people who can't shovel snow or install air-conditioners for themselves." So men, get out the snow shovel. Take your wife for a drive. Working out can work wonders. Go chop some wood.

- Women need to remind themselves that their prestige does not derive from what their husbands do.

- Get a joint checking account. I was astonished at how many female breadwinners worried that their husbands felt emasculated by having to ask them for money. Why should your husband have to ask you for money? Of course that's emasculating! Your earnings should go into a common account; you're married; you're a team. You should both have your own ATM cards. Repeat after me: You are a provider. So act like one.

- Men, stay flexible and interesting and always be moving forward. Women have a horror of stagnant men, and who can blame them?

Men staying home with children need to make sure they adapt and stay interesting. Read the newspaper. Stop stewing and feeling dissatisfied. Take up a hobby. "Dave just constantly wants to be actively doing, and learning new things, he has his hand in all these various activities," said Amy Antonellis of her fiancé. Similarly, Danny Hawkins is the kind of person who is always trying new ways of doing things, even just moving things around the house. "One of the things that makes Susan so good at her job is taking new information and changing her line of thought," he said. "We both have the thought that you're never perfect and you want to continue to improve." Embrace change. Stay interesting.

· Also, men! When you cook? Cook *for* her, not *at* her. It doesn't always have to be a performance. Sometimes, just make a salad.

Breadwinner Babies

A final question: How will children of women breadwinners find their own way forward? How will childhood be defined when mothers are the major earners? A couple of pieces of advice emerge here, as well. For one thing: fathers and mothers alike should help children understand that just because their mother is working doesn't mean she doesn't love them. This may seem obvious to you, reader, but it may not be obvious to children. This came up when I was talking to Ashlie Brown. Ashlie, who is in her twenties, grew up in Nebraska. Her dad worked as a farmer, and her mother was a teacher and later a school principal. This meant her dad was home most of the time, while her mother, who brought in the majority of the income, worked long hours during the school year. Ashlie says there was a time in adolescence when she assumed her mother didn't love them as much as her dad did, simply because her mother wasn't around as much.

She of course no longer thinks that, and has a great relationship with her mother. But looking back, Ashlie thinks her parents might have worked harder to correct this notion. It strikes her that the household did not adjust to suit her mother's schedule; if her mom was going to be late, they ate dinner without her, and there was not much conversation about why her mom was away. She thinks parents are well advised to reassure children about the many ways—including financial support—that love can be expressed.

It's also important that neither spouse lead children to think the situation is undesirable or even all that unusual. "I talk to him about how much I love what I'm doing," said Deborah Wahl Meyer, thinking about the impact of her breadwinning on her son. "I think the biggest thing I've learned is not to complain about work in front of him. If he hears me complaining—oh, I have to go to work—then it's a negative experience for him. When he sees me loving what I'm doing, energized and excited, then, even at eight years old, it's positive."

By far the majority of adult children I spoke with grew up feeling happy with the situation and grateful for the time they spent with their fathers. One of these is Stephanie Hawkins, older daughter of Danny and Susan, who when we spoke was majoring in theater at the University of Michigan and planning for a career as a stage manager. Stephanie said that growing up, she loved having her dad around. "He was the only guy on the PTA, the only dad I really saw around the school," she said. "I remember bragging a little—yeah, my dad's doing all this stuff. I get to hang out with my dad. It's definitely something I was proud of." Stephanie does remember feeling disconnected from her mother when she was in middle school, in part because Susan, being super-efficient, got distressed if Stephanie didn't get her assignments done immediately. But "it was nothing that was un-over-comeable," says Stephanie, who also felt very proud of her mother. "I always thought it was really cool that she was working and successful, and I grew up expecting that for myself. I expect to be successful and supported." She feels they are even closer now that she's in college, maybe because she is freer to work on her own schedule. "My mom's a go-getter: do everything early, then relax. That's not the way I functioned. It stressed her out. My sister is like my mom—she stresses out when things aren't done for two days into the future, which is why they haven't conflicted in that way." Danny thinks that he and Susan are wonderfully complementary—he is more low-key, she is more highly charged—and that it was good for their daughters to see that there are different ways to function effectively in the world.

And as Gary Hawkins can attest, parents can be a powerful example even when they are away. One parent can be a strong influence by being accessible and relaxed; another can do the same thing by being productive and happy. Girls are powerfully affected by their mother's example, and fulfilled mothers have a great deal of impact on the choices their own daughters make. Growing up with an accomplished mother, Stephanie Hawkins expects to be a breadwinner in her house. This created tension in her own relationship: she had a boyfriend who expected his wife would be the one doing the cooking and laundry, so she broke up with him. She doesn't have to be the sole breadwinner, but she wants an equal partnership. "I want someone who's willing to wash dishes."

Of course, children will be adversely affected if mothers are not paid a breadwinner's wage. Probably the greatest danger to children is if society continues to think working mothers are a temporary phenomenon or a niche subset of women or undesirable; if employers get away with paying women less than men, then families will suffer, and the model, no matter how emotionally satisfying for the children, will carry a subversive message: this is not sanctioned. Melissa Weaver, another adult child of a female breadwinner, contacted me to talk about her experience; her mother worked in city government and was the higher earner in their home. She remembers once when her mother, in her new job, overheard a member of the salary committee saying: "Well, it's not like she's the *breadwinner* of the family." She can only assume her mother in that instance was paid less than a man would have been. Melissa very much hopes that conversations like that are obsolete—she hopes women are recognized as breadwinners, and paid accordingly—and wanted to make it clear to readers of this book that her mother had been fully present during her childhood and that she never felt neglected.

The other danger lies in men who are underperforming. If men, particularly lower-income and working-class men, continue to falter; if we as a society are unable to imagine a new mission for men beyond providing; if men give up because they think that women have everything covered; if we don't find a way to keep more men in school; if women continue to feel these men are not worth partnering with, then home life will suffer and children will be the ones hardest hit. Studies show that men who aren't married to the mother of their children, and who can't contribute financially, are less likely to have a relationship with the children they father. This is bad for children and it's bound to have consequences. If one-half of America's children get to have newly intimate relationships with their fathers, and if the other half has no relationship at all, the gap between haves and have-nots will grow even wider. When fathers stay home by choice, that's one thing; when they fall out of the workforce and lose contact with their families, that's another. Men need to be able to sustain a sense of purpose and society needs to help them do it.

And if we manage that, here is another prediction: girls who have been raised with paternal involvement will have high expectations for how their husbands should treat them. Ashlie Brown recalled how her father always made her a big breakfast, and she remains convinced that attacking the day fortified by eggs and pancakes made all the difference in her success. She expects any man she marries to do the same. Children of breadwinning mothers will go into the future expecting parity in housework. They will look for men who will support them in their endeavors. This is what Rhonda McNally has seen in her three daughters: they expect to have husbands as engaged and hands-on as Hank. "He's not just a babysitter. They'll expect that, and I want them to expect that," says Rhonda. Leslie Ajlouny made a similar observation: before I arrived to interview her and Damon, she happened to mention to one of her son's friends that a writer was coming to interview them, explaining that it was because their family was considered a little different. The boy laughed when he heard this. It had never occurred to him that the Ajlounys were unusual, given the warmth of their household. "You should see my family," he commented. With all respect to Tolstoy, it seems increasingly true that not all happy families are happy in the same way. Yet different kinds of families can still be happy. So expect this: the next generation of breadwomen will be even more productive than this one.

Notes

Chapter One: The New Providers

Page

6   *Not that long ago, in 1970:* Using U.S. Census Bureau data, the Pew Research Center calculates that in 1970, 4 percent of wives ages 30 to 44 outearned their husbands, a proportion that had risen to 22 percent by 2007. Richard Fry and D'Vera Cohn, "Women, Men, and the New Economics of Marriage," *Social and Demographic Trends Report* (Washington, D.C.: Pew Research Center, January 19, 2010), 1, www.pewsocialtrends.org/2010/01/19/women-men-and-the-new-economics- of-marriage/.

6   *Some of these women were super-achievers:* Sara B. Raley, Marybeth J. Mattingly, and Suzanne M. Bianchi, in "How Dual Are Dual-Income Couples? Documenting Change from 1970 to 2001," *Journal of Marriage and Family* 68 (February 2006): 11–28; talk about super-achieving female breadwinners of the 1980s who were known as WASPS, or Wives as Senior Partners. But these were rare: Anne E. Winkler, in "Earnings of Husbands and Wives in Dual-Earner Families," *Monthly Labor Review* (April 1998): 42–48, looked at data from the early 1990s and found that even then, "nontraditional couples are especially common among dual-earner couples with low-wage husbands."

6   *Almost 40 percent of U.S. working wives:* Figures from the U.S. Bureau of Labor Statistics show that for couples with working wives, the proportion of wives outearning husbands has risen from 23.7 percent in 1987

to 37.7 percent in 2009, an all-time high. This includes all wives with any earnings at all, working full-time, part-time, or self-employed. Bureau of Labor Statistics, "Table 25: Wives Who Earn More than Their Husbands, 1987–2008," *Women in the Labor Force: A Databook,* 2010, 78, www.bls.gov/cps/wlftable25-2010.htm. Figures for 2009 were kindly provided to me by economist Mary Bowler of the BLS and posted online as this book was going to press at www.bls.gov/cps/wlf-table25-2011.pdf.

6   *Women occupy 51 percent:* Bureau of Labor Statistics, "Table 11: Employed Persons by Detailed Occupation and Sex, 2009 Annual Averages," *Women in the Labor Force: A Databook,* 2010, 28, www.bls.gov/cps/wlf-table11-2011.pdf. BLS labor force projections can be found in the version of T. Alan Lacey and Benjamin Wright, "Occupational Employment Projections to 2018," *Monthly Labor Review* (November 2009): 82–123, that was revised and re-posted December 22, 2010, www.bls.gov/opub/mlr/2009/11/art5full.pdf.

6   *By the year 2050, demographers forecast:* Albert Esteve and Iñaki Permanyer, demographers at the Centre d'Estudis Demogràfics, Barcelona, Spain, related this figure to the author in a Skype interview, April 11, 2011, and in email correspondence. They point out that the projections can be found in Wolfgang Lutz, Anne Goujon, Samir K.C., and Warren Sanderson, "Reconstruction of Populations by Age, Sex and Level of Educational Attainment for 120 Countries for 1970–2000," *Vienna Yearbook of Population Research 2007*: 193–235, and Samir K.C., Bilal Barakat, Anne Goujon, Vegard Skirbekk, Warren Sanderson, and Wolfgang Lutz, "Projection of Populations by Level of Educational Attainment, Age, and Sex for 120 Countries for 2005–2050," *Demographic Research* 22 (March 16, 2010): 383–472.

7   *"The trends are clear":* Gary Becker, telephone interview with author, May 30, 2011.

8   *She was raised in the Mormon Church:* "The Family: A Proclamation to the World," delivered in 1995 and included on the official website of the Church of Jesus Christ of Latter-day Saints, states, "By divine design, fathers are to preside over their families in love and righteousness and are responsible to provide the necessities of life and protection for their families. Mothers are primarily responsible for the nurture of their children." The Church of Jesus Christ of Latter-day Saints, "The Family: A Proclamation to the World," http://lds.org/library/display/0,4945,161-1-11-1,00.html.

9   *Of all the major cities where young women:* Conor Dougherty, "Young Women's Pay Exceeds Male Peers'," *Wall Street Journal,* September 1, 2010, http://online.wsj.com/article/SB10001424052748704421104575463790770831192.html.

11 *As countries all over the world:* In "The Decline of the Male Breadwinner: Explanations and Interpretations," Rosemary Crompton cites scholars who, observing the deindustrialization of many European countries and the rise of educated working women, in the 1990s predicted "a war between men and women" over issues like jobs, child care, and the domestic division of labor. Rosemary Crompton, ed., *Restructuring Gender Relations and Employment: The Decline of the Male Breadwinner* (Oxford: Oxford University Press, 1999), 17.

11 *"Men know that women are an over-match":* James Boswell, *The Journal of a Tour to the Hebrides, with Samuel Johnson, LL.D.* (Philadelphia: John F. Watson, 1810).

11 *In 2011, a study confirmed that women:* H. Colleen Stuart, Sue Moon, and Tiziana Casciaro, "The Oscar Curse: Status Dynamics and Gender Differences in Marital Survival," *Social Science Research Network,* January 27, 2011, http://ssrn.com/abstract=1749612.

12 *Google* Daily Mail—*the reliably conservative:* Sadie Nicholas, "Why Do Men Find the Female Breadwinner Utterly Terrifying?," *Mail Online,* June 17, 2008, www.dailymail.co.uk/femail/article-1026972/Why-men-female-breadwinner-utterly-terrifying.html.

13 *All measures confirm that men:* Francine D. Blau, "Trends in the Well-Being of American Women, 1970–1995," *Journal of Economic Literature* 36 (March 1998): 112–65. The discussion of husbands doing more housework is on pp. 150–55.

13 *"When culture runs up against economic trends":* Gary Becker, telephone interview with author, May 30, 2011.

Chapter Two: The Bargain

Page

20 *In 1929, when Virginia Woolf considered:* Virginia Woolf, *A Room of One's Own* (Orlando: Harcourt Brace, 1989), 37.

21 *"It is only for the last forty-eight years":* ibid., 22–23. The fact that married women for centuries had no property rights under British common law is reviewed in Matthias Doepke and Michèle Tertilt, "Women's Liberation: What's in It for Men?," *The Quarterly Journal of Economics* 124 (November 2009): 1541–91. Prior to 1830, the authors point out, married women in the United States and UK "essentially had no rights at all, as all legal authority rested with their husbands. This meant that a married woman could not own

property, she could not enter into contracts, she had no rights to her own earnings, she had no parental rights over her legitimate children, and she could not obtain a divorce" (p. 1542). They point out that in the UK, a series of reforms were carried out during the 19th century, first in child custody rules, then in divorce and in the realm of property with the Married Women's Property Act, "passed in 1870 and expanded in 1874 and 1882." The United States, they point out, underwent a similar evolution (pp. 1547–49).

22 *"She was intensely sympathetic":* Virginia Woolf, "Professions for Women," in *The Death of the Moth and Other Essays* (San Diego: Harcourt Brace, 1974), 237.

22 *"I need not hate any man":* Woolf, *A Room of One's Own,* 38.

22 *"Once a woman was married, there was":* Val D. Greenwood, *The Researcher's Guide to American Genealogy,* 3rd. ed. (Baltimore: Genealogical Publishing Co., 2000), 477. Greenwood adds, "One of the most difficult challenges faced by the genealogist is the challenge of identifying the women on his ancestral lines."

22 *While some argue that colonial society:* Marylynn Salmon, *Women and the Law of Property in Early America* (Chapel Hill: University of North Carolina Press, 1986). In her preface, Salmon notes: "My inquiry into the property rights of American women revealed above all else a picture of their enforced dependence, both before and after the Revolution" (p. xv).

22 *"After marriage, all of the personal property":* ibid., 15. Salmon's analysis of Puritanism is on p. 8, and a description of the wife sale is on p. 59.

23 *In colonial America, property:* Alice Kessler-Harris, *Out to Work: A History of Wage-Earning Women in the United States* (Oxford: Oxford University Press, 2003), makes the point that "for free, white, male immigrants to the colonies, land provided the major source of economic independence" and that most white and black women, and black men "did not hold land" (p. 3). She points out that the family was the "centerpiece of the economic system" and social order, and men were in charge of it (p. 4). She points out that male servants were paid more than female ones, but that the price of female slaves was higher than that of male ones (p. 10). She agrees with Salmon that married women's inability to own property "deprived women of economic independence, control of a household, and political influence" (pp. 12–13). And she points out that colonial women were barred from apprenticeships in the skilled trades on p. 13.

23 *Even when people married for love:* In *Marriage, a History: How Love Conquered Marriage* (New York: Penguin, 2006) the historian Stephanie Coontz

notes on p. 5: "In the eighteenth century, people began to adopt the radical new idea that love should be the most fundamental reason for marriage," unlike in earlier eras when other motives—political or familial alliances, say—often took priority.

23 *"We are the only animal species":* Charlotte Perkins Gilman, *Women and Economics* (New York: Cosimo, 2006), 3.

24 *When she developed depression:* In her introduction to a collection of Gilman's writings, Denise Knight notes that while pregnant with her daughter, Gilman sank into a "deep depression" and sought a cure from a leading Philadelphia "nerve specialist," Dr. Silas Weir Mitchell, who prescribed treatment that "required Gilman to live as domestic a life as possible, to have the baby with her at all times, and to never touch a pen, a paintbrush, or a pencil for the remainder of her life. Within months after returning home, she suffered a nervous breakdown." In Charlotte Perkins Gilman, *The Yellow Wall-Paper, Herland, and Selected Writings* (New York: Penguin, 2009), x.

24 *"When [man] became owner of the land":* Simone de Beauvoir, *The Second Sex* (New York: Vintage, 1989), 78. She argues that women were imperiling their selves and describes the "deal" on p. xxvii. And like Gilman and Woolf, she believed that being consigned to the home deformed women's personality, enabling the 20th century wife to "dawdle around the apartment in a wrapper" (p. 624).

25 *"[T]he proposed change would totally destroy":* Editorial, London *Times,* April 23, 1868, 8–9.

26 *If women objected, they were derided:* Kessler-Harris, *Out to Work,* 43. She addresses the "ruinous competition" argument on pp. 68–69.

26 *The point of keeping women out of lucrative work:* Kessler-Harris, ibid., discusses the domestic code on p. 49, saying that it "reflected earlier conceptions of women as the purer sex." She points out that the social order imposed a family structure that enforced the "subordination of women" on p. 50 and posits that the cult of womanhood developed in response to competition on p. 49. Similarly, Lynn Weiner in *From Working Girl to Working Mother: The Female Labor Force in the United States, 1820–1980* (Chapel Hill: University of North Carolina Press, 1985), 39–41, points out that all manner of forces enforced the "domestic ideology of the mid-nineteenth century," which held that women should be, pure, unspoiled, and "womanly." Stephanie Coontz, "When We Hated Mom," *New York Times,* May 7, 2011, www .nytimes.com/2011/05/08/opinion/08coontz.html?pagewanted=all, points out that the 19th century was the period in American culture when women

were viewed as occupying a "nobler sphere" apart from and above men's "bank-note world."

27 *To be sure, women weren't the only ones:* Kessler-Harris, *Out to Work*, on p. 51 points out that the domestic code obliged men to work ever harder and encouraged the idea that for his wife to earn income signified that he had failed. She points out that newspaper editorialists seemed to think that having a wife who depended on him kept men "sober and industrious." On p. 59, she points out that "[t]he belief that women belonged at home permitted employers to pay wages that were merely supplemental." On pp. 104–105, Weiner points out that it was believed that men shirked their own family duties when a wife worked and that having a working wife "deadens ambition in a man."

27 *"Contacts between fathers of urban families":* Elisabeth Badinter, *XY: On Masculine Identity* (New York: Columbia University Press, 1995), 86.

27 *Even now, 67 percent of Americans:* Pew Social Trends Staff, *The Decline of Marriage and Rise of New Families* (Washington, D.C.: Pew Research Center, November 18, 2010), www.pewsocialtrends.org/2010/11/18/the -decline-of-marriage-and-rise-of-new-families.

27 *The endurance of this idea is ironic:* Kessler-Harris, *Out to Work*, 29, 68.

28 *Once the mill girls "felt the jingle of silver":* ibid., 34.

28 *On average, most girls spent less than five years in the mill:* ibid., 36.

28 *As manufacturing expanded, more barriers:* Kessler-Harris, ibid., points out that as the 19th century progressed and the industrial labor force became much more heavily male dominated, "Male workers feared that the price of labor would fall" to the female standard, usually less than half what was paid to men. "Organized men insisted that wages paid to them would be higher if women were barred from the work force" (p. 69).

28 *Outside of the upper and middle classes:* ibid., 46–48. And on p. 121, Kessler-Harris points out that with the onset of immigration after the Civil War, many families required two workers to survive.

28 *Women for most of the 19th century:* ibid., 57–59.

28 *A moral code helped justify:* Weiner uses the term "future motherhood" and discusses protective legislation in *From Working Girl to Working Mother*, pp. 68–78.

28 *"Whenever the sexes work indiscriminately":* Kessler-Harris, *Out to Work*, 101. She talks about protective legislation on pp. 185–232.

29 *The economist Claudia Goldin notes:* Claudia Goldin, in a telephone interview with the author on July 5, 2010, pointed out that among the small cohort

of men and women who graduated from college in the early 20th century, the women were very well positioned for the workforce, but the playing field was not yet sufficiently level for them to make headway. "We would have seen female breadwinning a lot earlier" if it had been, she said. In "The Rising (and then Declining) Significance of Gender," a chapter in Francine D. Blau, Mary C. Brinton, and David B. Grusky, eds., *The Declining Significance of Gender?* (New York: Russell Sage, 2006), pp. 76–77, Goldin discusses the "high school movement," which endeavored to make a high school education more universal, encouraged literacy and numeracy, and better prepared both boys and girls for a white-collar workforce. She discusses the rise of office work, the growth of retail, the division of labor, and uses the term "white-collar counterpart of the industrial revolution" on p. 79. She cites the wage difference between men and women, and the premium for husbands, on p. 86. And she notes that there was no similar premium for married women.

29 *And World War I enabled women:* Kessler-Harris in *Out to Work* discusses wartime opportunities for women on pp. 219–36 and quotes the female banker on p. 232.

29 *The freedom of the 1920s:* Goldin, "The Rising (and then Declining) Significance of Gender," discusses marriage bars on p. 80. Erected by many school districts in the late 19th century, they were adopted by some offices in the 20th century, and spread during the Great Depression. She discusses women's inability to advance in offices on pp. 82–91.

30 *As the historian David Kennedy:* David M. Kennedy, *Freedom from Fear: The American People in Depression and War, 1929–1945* (New York: Oxford University Press, 1999), 27.

30 *"The wife who has her own income":* Kessler-Harris quotes the 20th century letter writer on p. 107. Weiner, *From Working Girl to Working Mother*, quotes Ernest Groves on p. 104

30 *As the sociologist Viviana Zelizer:* Viviana A. Zelizer, *The Social Meaning of Money: Pin Money, Paychecks, Poor Relief, and Other Currencies* (Princeton: Princeton University Press, 1997). She talks about the play *Chicken Feed* on pp. 36 and 37. She discusses the battle over allowances, including the *Ladies Home Journal* poll, on pp. 36–61.

31 *As Goldin shows, marriage bars:* Claudia Goldin, "Marriage Bars: Discrimination Against Married Women Workers, 1920s to 1950s," National Bureau of Economic Research, Working Paper No. 2747, October 1988, www.nber .org/papers/w2747, talks about marriage bars being extended during the

Depression on p. 10, as well as the issuing of a 1932 federal order that "mandated that executive branch officials, in the face of layoffs, fire workers whose spouses were employed by the federal government. The regulation almost always entailed the firing of married women, although many husbands could have been furloughed." On p. 11 she points out that the Depression "served to reinforce social norms that kept married women, particularly the emerging middle class, out of the labor force," and that economic recessions often provoke a social recession.

31 *Those women who did work:* Kessler-Harris, *Out to Work,* quotes Norman Cousins on p. 256 and talks about the inequitable WPA wage scale on 263.

31 *Interviewing 59 Depression-era families:* Mirra Komarovsky, *The Unemployed Man and His Family: The Effect of Unemployment upon the Status of the Man in Fifty-nine Families* (Walnut Creek, CA: AltaMira, 2004). The man who worries that his children no longer think as much of him is quoted on p. 14. The man who talks about losing something is quoted on p. 41; the man whose wife controls all the money is on p. 45. Komarovsky writes about patriarchal families on p. 59, women taking in boarders on pp. 30–31, "long-lasting and profound defeat" on p. 14, men who behaved better on p. 67, and men's preference to work on pp. 80–81. A man talks about a relief check being most humiliating, followed by a working wife, on p. 76.

32 *So strong was the breadwinning ethos:* Gardiner Harris, "The Public's Quiet Savior from Harmful Medicines," *New York Times,* September 13, 2010, www.nytimes.com/2010/09/14/health/14kelsey.html.

32 *The Depression "solidified their positions as workers":* Kessler-Harris, *Out to Work,* 271, 272.

32 *So did the Second World War:* Francine D. Blau, Marianne A. Ferber, and Anne E. Winkler, in *The Economics of Women, Men and Work,* 6th ed. (Boston: Prentice Hall, 2010), 116–18, discuss the measures put in place during World War II, such as day care, that made it easier for mothers to work. They show that returning veterans were usually able to reclaim their jobs from women; many day care centers were closed postwar; but that the wartime experience broke down attitudinal barriers and gave many women "a taste of the benefits of earning their own income." While many women did leave the workforce after the war, "a substantial number also remained." They credit historian William Chafe with the argument that it took a "cataclysmic event like World War II" to defeat the idea that women's place was in the home only. They point out that after the war, many working mothers were older

women, but that the overall proportion of mothers working would soar from the 1960s to the 1980s.

33 *During the 20th century, the proportion of married women:* Claudia Goldin, "The Role of World War II in the Rise of Women's Employment," *The American Economic Review* 81, no. 4 (September 1991): 741–56. Goldin talks about the view that World War II was a watershed for women, and a later revisionist theory which holds that the rise in the number of women working had more to do with an increase in education and white-collar work.

33 *In the 1950s, Simone de Beauvoir:* Beauvoir, *The Second Sex,* 679.

33 *And yet, the postwar period was one:* Coontz in *Marriage, a History,* points out on p. 228 that "from the 1940s through the 1960s, real wages rose rapidly across the population, fastest of all in the bottom half. More families than ever before could achieve a decent, if modest, standard of living on the wages of a single male breadwinner."

33 *Opportunities for women were emerging:* Goldin, in "The Rising (and then Declining) Significance of Gender," points out that between the 1940s and 1960s, well-educated women typically took jobs with a "flat" earning profile—teacher, social worker, nurse—meaning they could not expect much wage gain, and even ambitious women who wanted more than dead-end work were usually asked "Can you type?" when they applied for work, pp. 94–95.

33 *In 1942, in his overwrought:* Philip Wylie, *Generation of Vipers* (1942; repr., Illinois: Dalkey Archive Press, 1996). The book describes women as "an idle class, a spending class, a candy-craving class" (p. 52), argues that they "possess most of the wealth" (p. 53), and devotes a chapter (pp. 194–217) to the "rapacity of loving mothers."

34 *In that era, in a cohort of Californians:* Glen H. Elder, Jr., *Children of the Great Depression: Social Change in Life Experience* (Boulder: Westview, 1999). In his longitudinal study of children in California who were raised during the Great Depression, Elder points out on p. 161 that "a substantial number of the women with husbands from [families that suffered during the Depression] sacrificed their education in order to put them through college" and on p. 162 that over half the men who had grown up in the working class married women with less education. On p. 210 he points out that many women who did enter college in the middle of the 20th century left before graduating. On p. 211, he points out that over half the working-class girls had better-educated husbands; so did middle-class girls; women who stayed

in college too long became disadvantaged in the marriage market. On p. 219, he points out that women who were attractive were more likely to marry up and on p. 209 writes about the office as a marriage market. And Claudia Goldin, in "The Long Road to the Fast Track: Career and Family," *Annals of the American Academy of Political and Social Science* 596 (November 2004): 20–35, points out that women who graduated from college during the era of the baby boom—from the end of World War II to the 1960s—became mothers at a young age, and then, trying to start careers late, "became the frustrated group" that Betty Friedan made famous, pp. 24–25.

35 *That bargain would become known:* There is an excellent discussion of exchange theory in Liana C. Sayer, Paula England, Paul D. Allison, and Nicole Kangas, "She Left, He Left: How Employment and Satisfaction Affect Women's and Men's Decisions to Leave Marriages," *American Journal of Sociology* 116 (May 2011): 1982–2018.

35 *Among them was evolutionary psychology:* The literature on evolutionary psychology is by now vast. One seminal text is David M. Buss, *The Evolution of Desire* (New York: Basic Books, 1994). On p. 31, Buss notes that "women have evolved a preference for men who show signs of the ability to acquire resources and a disdain for men who lack ambition."

35 *In his landmark book,* A Treatise on the Family: In Chapter 2, "Division of Labor in Households and Families," Becker spells out his specialization theory, arguing on p. 38 that since "women have a comparative advantage over men in the household sector when they make the same investments in human capital, an efficient household with both sexes would allocate the time of women mainly to the household sector and the time of men mainly to the market sector." On p. 43, he writes, "Specialization of tasks, such as the division of labor between men and women, implies a dependence on others for certain tasks. Women have traditionally relied on men for provision of food, shelter, and protection, and men have traditionally relied on women for the bearing and rearing of children and the maintenance of the home. Consequently, both men and women have been made better off by a 'marriage,' the term for a written, oral, or customary long-term contract between a man and a woman to produce children, food, and other commodities in a common household." On p. 44, he also argues that marriage benefits women more than men: "[M]arriage law and contracts have mainly protected domestically specialized women against divorce, abandonment, and other unfair treatment." On p. 4, Becker notes that "even small amounts of market discrimination against women or small biological differences between men and

women can cause huge differences in the activities of husbands and wives." Gary S. Becker, *A Treatise on the Family*, enlarged ed. (Cambridge: Harvard University Press, 1991).

36   *But Becker saw:* On p. 78, in his supplement to Chapter 2 of *A Treatise on the Family*, Becker remarks on the rising earning power of women. Noting that husbands are doing more housework, he posits that women, being relieved of some domestic burden, now may have more of an incentive to invest in their careers. "The result could be a sizable increase in the relative earnings of married women and a sizable decline in their occupational segregation during the remainder of this century," he wrote. He continues with his forecasts, conjecturing that society could see a day where division of labor "would no longer be linked to sex: husbands would be more specialized to housework and wives to market activities in about half the marriages, and the reverse would occur in the other half." He continued to maintain the specialization would always be better for most couples, but a "person's sex would then no longer be a valid predictor of earnings and household activities." Rather, educational advantages could tip the scale in favor of women, p. 79.

Chapter Three: The Overtaking

Page

38   *Women make up nearly half:* In September 2011, women made up 49.4 percent of the total nonfarm employees, and 47.9 percent of all private employees. Bureau of Labor Statistics, "The Employment Situation—September 2011," www.bls.gov/news.release/archives/empsit10072011.pdf.

38   *The proportion of women:* These figures were provided to the author by Bureau of Labor Statistics economist Mitra Toossi, and can be found in Mitra Toossi, "A Behavioral Model for Projecting the Labor Force Participation Rate," *Monthly Labor Review*, May 2011, 31–32, www.bls.gov/opub/mlr/2011/05/art3full.pdf. They can also be found at Joanna Barsh and Lareina Yee, "Unlocking the Full Potential of Women in the US Economy," McKinsey & Company, April 2011, available at www.mckinsey.com/client_service/organization/latest_thinking/unlocking_the_full_potential.aspx.

38   *Of the 66 million women:* Bureau of Labor Statistics, "Table 20. Employed Persons by Full- and Part-Time Status and Sex, 1970–2009 annual averages," *Women in the Labor Force: A Databook*, 2010, http://bls.gov/cps/wlftable20-2010.htm.

38   *Eighty percent of college-educated:* Bureau of Labor Statistics, "Table 8. Em-

ployment Status of the Civilian Noninstitutional Population 25 to 64 Years of Age by Educational Attainment and Sex, 2009 Annual Averages," ibid., www .bls.gov/cps/wlftable8-2010.htm and Gary Becker, "The Revolution in the Economic Empowerment of Women," Becker-Posner blog, January 4, 2010, www.becker-posner-blog.com/2010/01/the-revolution-in-the-economic -empowerment-of-women-becker.html.

38 *The percentage of women with children:* Bureau of Labor Statistics, "Employment Status of Women by Presence and Age of Youngest Child, March 1975–2010," updated data at www.bls.gov/cps/wlf-table7-2011.pdf.

38 *As the economist David Autor has pointed out:* David Autor, "The Polarization of Job Opportunities in the U.S. Labor Market: Implications for Employment and Earnings," the Hamilton Project and Center for American Progress (April 2010), 2, www.brookings.edu/papers/2010/04_jobs_autor.aspx.

39 *Women are much more likely:* In 2008, 59 percent of working women worked full-time, year round, compared to 41 percent in 1970. Bureau of Labor Statistics, "Table 22. Work Experience of the Population by Sex and Full- and Part-Time Status, Selected Years, 1970–2008," *Women in the Labor Force*, 2, www.bls.gov/cps/wlftable22-2010.htm.

39 *As Catherine Rampell pointed out:* Catherine Rampell, "Rising Family Income: More Work, Not Raises," *New York Times Economix* blog, July 20, 2011, http:// economix.blogs.nytimes.com/2011/07/20/rising-family-income-more-work -not-raises.

39 *Back in the mid-1950s, virtually all:* David Brooks, "The Missing Fifth," *New York Times*, May 9, 2011, www.nytimes.com/2011/05/10/opinion/ 10brooks.html.

39 *Of the jobs expected to decline:* 2010 online revised edition of T. Alan Lacey and Benjamin Wright, "Occupational Employment Projections to 2018," *Monthly Labor Review* (November 2009): 82–123, bls.gov/opub/ mlr/2009/11/art5full.pdf.

39 *The Bureau of Labor Statistics projects:* This prediction is contained in a PowerPoint slide shared with the author on October 3, 2011, by BLS economist Mitra Toossi. It can also be found in Mitra Toossi, "Labor Force Projections to 2018: Older Workers Staying More Active," *Monthly Labor Review* (November 2009): 37, bls.gov/opub/mlr/2009/11/art3full.pdf.

39 *Among families with working wives:* Figures up to 2009 can be found in "Table 25. Wives Who Earn More than Their Husbands 1987–2009," *Women in the Labor Force*, www.bls.gov/cps/wlf-table25-2011.pdf.

39 *In 2009, the number of married women:* ibid., "Married-Couple Families by

Number and Relationships of Earners, 1967–2009," updated figures at www
.bls.gov/cps/wlf-table23-2011.pdf.

39 *Keep in mind, too:* Figures for births to unmarried mothers can be found in
U.S. Centers for Disease Control and Prevention, "Unmarried Childbear-
ing," 2008, available at www.cdc.gov/nchs/fastats/unmarry.htm. Figures for
the percentage of children under 18 living only with their mothers are in U.S.
Census Bureau, "C2. Household Relationship and Living Arrangements of
Children/1 Under 18 Years, by Age and Sex: 2010," *America's Families and
Living Arrangements*, 2010, www.census.gov/population/www/socdemo/
hh-fam/cps2010.html.

40 *They take the majority of associate's:* National Center for Education Statistics,
"Fast Facts," http://nces.ed.gov/fastfacts/display.asp?id=72.

40 *The seeds of this turnover were sown:* Claudia Goldin, "From the Valley to
the Summit: A Brief History of the Quiet Revolution That Transformed
Women's Work," *Regional Review*, Q4 (2004), pp. 5–12, points out that the
revolution of the 1970s was quieter than that of the 1960s, but had a "greater
long-run impact," p. 6. She notes that in 1968, when the National Longitudinal Survey asked young women what they would be doing at age 35, about
30 percent said they would be in the labor force. By 1975, about 65 percent
gave that answer. She refers to the late 1960s and early 1970s as a "turning point" for young women. She points out on p. 8 that in 1966, 75 percent of all female undergraduates were in female-intensive majors such as
education, literature and foreign languages, or home economics and social
services. She points out that by 1998, just 12 percent of women were majoring in education, compared to 40 percent in 1966. Between 1966 and
1988, the percentage of women majoring in business and management rose
from 2 percent to 22 percent. She points out that beginning in the early
1970s, female undergraduates "radically changed their concentrations." She
also points out on p. 9 that for both women and men, college enrollment
increased during the Vietnam War period, but that unlike enrollments for
men, those for women continued to rise after deferments ended. As for professional degrees: on p. 9, she points out that the early 1970s saw a big jump
in women applying to law, business, and medical schools. On pp. 10 and 11,
she attributes the radical change in women's planning and self-image to government antidiscrimination mandates, social change, and the birth control
pill. And she discusses trends in marriage delay on p. 10.

40 *"The big question that economists ask":* Claudia Goldin, telephone interview
with author, July 5, 2010.

41 *In the early 1900s, when there was a mass movement:* Claudia Goldin, Lawrence F. Katz, and Ilyana Kuziemko, "The Homecoming of American College Women: The Reversal of the College Gender Gap," *Journal of Economic Perspectives* 20 (Fall 2006): 133–56. The authors point out that from 1900 to 1930, "the ratio of male-to-female undergraduates in the United States was about at parity," but this was followed by a divergence as men's enrollment was encouraged and women's was not. After women caught up, the first group to outpace men were "the brightest and highest-achieving," but now the "leapfrogging" is found in all portions of the ability distribution.

41 *At the turn of the 20th century:* Kessler-Harris, *Out to Work*, points out that "More than 75 percent of the generation of college women who graduated before 1900 remained single," p. 113. Claudia Goldin, in "The Long Road to the Fast Track: Career and Family," *Annals of the American Academy of Political and Social Science* 596 (November 2004): 20–35, on p. 21 points out that women graduating from college in the first two decades of the 20th century were forced to choose either family or career. On p. 23, she points out that more than "30 percent of this cohort never married by age fifty, a rate that was four times that for their female counterparts who attended no college at all." In contrast, men who graduated from college married at the same rates as men who did not. Goldin points out that of college-educated women who did marry, about 30 percent had no children, which led to cultural anxieties about "race suicide" and contributed to the idea that college was inappropriate for women. Those college graduates who worked by and large became teachers. They also became librarians, social workers, and nurses, and spoke of all these as "higher callings."

41 *"Monstrous brains and puny":* The *Economist*, "Infertility and Inheritance," U.S. ed., June 10, 2000.

41 *In 1960, 65 percent of bachelor's degrees:* Claudia Buchmann and Thomas A. DiPrete, "The Growing Female Advantage in College Completion: The Role of Family Background and Academic Achievement," *American Sociological Review* 71, (August 2006): 515–41. Buchmann and DiPrete point out that parity was reached by women in 1982.

41 *During the Vietnam War, student:* David Autor, "The Polarization of Job Opportunities," p. 24, points out that "the Vietnam War artificially boosted college attendance during the 1970s" and that after the war, college enrollment rates "dropped sharply, particularly among males."

41 *In the 1970s, male college graduates outnumbered:* Gary S. Becker, William H. J. Hubbard, and Kevin M. Murphy, "Explaining the Worldwide Boom in

Higher Education of Women," *Journal of Human Capital* 4, no. 3 (Fall 2010), 203–41. They discuss the 1970s gender gap on p. 204.

42 *Among African Americans, women take 66 percent:* National Center for Education Statistics, "Fast Facts," http://nces.ed.gov/fastfacts/display.asp?id=72. In "The Growing Female Advantage in College Completion," p. 516, Buchmann and DiPrete point out that for African American women, the disparity is "a continuation of a long female-favorable trend," and show that as early as 1954, women were 58 percent of students at historically black colleges and universities. In 1974, when the Census Bureau began tracking degrees by race and gender, women earned 57 percent of degrees among African Americans.

42 *Between 1970 and 2008:* Autor, "The Polarization of Job Opportunities in the U.S. Labor Market." The quote from Autor is on p. 6.

42 *Now, it's among lower-income Americans:* In "The Homecoming of American College Women," Goldin et al. point out on p. 147 that, initially, gains by girls and young women were made in the "top quartile" of the socioeconomic distribution, where girls reached parity in college graduation in 1972. After this, gains by women occurred in all socioeconomic sectors, but proportional gains were greatest in the lower half of the socioeconomic status distribution. They point out that proportionally, the female advantage is greatest "for the children of families with low socioeconomic status."

42 *Among all Americans ages 25 to 29:* Wendy Wang and Kim Parker, "Women See Value and Benefits of College: Men Lag on Both Fronts, Survey Finds," Social and Demographic Trends Report, August 17, 2011 (Washington, D.C.: Pew Research Center), 1, www.pewsocialtrends.org/2011/08/17/women-see-value-and-benefits-of-college-men-lag-on-both-fronts-survey-finds/.

42 *By 2019, women are projected:* Peter Schmidt, "Men's Share of College Enrollments Will Continue to Dwindle, Federal Report Says," *The Chronicle of Higher Education*, May 27, 2010, http://chronicle.com/article/Mens-Share-of-College/65693/ .

42 *The imbalance is so worrisome:* Laura D'Andrea Tyson, "Education and Women in the Labor Market," *New York Times Economix* blog, March 11, 2011, http://economix.blogs.nytimes.com/2011/03/11/women-and-their-wages/.

43 *There was a point, not all that:* Sonia Goltz, an expert in wage inequality who teaches at Michigan Technological University, made this point and also made the analogy to the Tuskegee airmen in a telephone interview with author on August 3, 2010.

43 *Boys make up 60 percent of the children:* The figures in this paragraph can be found on pp. 320–23 of Claudia Buchmann, Thomas A. DiPrete, and Anne McDaniel, "Gender Inequalities in Education," *Annual Review of Sociology* 34 (2008): 319–37.

43 *Boys do less homework:* Judith Kleinfeld, "The State of American Boyhood," *Gender Issues* 26 (2009): 113–20 points out, "Boys are less likely to do homework and more likely to come to school unprepared."

43 *And in an area where they once trailed:* The figures in this paragraph can be found on pp. 320–23 of Buchmann, DiPrete, and McDaniel, "Gender Inequalities in Education."

43 *Looking at data from a survey of:* Betsey Stevenson and Justin Wolfers, "The Paradox of Declining Female Happiness," *American Economic Journal: Economic Policy* 1, no. 2 (2009): 190–255. The quote from Stevenson is from an in-person interview with author on August 6, 2010.

44 *"[N]on-cognitive skills are the key to explaining":* Becker et al., "Explaining the Worldwide Boom in Higher Education of Women" make this point on p. 226. The second quote is on page 233. They also point out that "women on average find school less difficult than men," and show that women have higher noncognitive abilities, and less variability among these abilities, than men do.

44 *College matters more than ever:* ibid.

44 *Studying the rise of women breadwinners in Europe:* Hans G. Bloemen and Elena Stancanelli, "Modelling the Employment and Wage Outcomes of Spouses: Is She Outearning Him?," Institute for the Study of Labor (IZA), Discussion Paper 3455, April 2008, www.iza.org/en/webcontent/publications/papers/viewAbstract?dp_id=3455.

44 *Other studies have found that in heterosexual:* Dan A. Black, Seth G. Sanders, and Lowell J. Taylor, "The Economics of Lesbian and Gay Families," *Journal of Economic Perspectives* 21 (Spring 2007): 53–70.

45 *Some argue, persuasively, that one:* Matthias Doepke and Michèle Tertilt, "Women's Liberation: What's in It for Men?," *Quarterly Journal of Economics* 124 (November 2009): 1541–91.

45 *"Although sons and daughters share":* Buchmann and DiPrete, "The Growing Female Advantage in College Completion," 517.

46 *According to a 2011 report by the Pew:* Wang and Parker, "Women See Value and Benefits of College."

46 *Alaska has the third highest college gender gap:* This statement, and the findings that follow, are from Judith Kleinfeld, "No Map to Manhood: Male

and Female Mindsets Behind the College Gender Gap," *Gender Issues* 26 (November 2009): 171–82.

48 *The "major change which occurred":* Buchmann and DiPrete, "Female College Advantage in College Completion," 527, 533.

49 *As Buchmann and DiPrete put it:* ibid., 535.

49 *In* Children of the Great Depression*:* Glen Elder, Jr., *Children of the Great Depression: Social Change in Life Experience* (Boulder: Westview, 1999), pp. 158–61, 186.

51 *A husband's long work hours:* Emily Fitzgibbons Shafer, "Wives' Relative Wages, Husbands' Paid Work Hours, and Wives' Labor Force Exit," *Journal of Marriage and Family* 73 (February 2011): 250–63, finds that "women married to men who work more than 45 hours per week are more likely to exit the labor force than are wives whose husbands work approximately 40 hours per week."

51 *Claudia Goldin and Lawrence Katz:* Claudia Goldin and Lawrence F. Katz, "The Career Cost of Family," paper prepared for the Sloan Conference Focus on Workplace Flexibility, Washington, D.C., November 30, 2010. On p. 12, they point out that for women MBAs, "the interaction of kids and high earning husbands" is what leads women to decrease their work time.

51 *But the good news:* University of Texas economist Christy Spivey, who is doing research in this area, shared her findings in an email to author, November 7, 2011.

51 *Laura D'Andrea Tyson has pointed out:* D'Andrea Tyson, "Education and Women in the Labor Market." Citing BLS figures, Tyson points out that "the real earnings of women with college degrees rose by 33 percent" between 1979 and 2009, compared to a 22 percent rise for college-educated men. Among Americans with high school diplomas and associate's degrees, real earnings rose for female workers and fell for males. Among Americans without a high school diploma, real earnings fell 9 percent for women and 28 percent for men. She points out that unemployment is consistently lower for workers with a college education.

52 *As the Bureau of Labor Statistics:* BLS, "Highlights of Women's Earnings in 2010," Report 1031, July 2011, 2, www.bls.gov/cps/cpswom2010.pdf.

52 *Apart from the most highly educated:* ibid., Chart 3, p. 7. This point is also made in Catherine Rampell, "Do You Earn More than Your Parents Did?," July 7, 2010, *New York Times Economix* blog, http://economix.blogs.nytimes .com/2010/07/07/do-you-earn-more-than-your-parents-did/.

52 *Women are going to continue:* Autor, "The Polarization of Opportunities in the

U.S. Labor Market," p. 20, points out the "long-term downward trend" in the percentage of men who are employed and the "more striking upward trend among females." The Bureau of Labor Statistics notes that, "From 2008 to 2018, the women's civilian labor force is projected to increase by 9.0 percent, or 6,462,000." Bureau of Labor Statistics, *Spotlight on Statistics: Women at Work* (March 2011), available at www.bls.gov/spotlight/2011/women/.

52 *The dramatic impact on household:* Kristin Smith, "Wives as Breadwinners: Wives' Share of Family Earnings Hits Historic High During the Second Year of the Great Recession," Carsey Institute, Fact Sheet No. 20, Fall 2010.

52 *A related study by Smith and a colleague:* Marybeth J. Mattingly and Kristin E. Smith, "Changes in Wives' Employment When Husbands Stop Working: A Recession-Prosperity Comparison," *Family Relations* 59 (October 2010): 343–57.

52 *In families where the husband:* Kristin Smith, "Increased Reliance on Wives as Breadwinners During the First Year of the Recession," *Carsey Institute,* Issue Brief No. 9, Fall 2009.

53 *In 2010, the consulting firm:* Conor Dougherty, "Young Women's Pay Exceeds Male Peers'," *Wall Street Journal,* September 1, 2010, http://online.wsj .com/article/SB10001424052748704421104575463790770831192.html.

53 *Demographer Andrew Beveridge:* Sam Roberts, "For Young Earners in Big City, a Gap in Women's Favor," *New York Times,* August 3, 2007, www .nytimes.com/2007/08/03/nyregion/03women.html?pagewanted=all.

53 *"We don't know what's going to":* James Chung, telephone interview with author, September 13, 2010.

53 *Between 2007 and 2009, men lost:* Dennis Caucon, "Women Gain as Men Lose Jobs," *USA Today,* September 3, 2009, www.usatoday.com/news/ nation/2009-09-02-womenwork_N.htm.

54 *In August 2009, the adult male unemployment:* Bureau of Labor Statistics, "The Employment Situation—August 2009," September 4, 2009, available at bls.gov/news.release/archives/empsit_09042009.pdf. Figures for September 2011 showed unemployment rates of 8.7 percent for women 16 and over, compared to 9.4 percent for their male counterparts. BLS, "The Employment Situation—September 2011," October 7, 2011, available at www.bls .gov/news.release/archives/empsit_10072011.pdf.

54 *It's been estimated that in the auto:* Christopher Rugaber, "Millions of Lost Jobs Won't Return," Associated Press article appearing online in *Main Street,* May 14, 2010, www.mainstreet.com/article/career/employment/millions -lost-jobs-wont-return.

54 *In a major paper written for the:* Autor, "The Polarization of Job Opportunities in the U.S. Labor Market."

55 *Projections made by the U.S. Bureau:* 2010 revised edition of T. Alan Lacey and Benjamin Wright, "Occupational Employment Projections to 2018."

55 *Claudia Goldin feels this will:* Claudia Goldin, telephone interview with author, July 5, 2010.

56 *According to the Bureau of Labor:* Bureau of Labor Statistics, "Spotlight on Statistics: Women at Work."

56 *The "wage gap" is not an exact comparison:* There is a painstaking analysis of the factors causing the gender wage gap in Francine D. Blau, Marianne A. Ferber, and Anne E. Winkler, *The Economics of Women, Men and Work*, 6th ed. (Boston: Prentice Hall, 2010), on pp. 141–49, 193–206 and 247–57.

56 *The wage gap has shrunk:* "Chart 1: Women's Earnings as a Percent of Men's, Full-Time Wage and Salary Workers, 1979–2010 Annual Averages," Bureau of Labor Statistics, *Highlights of Women's Earnings in 2010*, 6.

57 *In Puerto Rico, women:* David M. Getz, "Men's and Women's Earnings for States and Metropolitan Statistical Areas: 2009," *U.S. Census Bureau American Community Survey Briefs* (September 2010).

57 *Women food preparers and serving:* Bureau of Labor Statistics, "Spotlight on Statistics: Women at Work."

57 *Among 25- to 34-year-olds:* Bureau of Labor Statistics, *Highlights of Women's Earnings in 2010*, 1.

57 *The "penalties to family-conducive":* Goldin and Katz, "The Career Cost of Family," 1.

58 *The White House in 2011 announced:* The White House, Office of the Press Secretary, "The White House and National Science Foundation Announce New Workplace Flexibility Policies to Support America's Scientists and Their Families," September 26, 2011, www.whitehouse.gov/the-press -office/2011/09/26/white-house-and-national-science-foundation-announce -new-workplace-flexi.

58 *According to the U.S. Census Bureau:* Lynda Laughlin, "Maternity Leave and Employment Patterns: 1961–2008," *U.S. Census Bureau Current Population Reports* (October 2011), 14, www.census.gov/prod/2011pubs/p70-128 .pdf.

58 *Women are still thinking strategically:* Much of the data and analysis in this paragraph and the one that follows are from Goldin and Katz, "The Career Cost of Family." Their quote about veterinary medicine is on p. 10.

58 *Women now are 61 percent of veterinarians:* BLS, "Women in the Labor

Force," Table 11. Employed Persons by Detailed Occupation and Sex, 2009 Annual Averages."

59 *In Britain, women make up 56 percent:* BBC News, "Female Medics 'to Out-number Male,'" June 2, 2009, http://news.bbc.co.uk/2/hi/health/8077083 .stm. And Doreen Carvajal, "The Changing Face of Medical Care," *New York Times*, March 7, 2011, www.nytimes.com/2011/03/08/world/europe/ 08iht-ffdocs08.html?_r=2&pagewanted=all.

59 *The flip in some specialties:* Claudia Goldin, "A Pollution Theory of Discrimina-tion: Male and Female Differences in Occupations and Earnings," National Bureau of Economic Research, Working Paper 8985, June 2002, www.nber .org/papers/w8985. In this paper, Goldin makes the fascinating argument that for generations discrimination against women was "the consequence of a desire by men to maintain their occupational status or prestige, distinct from the desire to maintain their earnings." Men feared that if a woman entered an occupation, such as firefighting, she would bring down the status and thereby "pollute" it. When occupations become "credentialed"—when there is a test or license or set of credentials for entering—then the polluting quality of women becomes lessened.

60 *What's "really driving feminization":* Anne E. Lincoln, "The Shifting Supply of Men and Women to Occupations: Feminization in Veterinary Educa-tion," *Social Forces* 88 (2010): 1969–98. Lincoln's quotes are taken from her paper and from accompanying remarks published in Margaret Allen, "Veter-inary Medicine Shifts to More Women, Fewer Men: Pattern Will Repeat in Medicine, Law Fields," Southern Methodist University blog post, Novem-ber 1, 2010, in *SMU Research,* http://blog.smu.edu/research/2010/11/01/ veterinary-medicine-shifts-to-more-women-fewer-men-pattern-will-repeat-in-medicine-law-fields/.

60 *And the flip has already happened in psychology:* Benedict Carey, "Need Therapy? A Good Man Is Hard to Find," *New York Times*, May 21, 2011, www.nytimes.com/2011/05/22/health/22therapists.html?pagewanted=all.

61 *At the 2011 conference:* Anne McDaniel and Claudia Buchmann, "The Consequences of Career Choice: Family and Income Disparities Among Women in Science and Other Elite Professions," paper presented at the annual meeting of the Population Association of America, Washing-ton, D.C., April 1, 2001, available at paa2011.princeton.edu/download .aspx?submissionId=111799.

61 *Four out of 10 babies:* U.S. Centers for Disease Control and Prevention, "Percent of live births to unmarried mothers: United States, each state,

preliminary 2009," *Stats of the States, 2009,* www.cdc.gov/nchs/pressroom/stats_states.htm.

62 *When I asked McDaniel:* Anne McDaniel, telephone interview with author, April 8, 2011.

62 *Just 66 percent of men in the prime:* Michael Greenstone and Adam Looney, "Have Earnings Actually Declined?," *Up Front* blog, Brookings Institution's the Hamilton Project, March 4, 2011, www.brookings.edu/opinions/2011/0304_jobs_greenstone_looney.aspx.

62 *In 2006, Louis Uchitelle and David Leonhardt:* Louis Uchitelle and David Leonhardt, "Men Not Working, and Not Wanting Just Any Job," *New York Times,* July 31, 2006, www.nytimes.com/2006/07/31/business/31men.html?pagewanted=all.

62 *"Every one of the women had gone":* David Leonhardt, "Mark Penn on 'Guys Left Behind,'" *New York Times Economix* blog, June 1, 2009, http://economix.blogs.nytimes.com/2009/06/01/mark-penn-on-guys-left-behind/.

62 *During the 1990s, it was the most educated men:* Jay Stewart, "What Do Male Nonworkers Do?," U.S. Bureau of Labor Statistics, Working Paper No. 371, April 2004, www.bls.gov/osmr/pdf/ec040010.pdf.

63 *A 2008 workforce survey:* Ellen Galinsky, Kerstin Aumann, and James T. Bond, "Times Are Changing: Gender and Generation at Work and at Home," *Families and Work Institute National Study of the Changing Workforce 2008,* www.familiesandwork.org.

64 *The "dramatic change in labor force participation":* Gary Becker, "The Revolution in the Economic Empowerment of Women," *Becker-Posner* blog, January 4, 2010, www.becker-posner-blog.com/2010/01/the-revolution-in-the-economic-empowerment-of-women-becker.html.

64 *In the European Union, as a* Newsweek: Jessica Bennett and Jesse Ellison, "Women Will Rule the World," *Newsweek/The Daily Beast,* July 6, 2010, www.thedailybeast.com/newsweek/2010/07/06/women-will-rule-the-world.html.

64 *In Japan and Britain:* Tanith Carey, "The Survival Guide for Breadwinning Wives," *Mail Online,* October 13, 2011, www.dailymail.co.uk/femail/article-2048459/Survival-guide-breadwinning-wives-1-4-earn-husbands.html. Chico Harlan, "Japan's Young Men Seek a New Path," *Washington Post,* October 24, 2010. www.washingtonpost.com/wp-dyn/content/article/2010/10/24/AR2010102403342.html.

64 *In South Korea:* "The Flight from Marriage," *Economist,* August 20, 2011, www.economist.com/node/21526329.

64 *Women are 25 percent of breadwinners in the U.K.:* Bloemen and Stan-canelli, "Modelling the Employment and Wage Outcomes of Spouses: Is She Outearning Him?" and Julia Llewellyn Smith, "Female Breadwinners: When Mum Makes More," *Telegraph*, September 11, 2011, www.telegraph .co.uk/relationships/8754984/Female-Breadwinners-When-Mum-makes -more.html.

64 *And women around the world:* The figures in this paragraph, and many of the observations in the subsequent paragraph, are from an author telephone interview with Anne McDaniel, April 8, 2011, and from a working paper by Anne McDaniel, "The Gender Gap in Higher Education: A Cross-National Analysis of 131 Countries," provided to the author by McDaniel. Becker et al., in "Explaining the Worldwide Boom in Higher Education of Women," point out that both richer and poor countries have seen "sharp growth in higher education since 1970," to the point where 27 percent of 30- to 34-year-olds in richer countries have college education, up from 12 percent in 1970; in poor countries, it was 11 percent in 2010, "up from less than 3 percent in 1970." They point out that in rich and poor countries alike, "most of the growth in higher education is due to women."

65 *Anju Malhotra, a vice president at:* Anju Malhotra, in-person interview with author, May 27, 2011.

66 *MIT economist Esther Duflo has done groundbreaking work:* Esther Duflo, "Grandmothers and Granddaughters: Old Age Pension and Intra-household Allocation in South Africa," *World Bank Economic Review* 17, no. 1 (2003): 1–25. S. Lundberg, R. Pollak, and T. Wales, "Do Husbands and Wives Pool Their Resources?: Evidence from the United Kingdom Child Benefit," *Journal of Human Resources* 32, no. 3 (Summer 1997): 463–80.

66 *"The World Economic Forum has estimated":* Bennett and Ellison, "Women Will Rule the World."

66 *To the extent that married men's finances have improved:* Pew Research Center, "Women, Men, and the New Economics of Marriage."

Chapter Four: The New Rules of Mating

Page

70 *In a sense, as sociologist Andrew Cherlin:* Cherlin, who has written widely on this topic, made this point in a telephone interview with author, spring 2009.

70 *It is one reason social and income inequality:* Christine R. Schwartz, "Earnings Inequality and the Changing Association Between Spouses' Earnings,"

American Journal of Sociology 115, (March 1, 2010): 1524–57. This study looks at the trend of marriages increasingly consisting of two high-earning or low-earning partners. The paper explores the impact of this trend on inequality across families, and finds that "increases in earnings inequality would have been about 25%–30% lower" had the trend not emerged. Another study, Christine R. Schwartz and Robert D. Mare, "Trends in Educational Assortative Marriage from 1940 to 2003," *Demography* 42 (November 2005): 621–46, also makes this point. The authors point out that for women the heyday of marrying up educationally was the 1970s. The trend toward educational homogamy—like marrying like—increased from 1960 to 2003. These trends, they point out, "are consistent with a growing social divide between those with very low levels of education and those with more education in the United States." Andrew Cherlin also made this point in a telephone interview with author: educated couples are "consolidating their gains" compared to lower-income Americans.

70 *A new theory among people who look:* Justin Garcia, telephone interview with author, February 8, 2011. And in a telephone interview with author on February 22, 2011, Helen Fisher pointed out that during our hunter-gatherer phase, "the double income family is the rule."

71 *Some speed dating studies:* Raymond Fisman, Sheena S. Iyengar, Emir Kamenica, and Itamar Simonson, "Gender Differences in Mate Selection: Evidence from a Speed Dating Experiment," *The Quarterly Journal of Economics* 121 (2006): 673–97.

72 *A powerful body of work shows that women:* Schwartz and Mare, "Trends in Educational Assortative Marriage from 1940 to 2003," point out that, "As women's labor force participation and earnings have increased, men may have begun to compete for high-earning, highly educated women as women have traditionally competed for high-earning men," and cite a number of scholars whose work supports this finding.

72 *There are economists who argue:* Raquel Fernandez, Alessandra Fogli, and Claudia Olivetti, "Marrying Your Mom: Preference Transmission and Women's Labor and Education Choices," National Bureau of Economic Research, Working Paper 9234, October 2002. The paper argues that "the evolution of male preferences contributed to the dramatic increase in the proportion of working and educated women in the population over time."

72 *For the dating website Match.com:* "Everything You Think You Know About Single Is Wrong," match.com blog post, February 4, 2011, http://blog.match

.com/2011/02/04/everything-you-think-you-know-about-singles-is-wrong
-we-separate-fact-from-fiction-with-the-first-comprehensive-study-of-singles
-in-america/.

72 *"I think the idea that men just want to":* Justin Garcia, telephone interview
with author, Feb. 8, 2011.

74 *"It's a time of dramatic adjustment":* Helen Fisher, telephone interview with
author, Feb. 22, 2011.

75 *Women have two options:* Actually, you could argue that they have three. In
"The Growing Female Advantage in College Completion," p. 517, Buchmann and DiPrete point out that the current educational disparity could
cause women to marry down, not marry, or delay marriage. Claudia Buchmann and Thomas A. DiPrete, "The Growing Female Advantage in College
Completion: The Role of Family Background and Academic Achievement,"
American Sociological Review 71 (August 2006): 515–41.

75 *All women could follow the example:* Donna L. Franklin, *What's Love Got to Do
with It? Understanding and Healing the Rift Between Black Men and Women*
(New York: Simon & Schuster, 2000). Franklin points out on p. 165 that even
in 1960, black women constituted a much higher proportion of the black professional class than white women did in the white professional class, and that
"the very success of black women in the professions made it harder for them
to maintain the traditional feminine role in relationships with their men." She
says many black men "subscribe to the 'ideal' of male dominance. In effect, they
expect their wives to be at once feminine and submissive yet strong enough
to shoulder their double burden of family responsibilities and work," p. 195.
Holly E. Furdyna, M. Belinda Tucker, and Angela D. James, in "Relative Spousal Earnings and Marital Happiness Among African American and White
Women," *Journal of Marriage and Family* 70 (May 2008): 332–44, point out
that "African American women have played more significant economic roles
within families for some time." In 1910, 55 percent of black women were employed compared to just 20 percent of white women. They point out that black
husbands "express lower family satisfaction when performing most in-home
chores" even though they are more likely than white husbands to do them.
Black women are more likely than white women to earn as much or more than
their husbands, but they are more likely to think men should be providers.
And in another paper, four sociologists point out that black women worked,
historically, because black families had lower incomes but also because paid
work was not as socially stigmatized for black women as for white ones. They
point out that most college-educated black women, like white ones, worked as

teachers from 1940 through the 1970s. Moreover, for college-educated black men, the barriers to high-status jobs were enormous; so black women had more of an incentive to attend college than black men did. Anne McDaniel, Thomas A. DiPrete, Claudia Buchmann, and Uri Shwed, "The Black Gender Gap in Educational Attainment: Historical Trends and Racial Comparisons," *Demography* 48 (2011): 889–914.

76 *Partly in response, observes the sociologist:* Brad Wilcox, telephone interview with author, January 13, 2011.

76 *More than 70 percent of African American:* Kirsten West Savali, "72 Percent of African-American Children Born to Unwed Mothers," *Huffington Post*, November 8, 2010, www.bvblackspin.com/2010/11/08/72-percent-of-african -american-child ren-born-to-unwed-mothers/. The statistics on marriage and divorce are from Ralph Richard Banks, *Is Marriage for White People? How the African American Marriage Decline Affects Everyone* (New York: Dutton, 2011).

77 *Same-sex couples are more:* Christine Schwartz and Nikki L. Graf, "Assortative Matching Among Same-Sex and Different-Sex Couples in the United States, 1990–2000," *Demographic Research* 21 (December 8, 2009): 843–78, available at www.demographic-research.org. Naveen Jonathan, in "Carrying Equal Weight: Relational Responsibility and Attunement Among Same-Sex Couples," in Carmen Knudson-Martin and Anne Rankin Mahoney, eds, *Couples, Gender and Power: Creating Change in Intimate Relationships* (New York: Springer, 2009), pp. 79–103, points out that same-sex couples, while not impervious to economic power issues, tend to be more equitable and labor is not allocated along traditional gender lines.

77 *Interestingly, lesbians—who know:* Dan A. Black, Seth G. Sanders, and Lowell J. Taylor, "The Economics of Lesbian and Gay Families," *Journal of Economic Perspectives*, 21 (Spring 2007), 53–70.

77 *In 1960, 72 percent of adult Americans:* Pew Research Center, "The Decline of Marriage and Rise of New Families," *Social and Demographic Trends Report*, Nov. 18, 2010, www.pewresearch.org/pubs/1802/decline-marriage-rise -new-families.

78 *In 2007, 28 percent of American wives:* Richard Fry and D'Vera Cohn, "Women, Men, and the New Economics of Marriage," Pew Research Center, *Social and Demographic Trends Report,* 2010, 1, www.pewsocialtrends .org/2010/01/19/women-men-and-the-new-economics-of-marriage/.

78 *Up to now, studies have shown that marriages:* Schwartz and Mare, "Trends in Educational Assortative Marriage from 1940 to 2003," p. 636.

78 *Sociologist Annette Lareau:* Annette Lareau, *Unequal Childhoods: Class, Race, and Family Life* (Berkeley: University of California Press, 2003).

78 *Betsey Stevenson, chief economist for the U.S. Labor Department:* In-person interview with author, August 6, 2010.

Chapter Five: Competition and Undermining

Page

89 *And in 2011, a writer named Aaron Gouveia:* Aaron Gouveia, "The Breadwinner," *Good Men Project* blog, May 22, 2011, http://goodmenproject.com/featured-content/the-breadwinner-2/.

90 *In 2003, researchers in Finland:* Marika Jalovaara, "The Joint Effects of Marriage Partners' Socioeconomic Positions on the Risk of Divorce," *Demography* 40 (February 2003): 67–81.

90 *In 2009, researchers in Germany:* Kornelius Kraft and Stefanie Neimann, "Effect of Labor Division Between Wife and Husband on the Risk of Divorce: Evidence from German Data," Institute for the Study of Labor (IZA), Discussion Paper 4515, October 2009.

90 *In the United States, sociologist Jay Teachman:* Jay Teachman, "Wives' Economic Resources and Risk of Divorce," *Journal of Family Issues* 31 (October 2010): 1305–23.

91 *And in 2010, Christin Munsch:* Christin Munsch, "The Effect of Unemployment and Relative Income Disparity on Infidelity for Men and Women," paper presented at annual meeting of the American Sociological Association, Atlanta, Georgia, August 16, 2010, shared by author in an email exchange on April 7, 2011.

91 *In an interview, Munsch allowed:* Nitasha Tiku, "Husbands Outsource Sexual Fulfillment so as Not to Burden Hardworking Wives," *New York Magazine* "Daily Intel," August 16, 2010, http://nymag.com/daily/intel/2010/08/freeloading_husbands_outsource.html.

91 *"I can think of many, many examples":* Carmen Knudson-Martin, telephone interview with author, January 14, 2011.

91 *Mira Kirshenbaum, clinical director:* Mira Kirshenbaum, author of numerous books, including most recently *I Love You but I Don't Trust You*, email exchange with author, September 24, 2011.

92 *Veronica Tichenor, a sociologist:* Veronica Tichenor, "Maintaining Men's Dominance: Negotiating Identity and Power When She Earns More," *Sex Roles* 53 (August 2005): 191–205.

92 *Jay Teachman thinks:* Jay Teachman, telephone interview with author, September 30, 2010.

92 *The economist Fran Blau:* Francine D. Blau, "Trends in the Well-Being of American Women, 1970–1995."

92 *And the Pew Research Center found:* Richard Fry and D'Vera Cohn, "Women, Men, and the New Economics of Marriage," Pew Research Center, *Social and Demographic Trends Report*, 2010, 18, www.pewsocialtrends.org/2010/01/19/women-men-and-the-new-economics-of-marriage/.

94 *"If you ask people—how do you feel":* The description of Tesser's work is taken from a telephone interview with Abraham Tesser, March 3, 2011, and from several papers by Tesser and colleagues. These include: Abraham Tesser, Murray Millar, and Janet Moore, "Some Affective Consequences of Social Comparison and Reflection Processes: The Pain and Pleasure of Being Close," *Journal of Personality and Social Psychology* 54 (1988): 49–61. Also Steven R. H. Beach, Abraham Tesser, Frank D. Fincham, Deborah Jones, Debra Johnson, and Daniel Whitaker, "Pleasure and Pain in Doing Well, Together: An Investigation of Performance-Related Affect in Close Relationships," *Journal of Personality and Social Psychology* 74 (1998): 923–38. And Steven R. H. Beach, Daniel Whitaker, Deborah Jones, and Abraham Tesser, "When Does Performance Feedback Prompt Complementarity in Romantic Relationships?," *Personal Relationships* 8 (2001), 231–48. There is an excellent discussion of social comparison in marriage in Shankar Vedantam, *The Hidden Brain: How Our Unconscious Minds Elect Presidents, Control Markets, Wage Wars, and Save Our Lives* (New York: Spiegel & Grau, 2010), 33–42.

95 *"When couples find themselves":* Beach et al., "Pleasure and Pain in Doing Well, Together," 935.

95 *"People are obsessed with what other people":* Lamar Pierce, telephone interview with author, December 14, 2010.

96 *Similarly, in 2011, when National Public Radio:* Tamara Keith, "Finding Love While Searching for Work," National Public Radio, May 25, 2011, www.npr.org/2011/05/25/136402638/finding-love-while-searching-for-work.

96 *A 2010 paper coauthored:* Ronit Waismel-Manor and Pamela Tolbert, "The Impact of Relative Earnings Among Dual-Earner Couples on Career Satisfaction and Family Satisfaction," paper presented at the International Sociological Association meeting in Gothenburg, Sweden, July 2010.

97 *Similarly, in 2011, a psychological study:* Jennifer Spoor and Michael Schmitt, " 'Things Are Getting Better' Isn't Always Better: Considering Women's

Progress Affects Perceptions of and Reactions to Contemporary Gender Inequality," *Basic and Applied Social Psychology* 33 (2011), 24–36.

98 *Thus, the question of who is good:* Beach et al., "Pleasure and Pain in Doing Well, Together," 935.

99 *"The biggest cost of income comparison":* Lamar Pierce, telephone interview with author, December 14, 2010.

102 *In 2008, Souha Ezzedeen:* Souha Ezzedeen and Kristen Grossnickle Ritchey, "The Man Behind the Woman: A Qualitative Study of the Spousal Support Received and Valued by Executive Women," *Journal of Family Issues* 29 (2008):1107–35, http://jfi.sagepub.com/cgi.content/abstract/29/9/1107.

105 *A social comparison study published in 2008 confirmed:* Rebecca T. Pinkus, Penelope Lockwood, Ulrich Schimmack, and Marc A. Fournier, "For Better and for Worse: Everyday Social Comparisons Between Romantic Partners," *Journal of Personality and Social Psychology* 95 (November 2008): 1180–1201.

108 *Sociologists Ilana Demantas and Kristen Myers:* Ilana Demantas and Kristen Myers, " 'It's a Blessing That My Wife Works': Balancing Masculinity and Economic Dependence on Women During Unsettled Times," paper presented at the annual meeting of the American Sociological Association, August 23, 2011, Las Vegas, NV.

Chapter Six: Let Go, and Lexapro

Page

111 *Even now, about half of men say:* "20/50: The Esquire Survey of American Men," *Esquire*, September 2010. Forty-seven percent of 20-year-old men and 55 percent of fifty-year-old men felt a wife could do whatever she liked. Somewhat surprisingly, 20 percent of younger men felt a wife should stay home and take care of the kids, compared to 14 percent of older men, who presumably knew better the value of a wife's paycheck, www.esquire.com/features/facts-about-men-1010.

116 *A study presented by sociologist Karen Kramer at the 2011 Population:* Karen Z. Kramer and Amit Kramer, "The Relationship Between Economic Downturns and the Proportion of Stay-at-Home Father Households," working paper and PowerPoint presentation at the annual convention of the Population Association of America, Washington, D.C., April 2011.

120 *The best-known articulation of this:* Arlie Russell Hochschild with Anne Ma-chung, *The Second Shift* (New York: Penguin, 2003).

120 *In 2011, Oriel Sullivan:* Oriel Sullivan, "An End to Gender Display Through the Performance of Housework? A Review and Reassessment of the Quantitative Literature Using Insights from the Qualitative Literature," *Journal of Family Theory and Review* 3 (March 2011): 1–13.

121 *In an accompanying essay:* Paula England, "Missing the Big Picture and Making Much Ado About Almost Nothing: Recent Scholarship on Gender and Household Work," *Journal of Family Theory and Review* 3 (March 2011): 23–26. The gender deviance neutralization idea has a complicated trajectory, England shows, beginning with a study in 1994 which was interpreted to mean that "when men are unemployed or earn less than their wives, they respond by reducing their housework." She points out that later studies amplified the idea, suggesting that women increase their own housework when they outearn their husbands. She allows now that this may have been a "mistaken inference resulting from incorrectly specified equations," and points to work by Sanjiv Gupta showing that the women who do more housework are lower-income women who can't afford to pay for help. "I contributed to what I now regard as the undue attention to the phenomenon of compensatory gender display," she writes, and points out that work by her, Liana Sayer, and others suggests that husbands on average spend more hours per week in paid work plus housework than wives do, though the second shift is worst for mothers of young children working full-time.

121 *And men still bear the brunt:* Liana C. Sayer, Paula England, Paul D. Allison, and Nicole Kangas, "She Left, He Left: How Employment and Satisfaction Affect Women's and Men's Decisions to Leave Marriages," *American Journal of Sociology* 116 (May 2011): 1982–2018.

121 *Once upon a time, men with a domestic side:* Susan Faludi, *Backlash: The Undeclared War Against American Women* (New York: Three Rivers, 2006).

Chapter Seven: Stigma and Female Earning

Page

144 *This argument has been set forth:* Among the works that explore the idea of masculinity as a public construct are Elisabeth Badinter, *XY: On Masculine Identity* (New York: Columbia University Press, 1995); David D. Gilmore, *Manhood in the Making: Cultural Concepts of Masculinity* (New Haven: Yale

University Press, 1990); Michael Kimmel, *Manhood in America: A Cultural History* (New York: Oxford University Press, 2006).

144 *To take just one recent example:* Jennifer K. Bosson and Joseph A. Vandello, "Precarious Manhood and Its Links to Action and Aggression," *Current Directions in Psychological Science* 20 (April 2011): 82–86.

144 *As early as the 1950s,* Look *magazine:* Stephanie Coontz, *A Strange Stirring: The Feminine Mystique and American Women at the Dawn of the 1960s* (New York: Basic Books, 2011), p. 78.

145 Foreign Policy *published a piece:* Reihan Salam, "The Death of Macho," *Foreign Policy*, July/August 2009, www.foreignpolicy.com/articles/2009/06/18/the_death_of_macho; Hanna Rosin, "The End of Men," *Atlantic*, July/August 2010, www.theatlantic.com/magazine/archive/2010/07/the-end-of-men/8135/#.

145 *The 2011–2012 TV season:* For two takes on television's current obsession with manhood, see Amanda Marcotte, "How to Make a Critically Acclaimed TV Show About Masculinity," *Jezebel*, September 7, 2011, http://jezebel.com/5837945/how-to-make-a-critically-acclaimed-tv-show-about-masculinity; and Jessica Grose, "The New Girls: Fall TV Is Full of Emasculated Men. Does That Mean It's Also Full of Empowered Women?," *Slate*, September 8, 2011, www.slate.com/articles/arts/culturebox/2011/09/the_new_girls.html.

147 *This is a durable if increasingly vexed directive:* Barbara J. Harris, *English Aristocratic Women, 1450–1550: Marriage and Family, Property and Careers* (Oxford: Oxford University Press, 2002).

148 *Churches may have good reason to preach the ideal:* W. Bradford Wilcox made these points in a telephone interview with the author on January 13, 2011.

148 *In a 2011 blog post to a Christian website:* Karen Swallow Prior, "Confessions of a Breadwinner Wife," *Her.meneutics*, May 3, 2011. http://blog.christianitytoday.com/women/2011/05/confessions_of_a_breadwinner_w.html.

149 *In 2006, when Minnesota Republican Michele Bachmann:* Jason Horowitz, "Michele Bachmann's Husband Shares Her Strong Conservative Values," *Washington Post*, July 5, 2011, www.washingtonpost.com/lifestyle/style/michele-bachmanns-husband-shares-her-strong-conservative-values/2011/06/21/gIQAyNmvzH_story.html. And Shushannah Walshe, "Michele Bachmann 'Submissive' Wife Idea a Matter of Interpretation," *ABC News*, August 12, 2011, http://abcnews.go.com/Politics/michele-bachmann-submissive-wife-belief-matter-interpretation/story?id=14292494#.Tukp7UqKWUc.

Chapter Eight: Sex and the Self-Sufficient Girl

Page

155 *The theory is based:* Russell D. Clark III and Elaine Hatfield, "Gender Differences in Receptivity to Sexual Offers," *Journal of Psychology and Human Sexuality* 2 (1989): 39–55. In their 2010 book *Sex at Dawn: The Prehistoric Origins of Modern Sexuality,* Christopher Ryan and Cacilda Jethá (New York: HarperCollins, 2010) note the remarkable staying power of the Florida State study, even as they refute the theory that women don't enjoy sex as much as men do, on pp. 47–52.

156 *"Sex is a female resource":* Roy F. Baumeister and Kathleen Vohs, "Sexual Economics: Sex as Female Resource for Social Exchange in Heterosexual Interactions," *Personality and Social Psychology Review* 8, (2004), 339–63.

156 *"If women were more fully in charge":* This quote is from Mark Regnerus, "Sex Is Cheap: Why Young Men Have the Upper Hand in Bed, even When They're Failing in Life," *Slate,* February 25, 2011, www.slate.com/articles/double_x/doublex/2011/02/sex_is_cheap.html.

157 *Now, it may be true that women don't think:* Pamela Paul, "When Thoughts Turn to Sex, or Not," *New York Times,* December 9, 2011, notes that an upcoming study in *The Journal of Sex Research* found that male undergraduates don't think about sex nearly as frequently as they are said to, and that they think just as much about food and sleep. www.nytimes.com/2011/12/11/fashion/sex-on-the-brain-studied.html?_r=1.

157 *A report using data from the National Survey of Family Growth:* Anjani Chandra, William D. Mosher, Casey Copen, and Catlainn Sionean, "Sexual Behavior, Sexual Attraction, and Sexual Identity in the United States: Data from the 2006–2008 National Survey of Family Growth," National Health Statistics Reports, No. 36, National Center for Health Statistics, March 2011, 15.

160 *Lamar Pierce, the business professor:* Michael S. Dahl and Lamar Pierce, "In Sickness and in Wealth: Psychological and Sexual Costs of Income Comparison in Marriage," working paper, shared with author by Lamar Pierce.

161 *Talking about the study in an interview:* Lamar Pierce, telephone interview with author, December 14, 2010.

161 *The "first man I dated after separating":* Gail Konop Baker, "Do Women Now Want Sex More than Men?," *Huffington Post,* September 23, 2011, www

.huffingtonpost.com/gail-konop-baker/women-want-sex-more-than-men
_b_977416.html.

161 *But in other cases:* Judy Kuriansky, telephone interview with author, spring 2009.

162 *Mira Kirshenbaum, clinical director:* Mira Kirshenbaum, email with author, September 24, 2011.

162 *Men, for example, experience a drop:* Pam Belluck, "Fatherhood Cuts Testosterone, Study Finds, For Good of the Family," New York Times, September 13, 2011, A1.

162 *I had a conversation about the possible:* A description of Karasu's alpha male therapy sessions can be found in Melinda Beck, "Are Alpha Males Healthy? Aggressiveness Aids Rise to the Top, but the Stress Can Harm a Body," *Wall Street Journal*, September 13, 2011, D1. Karasu's comments are from a telephone interview with this author, September 14, 2011.

164 *That communication is a crucial aspect:* Michelle J. Hindin and Carie J. Muntifering, "Women's Autonomy and Timing of Most Recent Sexual Intercourse in Sub-Saharan Africa: A Multi-Country Analysis," *Journal of Sex Research* 48 (2011) 1–9. Hindin's comments were made in a telephone interview with the author on October 7, 2011.

169 *This research has found that women:* Constance T. Gager and Scott T. Yabiku, "Who Has the Time? The Relationship Between Household Labor Time and Sexual Frequency," *Journal of Family Issues* 31 (2010):135–163, http://jfi.sage pub.com/content/31/2/135.

170 *"We're at a point of historical flux":* Justin Garcia, telephone conversation with author, February 8, 2011.

Chapter Nine: Desirable Women

Page

178 *A study published in 2001 by University of Texas:* David Buss, Todd K. Shackelford, Lee A. Kirkpatrick, and Randy J. Larsen, "A Half Century of Mate Preferences: The Cultural Evolution of Values," *Journal of Marriage and Family* 63 (May 2001): 491–503. The paper found that over a period spanning almost sixty years, "Both sexes increased the importance they attach to physical attractiveness in a mate. Both sexes, but especially men, increased the importance they attach to mates with good financial prospects. Domestic skills in a partner plummeted in importance for men. Mutual attraction and love climbed in importance for both sexes.

The sexes converged in the ordering of the importance of different mate qualities."

178 *Demographer Christine Schwartz agreed:* Christine R. Schwartz, "Earnings Inequality and the Changing Association between Spouses' Earnings," *American Journal of Sociology* 115 (March 1, 2010), 1524–57.

179 *But Ran Abramitzky, an economist:* Ran Abramitzky shared the origins of his project in a telephone interview with author, September 2, 2010. Ran Abramitzky, Adeline Delavande, and Luis Vasconcelos, "Marrying Up: The Role of Sex Ratio in Assortative Matching," *American Economic Journal: Applied Economics* 3 (July 2011): 124–57, http://aeaweb.org/articles .php?doi=10.1257/app.3.3.124.

183 *Stevenson argues that times have changed:* Adam Isen and Betsey Stevenson, "Women's Education and Family Behavior: Trends in Marriage, Divorce and Fertility," in John Shoven, ed., *Demography and the Economy* (Chicago: University of Chicago Press, 2011).

185 *In an interview, economist Betsey Stevenson:* In-person interview with author, August 6, 2010.

185 *When people are in close and supportive marriages:* Rebecca T. Pinkus, Penelope Lockwood, Ulrich Schimmack, and Marc A. Fournier, "For Better and for Worse: Everyday Social Comparisons Between Romantic Partners," *Journal of Personality and Social Psychology* 95 (2008):1180–1201.

Chapter Ten: The New World of Nonmarriage Choices

Page

190 *This country, like much of Europe:* D'Vera Cohn, Jeffrey Passel, Wendy Wang, and Gretchen Livingston, "Barely Half of US Adults are Married—A Record Low," Pew Social and Demographic Trends Report, Dec. 14, 2011, http://www.pewsocialtrends.org/2011/12/14/barely-half-of-u-s-adults-are -married-a-record-low.

191 *Births to single mothers:* Pew Research Center, "The Decline of Marriage and Rise of New Families" (Washington, D.C.: Pew Research Center, November 18, 2010), www.pewsocialtrends.org/2010/11/18/the-decline-of-marriage -and-rise-of-new-families/2/#ii-overview.

192 *Those who remarry fastest:* Betsey Stevenson, telephone interview with author, and in Adam Isen and Betsey Stevenson, "Women's Education and Family Behavior: Trends in Marriage, Divorce and Fertility," in John Shoven, ed., *Demography and the Economy* (Chicago: University of Chicago Press, 2010).

193 *Somewhat paradoxically, working- and:* Pamela J. Smock, Wendy D. Manning, and Meredith Porter, " 'Everything's There Except Money': How Money Shapes Decisions to Marry Among Cohabitors," *Journal of Marriage and Family* 67 (August 2005): 680–96.

197 *That future is already visible:* James Chung and Sally Johnstone, "A Glimpse into the Postcrash Environment," *Urban Land*, March/April 2010, 42–44, http://urbanland.uli.org/Articles/2010/MarApr/Chung.

200 *Back in 1964, the sociologist Milton Gordon:* Elizabeth Aura McClintock makes the point about Milton Gordon and the factors that delayed his prediction coming true, in "When Does Race Matter? Race, Sex, and Dating at an Elite University," *Journal of Marriage and Family* 72 (February 2010): 45–72. This article includes the results of her interracial hookups at Stanford University. McClintock talked about her findings in a telephone interview with author, April 11, 2011.

200 *Among Hispanics, college-educated women:* Sharon M. Lee and Barry Edmonston, "New Marriages, New Families: U.S. Racial and Hispanic Intermarriage," *Population Bulletin* 60 (June 2005), 26, www.prb.org/pdf05/60.2NewMarriages. pdf.

201 *In 2011, Zhenchao Qian and Daniel Lichter:* Zhenchao Qian and Daniel Lichter, "Changing Patterns of Interracial Marriage in a Multiracial Society," *Journal of Marriage and Family* 73 (October 2011): 1065–84. Qian's comments appear in a press release issued by EurekAlert! on September 15, 2011.

Chapter Eleven: The View from Abroad

Page

208 *It is the dog days of August:* Data on marriage rates, konkatsu, and Japan's shrinking population can be found in: Miho Inada, "Japan Has a New Name for the Mating Game: Konkatsu," *Wall Street Journal*, June 29, 2009, http://online.wsj.com/article/SB124623617832566695.html, and Venessa Wong, "Shrinking Societies: The Other Population Crisis," *Businessweek*, August 12, 2010, http://www.businessweek.com/lifestyle/content/aug2010/bw20100812_825983.htm.

208 *Other Asian countries are seeing:* "The Flight from Marriage," *The Economist*, August 20, 2011, http://www.economist.com/node/21526350.

209 *Esteve and two colleagues have:* Albert Esteve and Iñaki Permanyer, demographers at the Centre d'Estudis Demogràfics, Barcelona, Spain, related this figure in a Skype interview with author, April 11, 2011, and email corre-

spondence with author. They shared their dynamic chart and a copy of the working paper they presented at the 2011 Population Association of America conference: Albert Esteve, Joan Garcia-Roman, and Iñaki Permanyer, "Union Formation Implications of the Gender-Gap Reversal in Education: The End of Hypergamy?" They point out that the chart is based on projections that appear in Wolfgang Lutz, Anne Goujon, Samir K.C., and Warren Sanderson, "Reconstruction of Populations by Age, Sex and Level of Educational Attainment for 120 Countries for 1970–2000," *Vienna Yearbook of Population Research 2007:* 193–235, and Samir K.C., Bilal Barakat, Anne Goujon, Vegard Skirbekk, Warren Sanderson, Wolfgang Lutz, "Projection of Populations by Level of Educational Attainment, Age and Sex for 120 Countries for 2005–2050, *Demographic Research* 22 (March 16, 2010): 383–472.

210 *Elsewhere, in parts of Europe, marriage:* Gardiner Harris, "Out-of-Wedlock Birthrates Are Soaring, US Reports," *New York Times,* May 13, 2009, http://www.nytimes.com/2009/05/13health/13mothers.htlm.

210 *Nearly a third of Japanese women:* These figures and the figures that follow, as well as the 2003 survey of Beijing women, are taken from two articles that appeared in *The Economist*: "Asia's Lonely Hearts: Women Are Rejecting Marriage in Asia. The Social Implications Are Serious," August 20, 2011, www.economist.com/node/21526350; and "The Flight from Marriage," August 20, 2011, www.economist.com/node/21526329.

211 *In Japan, single women under 30:* "Income of Young Japanese Women Tops That of Men," Reuters, Oct. 15, 2010, http://www.reuters.com/article/2010/10/15/us-japan-income-idUSTRE69E15R20101015.

211 *A number of studies have concluded that well-educated:* James Raymo, "Later Marriages or Fewer? Changes in the Marital Behavior of Japanese Women," *Journal of Marriage and Family* 60 (November 1998): 1023–34, points out that women in Japan say they want to marry, but also may be buying their way out of marriage. And James M. Raymo and Miho Iwasawa, "Marriage Market Mismatches in Japan: An Alternative View of the Relationship Between Women's Education and Marriage," *American Sociological Review* 70 (October 2005): 801–22, point out that the decline in marriage in Japan reflects both the "increasing economic independence [of Japanese women] and continued economic dependence on men."

212 *"In the past we had":* In-person interview with author, August 7, 2009.

214 *Toko Shirakawa, a Japanese journalist:* In-person interview with author, August 17, 2009

214 *The sociologist Masahiro Yamada:* In-person interview with author, August 13, 2009.

215 *One of these imaginative businessmen:* In-person interview with author, August 5, 2009.

216 *As a result of the upending of the old:* There are various accounts of Japan's traumatized men and their behavior; they include Chico Harlan, "Japan's Young Men Seek a New Path," *Washington Post*, October 24, 2010; and Daisuke Wakabayashi, "Only in Japan, Real Men Go to a Hotel with Virtual Girlfriends," *Wall Street Journal*, August 31, 2010. The data on sex are in Roland Kelts, "Japan Leads the Way in Sexless Love," *The Guardian*, Dec. 27, 2011. www.guardian.co.uk/commentisfree/2011/dec/27/japan-men-sexless-love.

218 *Hyunok Lee, a South Korean sociologist:* Hyunok Lee shared her research on rural bachelors at the 2011 Population Association of America conference in Washington, D.C., and in a telephone interview with author, April 16, 2011.

219 *In 2010, the New York Times:* Seth Mydans, "Udon Thani Journal: Drawing Western Men with Marriage in Mind," *New York Times*, September 28, 2010, A9.

Chapter Twelve: Our Female Future

Page

224 *Women "suffered no penalties":* Francine M. Deutsch, Josipa Roksa, and Cynthia Meeske, "How Gender Counts When Couples Count Their Money," *Sex Roles* 48 (April 2003): 291–304.

224 *Another found that women:* Rebecca Meisenbach, "The Female Breadwinner: Phenomenological Experience and Gendered Identity in Work/Family Spaces," *Sex Roles* 62 (2010): 2–19.

239 *This is already the case in Scandinavian:* Nathan Hegedus, "Snack Bags and a Regular Paycheck: The Happy Life of a Swedish Dad," *Slate*, August 31, 2010.

239 *Slightly more than a century:* Elisabeth Badinter, *XY: On Masculine Identity* (New York: Columbia University Press, 1995), 14.

240 *"The kitchen is the new garage":* Vidya Rao, "Home Kitchens Heat Up as More Men Start Cooking," *Today.com*, April 11, 2011, http://today.msnbc.msn.com/id/42482506/ns/today-food/t/home-kitchens-heat-more-men-start-cooking.

240 *In the past two years, at:* Dana Schuster, "Dudes Do Food," *New York Post*,

February 2, 2011, www.nypost.com/p/lifestyle/food/dudes_do_food_xte PA6TzRhmH6bxXVENtkO.

242 *Anthropologist David Gilmore, in his book:* David D. Gilmore, *Manhood in the Making: Cultural Concepts of Masculinity,* (New Haven: Yale University Press, 1990).

243 *Bachmann once blocked a fan from:* James Hohmann and Byron Tau, "Marcus Bachmann, Campaign Spouse," *Politico.com,* July 4, 2011, www.politico .com/news/stories/0711/58291.html.

244 *The writer Aaron Traister:* Aaron Traister, "Dude, Man Up and Start Acting like a Mom," *Salon.com,* June 9, 2009, www.salon.com/2009/06/09/man _up/.

247 *Studies show men who aren't married to the:* Men, when unable to provide, are not only less likely to marry, but more likely to lose contact with their children, contributing to a divergence in the destinies of American children, point out Suzanne Bianchi and Melissa Milkie in "Work and Family Research in the First Decade of the 21st Century," *Journal of Marriage and Family* 72 (June 2010): 705–725.

Bibliography

Books

Badinter, Elisabeth. *XY: On Masculine Identity*. New York: Columbia University Press, 1995.

Banks, Ralph Richard. *Is Marriage for White People? How the African American Marriage Decline Affects Everyone*. New York: Dutton, 2011.

Becker, Gary S. *A Treatise on the Family*. Enlarged ed. Cambridge: Harvard University Press, 1993.

Blau, Francine D., Marianne A. Ferber, and Anne E. Winkler, eds. *The Economics of Women, Men, and Work*. 6th ed. Boston: Prentice Hall, 2010.

Blau, Francine D., Mary C. Brinton, and David B. Grusky, eds. *The Declining Significance of Gender?* New York: Russell Sage, 2006.

Boswell, James. *The Journal of a Tour to the Hebrides, with Samuel Johnson, LL.D.* Philadelphia: John F. Watson, 1810.

Buss, David M. *The Evolution of Desire: Strategies of Human Mating*. New York: Basic Books, 1994.

Cahn, Naomi, and June Carbone. *Red Families v. Blue Families: Legal Polarization and the Creation of Culture*. Oxford: Oxford University Press, 2010.

Cherlin, Andrew. *The Marriage-Go-Round: The State of Marriage and the Family in America Today*. New York: Vintage, 2010.

Collins, Gail. *When Everything Changed: The Amazing Journey of American Women from 1960 to the Present*. New York: Little, Brown, 2009.

Coontz, Stephanie. *Marriage, a History: How Love Conquered Marriage.* New York: Penguin, 2006.

———. *A Strange Stirring: The Feminine Mystique and American Women at the Dawn of the 1960s.* New York: Basic Books, 2011.

Crompton, Rosemary, ed. *Restructuring Gender Relations and Employment: The Decline of the Male Breadwinner.* Oxford: Oxford University Press, 1999.

De Beauvoir, Simone. *The Second Sex.* Translated and edited by H. M. Parshley. New York: Vintage Books, 1989.

Donohue, John, ed. *Man with a Pan: Culinary Adventures of Fathers Who Cook for Their Families.* Chapel Hill: Algonquin, 2011.

Elder, Glen H., Jr. *Children of the Great Depression: Social Change in Life Experience.* 1974. Reprint, Colorado: Westview, 1999.

Faludi, Susan. *Backlash: The Undeclared War Against American Women.* New York: Three Rivers, 2006.

Franklin, Donna L. *What's Love Got to Do with It? Understanding and Healing the Rift between Black Men and Women.* New York: Simon & Schuster, 2000.

Friedan, Betty. *The Feminine Mystique.* New York: W.W. Norton, 2001.

Gilman, Charlotte Perkins. *The Yellow Wall-Paper, Herland, and Selected Writings.* Edited with an introduction and notes by Denise D. Knight. New York: Penguin, 2009.

———. *Women and Economics.* New York: Cosimo, 2006.

Gilmore, David D. *Manhood in the Making: Cultural Concepts of Masculinity.* New Haven: Yale University Press, 1990.

Greenwood, Val D. *The Researcher's Guide to American Genealogy.* 3rd ed. Baltimore: Genealogical Publishing Co., 2007.

Harris, Barbara J. *English Aristocratic Women: 1450–1550: Marriage and Family, Property and Careers.* Oxford: Oxford University Press, 2002.

Hochschild, Arlie Russell, with Anne Machung. *The Second Shift.* New York: Penguin, 2003.

Hood, Jane C., ed. *Men, Work, and Family.* Newbury Park: Sage Publications, 1993.

Hymowitz, Kay. *Manning Up: How the Rise of Women Has Turned Men into Boys.* New York: Basic Books, 2011.

Kennedy, David M. *Freedom from Fear: The American People in Depression and War, 1929–1945.* New York: Oxford University Press, 1999.

Kessler-Harris, Alice. *Out to Work: A History of Wage-Earning Women in the*

United States. 20th anniversary ed. Oxford: Oxford University Press, 2003.

Kimmel, Michael. *Manhood in America: A Cultural History.* 2nd ed. New York: Oxford University Press, 2006.

Knudson-Martin, Carmen, and Anne Rankin Mahoney, eds. *Couples, Gender, and Power: Creating Change in Intimate Relationships.* New York: Springer, 2009.

Komarovksy, Mirra. *Dilemmas of Masculinity: A Study of College Youth.* 1976. Reprint, Walnut Creek: AltaMira, 2004.

———. *The Unemployed Man and His Family: The Effect of Unemployment upon the Status of the Man in Fifty-nine Families.* 1940. Reprint, Walnut Creek: AltaMira, 2004.

Lareau, Annette. *Unequal Childhoods: Class, Race, and Family Life.* Berkeley: University of California Press, 2003.

Regnerus, Mark, and Jeremy Uecker. *Premarital Sex in America: How Young Americans Meet, Mate, and Think about Marrying.* Oxford: Oxford University Press, 2011.

Rotundo, E. Anthony. *American Manhood: Transformations in Masculinity from the Revolution to the Modern Era.* New York: Basic Books, 1993.

Ryan, Christopher, and Cacilda Jethá. *Sex at Dawn: The Prehistoric Origins of Modern Sexuality.* New York: HarperCollins, 2010.

Salmon, Marylynn. *Women and the Law of Property in Early America.* Chapel Hill: University of North Carolina Press, 1986.

Vedantam, Shankar. *The Hidden Brain: How Our Unconscious Minds Elect Presidents, Control Markets, Wage Wars, and Save Our Lives.* New York: Spiegel & Grau, 2010.

Weiner, Lynn. *From Working Girl to Working Mother: The Female Labor Force in the United States, 1820–1980.* Chapel Hill: University of North Carolina Press, 1985.

Wilson, William Julius. *When Work Disappears: The World of the New Urban Poor.* New York: Vintage, 1997.

Woolf, Virginia. *A Room of One's Own.* Orlando: Harcourt Brace, 1989.

———. *The Death of the Moth and Other Essays.* San Diego: Harcourt Brace, 1970.

Wylie, Philip. *Generation of Vipers.* 1942. Reprint, Normal, Ill.: Dalkey Archive Press, 1996.

Zelizer, Viviana A. *The Social Meaning of Money: Pin Money, Paychecks, Poor Relief, and Other Currencies.* Princeton: Princeton University Press, 1997.

Selected Newspaper Articles

BBC News. "Female Medics 'to Outnumber Male.'" June 2, 2009, news.bbc .co.uk/2/hi/health/8077083.stm.

Beck, Melinda. "Are Alpha Males Healthy? Aggressiveness Aids Rise to the Top, but the Stress Can Harm a Body." *Wall Street Journal*, September 13, 2011, D1.

Brooks, David. "The Missing Fifth." *New York Times*, May 9, 2011, www.nytimes .com/2011/05/10/opinion/10brooks.html.

Carey, Benedict. "Need Therapy? A Good Man Is Hard to Find." *New York Times*, May 21, 2011, www.nytimes.com/2011/05/22/health/22therapists .html?pagewanted=all.

Carey, Tanith. "The Survival Guide for Breadwinning Wives." *Mail Online*, October 13, 2011, www.dailymail.co.uk/femail/article-2048459/Survival -guide-breadwinning-wives-1-4-earn-husbands.html.

Carvajal, Doreen. "The Changing Face of Medical Care." *New York Times*, March 7, 2011, www.nytimes.com/2011/03/08/world/europe/08iht-ffdocs08.html? _r=2&pagewanted=all.

Caucon, Dennis. "Women Gain as Men Lose Jobs." *USA Today*, September 3, 2009, www.usatoday.com/news/nation/2009-09-02-womenwork_ N.htm.

Coontz, Stephanie. "When We Hated Mom." *New York Times*, May 7, 2011, www.nytimes.com/2011/05/08/opinion/08coontz.html?pagewanted=all.

Dougherty, Conor. "Young Women's Pay Exceeds Male Peers'." *Wall Street Journal*, September 1, 2010, http://online.wsj.com/article/SB100014240527487 04421104575463790770831192.html.

Harlan, Chico. "Japan's Young Men Seek a New Path." *Washington Post*, October 24, 2010, www.washingtonpost.com/wp-dyn/content/article/2010/10/24/ AR2010102403342.html.

Harris, Gardiner. "The Public's Quiet Savior from Harmful Medicines." *New York Times*, September 13, 2010, www.nytimes.com/2010/09/14/health/14kelsey .html.

Horowitz, Jason. "Michele Bachmann's Husband Shares Her Strong Conservative Values." *Washington Post*, July 5, 2011, www.washingtonpost.com/ lifestyle/style/ michele-bachmanns-husband-shares-her-strong-conservative -values/2011/06/21/gIQAyNmvzH_story.html.

Mydans, Seth. "Udon Thani Journal: Drawing Western Men with Marriage in Mind." *New York Times*, September 28, 2010, A9.

Nicholas, Sadie. "Why Do Men Find the Female Breadwinner Utterly Terrifying?," *Mail Online*, June 17, 2008, www.dailymail.co.uk/femail/article-1026972/Why-men-female-breadwinner-utterly-terrifying.html.

Paul, Pamela. "When Thoughts Turn to Sex, or Not." *New York Times*, December 9, 2011, www.nytimes.com/2011/12/11/fashion/sex-on-the-brain-studied.html?_r=1.

Roberts, Sam. "For Young Earners in Big City, a Gap in Women's Favor." *New York Times*, August 3, 2007, www.nytimes.com/2007/08/03/nyregion/03women.html?pagewanted=all.

Rugaber, Christopher. "Millions of Lost Jobs Won't Return." Associated Press article appearing online in *Main Street*, May 14, 2010, www.mainstreet.com/article/career/employment/millions-lost-jobs-wont-return.

Schmidt, Peter. "Men's Share of College Enrollments Will Continue to Dwindle, Federal Report Says." *The Chronicle of Higher Education*, May 27, 2010, http://chronicle.com/article/Mens-Share-of-College/65693/.

Smith, Julia Llewellyn. "Female Breadwinners: When Mum Makes More," *Telegraph*, September 11, 2011, www.telegraph.co.uk/relationships/8754984/Female-Breadwinners-When-Mum-makes-more.html.

Uchitelle, Louis, and David Leonhardt. "Men Not Working, and Not Wanting Just Any Job," *New York Times*, July 31, 2006, www.nytimes.com/2006/07/31/business/31men.html?pagewanted=all.

Wakabayashi, Daisuke. "Only in Japan, Real Men Go to a Hotel with Virtual Girlfriends," *Wall Street Journal*, August 31, 2010.

Walshe, Shushannah. "Michele Bachmann 'Submissive' Wife Idea Matter of Interpretation," *ABC News*, August 12, 2011, http://abcnews.go.com/Politics/michele-bachmann-submissive-wife-belief-matter-interpretation/story?id=14292494#.Tukp7UqKWUc.

Selected Magazine Articles, Print and Online

Bennett, Jessica, and Jesse Ellison. "Women Will Rule the World." *Newsweek/The Daily Beast*, July 6, 2010, www.thedailybeast.com/newsweek/2010/07/06/women-will-rule-the-world.html.

Chung, James, and Sally Johnstone. "A Glimpse into the Postcrash Environment." *Urban Land*. March/April 2010, 42–44, http://urbanland.uli.org/Articles/2010/MarApr/Chung.

Economist. "Asia's Lonely Hearts: Women Are Rejecting Marriage in Asia. The Social Implications Are Serious." August 20, 2011, www.economist.com/

node/21526350, and "The Flight from Marriage." August 20, 2011, and www.economist.com/node/21526329.

Esquire, "20/50: The Esquire Survey of American Men." *Esquire*, September 2010.

Grose, Jessica. "The New Girls: Fall TV Is Full of Emasculated Men. Does That Mean It's Also Full of Empowered Women?" *Slate*, September 8, 2011, www.slate.com/articles/arts/culturebox/2011/09/the_new_girls.html.

Hegedus, Nathan. "Snack Bags and a Regular Paycheck: The Happy Life of a Swedish Dad." *Slate*, August 31, 2010.

Hohmann, James and Byron Tau. "Marcus Bachmann, Campaign Spouse." *Politico.com*, July 4, 2011, www.politico.com/news/stories/0711/58291.html.

Keith, Tamara. "Finding Love While Searching for Work." National Public Radio, May 25, 2011, www.npr.org/2011/05/25/136402638/finding-love-while-searching-for-work.

Marcotte, Amanda. "How to Make a Critically Acclaimed TV Show About Masculinity." *Jezebel*, September 7, 2011, http://jezebel.com/5837945/how-to-make-a-critically-acclaimed-tv-show-about-masculinity.

Rao, Vidya. "Home Kitchens Heat Up as More Men Start Cooking." *Today.com*, April 11, 2011, www.economist.com/node/21526329.

Regnerus, Mark. "Sex Is Cheap: Why Young Men Have the Upper Hand in Bed, Even When They're Failing in Life." *Slate*, February 25, 2011, www.slate.com/articles/double_x/doublex/2011/02/sex_is_cheap.html

Rosin, Hanna. "The End of Men." *Atlantic*, July/August 2010, www.theatlantic.com/magazine/archive/2010/07/the-end-of-men/8135/#.

Salam, Reihan. "The Death of Macho." *Foreign Policy*, July/August 2009, www.foreignpolicy.com/articles/2009/06/18/the_death_of_macho.

Schuster, Dana. "Dudes Do Food." *New York Post*, February 2, 2001, www.nypost.com/p/lifestyle/food/dudes_do_food_xtePA6TzRhmH6bxXVENtkO.

Tiku, Nitasha. "Husbands Outsource Sexual Fulfillment so as Not to Burden Hard-working Wives." *New York Magazine* "Daily Intel," August 16, 2010, http://nymag.com/daily/intel/2010/08/freeloading_husbands_outsource.html.

Traister, Aaron. "Dude, Man Up and Start Acting like a Mom." *Salon.com*, June 9, 2009, www.salon.com/2009/06/09/man_up/.

Selected Blog Posts and Websites

Baker, Gail Konop. "Do Women Now Want Sex More than Men?" *Huffington Post*, September 23, 2011, www.huffingtonpost.com/gail-konop-baker/women-want-sex-more-than-men_b_977416.html.

Becker, Gary. "The Revolution in the Economic Empowerment of Women." *Becker-Posner* blog, January 4, 2010, www.becker-posner-blog.com/2010/01/the-revolution-in-the-economic-empowerment-of-women-becker.html.

D'Andrea Tyson, Laura. "Education and Women in the Labor Market." *New York Times Economix* blog, March 11, 2011, http://economix.blogs.nytimes.com/2011/03/11/women-and-their-wages/.

Gouveia, Aaron. "The Breadwinner." *Good Men Project* blog, May 22, 2011, goodmenproject.com/featured-content/the-breadwinner-2/.

Greenstone, Michael, and Adam Looney. "Have Earnings Actually Declined?" *Up Front* blog, Brookings Institution's the Hamilton Project, March 4, 2011, www.brookings.edu/opinions/2011/0304_jobs_greenstone_looney.aspx.

Leonhardt, David. "Mark Penn on 'Guys Left Behind.'" *New York Times Economix* blog, June 1, 2009, http://economix.blogs.nytimes.com/2009/06/01/mark-penn-on-guys-left-behind/.

Match.com. "Everything You Think You Know About Single Is Wrong." Match.com blog post, February 4, 2011, http://blog.match.com/2011/02/04/everything-you-think-you-know-about-singles-is-wrong-we-separate-fact-from-fiction-with-the-first-comprehensive-study-of-singles-in-america/.

Prior, Karen Swallow. "Confessions of a Breadwinner Wife," Her.meneutics, May 3, 2011. http://blog.christianitytoday.com/women/2011/05/confessions_of_a_breadwinner_w.html.

Rampell, Catherine. "Do You Earn More than Your Parents Did?," July 7, 2010, *New York Times Economix* blog, http://economix.blogs.nytimes.com/2010/07/07/do-you-earn-more-than-your-parents-did/.

———. "Rising Family Income: More Work, Not Raises." *New York Times Economix* blog, July 20, 2011, http://economix.blogs.nytimes.com/2011/07/20/rising-family-income-more-work-not-raises/.

Savali, Kirsten West. "72 Percent of African-American Children Born to Unwed Mothers." *Huffington Post*, November 8, 2010, www.bvblackspin.com/2010/11/08/72-percent-of-african-american-children-born-to-unwed-mothers/.

Academic Papers

Abramitzky, Ran, Adeline Delavande, and Luis Vasconcelos. "Marrying Up: The Role of Sex Ratio in Assortative Matching." *American Economic Journal: Applied Economics* 3 (July 2011): 125–57, http://aeaweb.org/articles.php?doi=10.1257/app.3.3.124.

Baumeister, Roy F. and Kathleen Vohs. "Sexual Economics: Sex as Female Resource for Social Exchange in Heterosexual Interactions." *Personality and Social Psychology Review* 8, no. 4 (2004), 339–63.

Beach, Steven R. H., Abraham Tesser, Frank D. Fincham, Deborah Jones, Debra Johnson, and Daniel Whitaker. "Pleasure and Pain in Doing Well, Together: An Investigation of Performance-Related Affect in Close Relationships." *Journal of Personality and Social Psychology* 74 (1998): 923–38.

Beach, Steven R. H., Daniel Whitaker, Deborah Jones, and Abraham Tesser. "When Does Performance Feedback Prompt Complementarity in Romantic Relationships?" *Personal Relationships* 8 (2001), 231–48.

Becker, Gary, William H. J. Hubbard, and Kevin M. Murphy. "Explaining the Worldwide Boom in Higher Education of Women." *Journal of Human Capital* 4 (Fall 2010), 203–41.

Bianchi, Suzanne M., and Melissa A. Milke. "Work and Family Research in the First Decade of the 21st Century." *Journal of Marriage and Family* 72 (June 2010): 705–25.

Black, Dan A., Seth G. Sanders, and Lowell J. Taylor. "The Economics of Lesbian and Gay Families." *Journal of Economic Perspectives*, 21 (Spring 2007), 53–70.

Blau, Francine D. "Trends in the Well-being of American Women, 1970–1995." *Journal of Economic Literature* 36 (March 1998): 112–65.

Bloemen, Hans G., and Elena Stancanelli. "Modelling the Employment and Wage Outcomes of Spouses: Is She Outearning Him?" Institute for the Study of Labor (IZA), Discussion Paper 3455, April 2008, www.iza.org/en/webcontent/publications/papers/viewAbstract?dp_id=3455.

Bosson, Jennifer K. and Joseph A. Vandello. "Precarious Manhood and Its Links to Action and Aggression." *Current Directions in Psychological Science* 20 (April 2011): 82.

Buchmann, Claudia, and Thomas A. DiPrete. "The Growing Female Advantage in College Completion: The Role of Family Background and Academic Achievement." *American Sociological Review* 71 (August 2006): 515–41.

Buchmann, Claudia, Thomas A. DiPrete, and Anne McDaniel. "Gender Inequalities in Education." *Annual Review of Sociology* 34 (2008): 319–37.

Buss, David, T. K. Shackelford, L. A. Kirkpatrick, and R. J. Larsen. "A Half Century of Mate Preferences: The Cultural Evolution of Values." *Journal of Marriage and Family* 63 (May 2001): 491–503.

Chandra, Anjani, William D. Mosher, Casey Copen, and Catlainn Sionean. "Sexual Behavior, Sexual Attraction, and Sexual Identity in the United States: Data from the 2006–2008 National Survey of Family Growth." National Health Statistics Reports, No. 36, National Center for Health Statistics, March 2011, 15.

Clark, Russell D., III, and Elaine Hatfield. "Gender Differences in Receptivity to Sexual Offers." *Journal of Psychology and Human Sexuality* 2 (1989): 39–55.

Dahl, Michael S., and Lamar Pierce. "In Sickness and in Wealth: Psychological and Sexual Costs of Income Comparison in Marriage." Working paper, shared with author by Lamar Pierce.

Demantas, Ilana, and Kristen Myers. " 'It's a Blessing That My Wife Works': Balancing Masculinity and Economic Dependence on Women During Unsettled Times." Paper presented at the annual meeting of the American Sociological Association in August 2011.

Deutsch, Francine M., Josipa Roksa, and Cynthia Meeske. "How Gender Counts When Couples Count Their Money." *Sex Roles* 48 (April 2003): 291–304.

Doepke, Matthias, and Michèle Tertilt. "Women's Liberation: What's in It for Men?" *The Quarterly Journal of Economics* 124 (November 2009): 1541–91.

Duflo, Esther. "Grandmothers and Granddaughters: Old Age Pension and Intra-household Allocation in South Africa." *World Bank Economic Review* 17, no. 1 (2003): 1–25.

England, Paula. "Missing the Big Picture and Making Much Ado About Almost Nothing: Recent Scholarship in Gender and Household Work." *Journal of Family Theory and Review* 3 (March 2011): 23–26.

Esteve, Albert, Joan Garcia-Roman, J., and Iñaki Permanyer. "Union Formation Implications of the Gender-Gap Reversal in Education: The End of Hypergamy?" Working paper presented at Population Association of America annual meeting in Washington, D.C., in April 2011.

Ezzedeen, Souha, and Kristen Grossnickle Ritchey. "The Man Behind the Woman: A Qualitative Study of the Spousal Support Received and Valued by Executive Women." *Journal of Family Issues* 29 (2008):1007, http://jfi .sagepub.com/cgi.content/abstract/29/9/1107.

Fernandez, Raquel, Alessandra Fogli, and Claudia Olivetti. "Marrying Your Mom: Preference Transmission and Women's Labor and Education Choices." National Bureau of Economic Research, Working Paper 9234, October 2002.

Fisman, Raymond, Sheena S. Iyengar, Emir Kamenica, and Itamar Simonson. "Gender Differences in Mate Selection: Evidence from a Speed Dating Experiment." *The Quarterly Journal of Economics* 121 (2006): 673–97.

Furdyna, Holly E., M. Belinda Tucker, and Angela D. James. "Relative Spousal Earnings and Marital Happiness Among African American and White Women." *Journal of Marriage and Family* 70 (May 2008): 332–44.

Gager, Constance T. and Scott T. Yabiku. "Who Has the Time? The Relationship Between Household Labor Time and Sexual Frequency." *Journal of Family Issues* 13 (2010):135, http://jfi.sagepub.com/content/31/2/135.

Goldin, Claudia. "A Pollution Theory of Discrimination: Male and Female Differences in Occupations and Earnings." National Bureau of Economic Research, Working Paper 8985, June 2002, www.nber.org/papers/w8985.

———. "From the Valley to the Summit: A Brief History of the Quiet Revolution That Transformed Women's Work." *Regional Review* Q4 (2004): 5–12.

———. "Marriage Bars: Discrimination Against Married Women Workers, 1920s to 1950s." National Bureau of Economic Research, Working Paper 2747, October 1988, www.nber.org/papers/w2747.

———. "The Long Road to the Fast Track: Career and Family." *Annals of the American Academy of Political and Social Science* 596 (November 2004): 20–35.

———. "The Role of World War II in the Rise of Women's Employment." *The American Economic Review* 81, no. 4 (September 1991): 741–56.

Goldin, Claudia, and Lawrence Katz. "Transitions: Career and Family Life Cycles of the Educational Elite." *American Economic Review: Papers and Proceedings*, 98.2 (2008): 363–69.

Goldin, Claudia, Lawrence F. Katz, and Ilyana Kuziemko. "The Homecoming of American College Women: The Reversal of the College Gender Gap." *Journal of Economic Perspectives* 20 (Fall 2006): 133–56.

Hindin, Michelle J., and Carie J. Muntifering. "Women's Autonomy and Timing of Most Recent Sexual Intercourse in Sub-Saharan Africa: A Multi-Country Analysis." *Journal of Sex Research* 48 (2011): 1–9.

Isen, Adam, and Betsey Stevenson. "Women's Education and Family Behavior: Trends in Marriage, Divorce and Fertility." In John Shoven, ed., *Demography and the Economy* (Chicago: University of Chicago Press, 2010).

K.C., Samir, Bilal Barakat, Anne Goujon, Vegard Skirbekk, Warren Sanderson, and Wolfgang Lutz. "Projection of Populations by Level of Educational Attainment, Age, and Sex for 120 Countries for 2005–2050," *Demographic Research* 22 (March 16, 2010): 383–472.

Kleinfeld, Judith. "No Map to Manhood: Male and Female Mindsets Behind the College Gender Gap." *Gender Issues* 26 (November 2009): 171–82.

———. "The State of American Boyhood." *Gender Issues* 26 (2009): 113–20.

Kraft, Kornelius, and Stefanie Neimann. "Effect of Labor Division Between Wife and Husband on the Risk of Divorce: Evidence from German Data." Institute for the Study of Labor (IZA), Discussion Paper 4515, October 2009.

Kramer, Karen Z., and Amit Kramer. "The Relationship Between Economic Downturns and the Proportion of Stay-at-Home Father Households." Working paper and PowerPoint presentation at the annual convention of the Population Association of America, Washington, D.C., April 2011.

Jalovaara, Marika. "The Joint Effects of Marriage Partners' Socioeconomic Positions on the Risk of Divorce." *Demography* 40 (February 2003): 67–81.

Lincoln, Anne E. "The Shifting Supply of Men and Women to Occupations: Feminization in Veterinary Education." *Social Forces* 88 (2010): 1969–98.

Lundberg, S., R. Pollak, and T. Wales. "Do Husbands and Wives Pool Their Resources: Evidence from the U.K. Child Benefit." *Journal of Human Resources* 32 (Summer 1997): 463–80.

Lutz, Wolfgang, Anne Goujon, Samir K.C., and Warren Sanderson. "Reconstruction of Populations by Age, Sex and Level of Educational Attainment for 120 Countries for 1970–2000." *Vienna Yearbook of Population Research* 2007: 193–235.

Mattingly, Marybeth J., and Kristin E. Smith. "Changes in Wives' Employment When Husbands Stop Working: A Recession-Prosperity Comparison." *Family Relations* 59 (October 2010): 343–57.

McClintock, Elizabeth Aura. "When Does Race Matter? Race, Sex, and Dating at an Elite University." *Journal of Marriage and Family* 72 (February 2010): 45–72.

McDaniel, Anne. "The Gender Gap in Higher Education: A Cross-National Analysis of 131 Countries." Working papers, shared by author.

McDaniel, Anne, and Claudia Buchmann. "The Consequences of Career Choices: Family and Income Disparities Among Women in Science and Other Elite Professions." Working paper presented at the annual meeting of the Population Association of America, Washington, D.C., March 19, 2011, available at paa2011.princeton.edu/download.aspx?submissionId=111799.

McDaniel, Anne, Thomas A. DiPrete, Claudia Buchmann, and Uri Shwed. "The Black Gender Gap in Educational Attainment: Historical Trends and Racial Comparison." *Demography* 48 (2011): 889–914.

Meisenbach, Rebecca. "The Female Breadwinner: Phenomenological Experience and Gendered Identity in Work/Family Spaces." *Sex Roles* 62 (2010): 2–19.

Munsch, Christin. "The Effect of Unemployment and Relative Income Disparity on Infidelity for Men and Women." Paper presented at annual meeting of the American Sociological Association, Atlanta, Georgia, August 16, 2010.

Pinkus, Rebecca T., Penelope Lockwood, Ulrich Schimmack, and Marc A. Fournier. "For Better and for Worse: Everyday Social Comparisons Between

Romantic Partners." *Journal of Personality and Social Psychology* 95 (November 2008): 1180–1201.

Qian, Zhenchao, and Daniel Lichter. "Changing Patterns of Interracial Marriage in a Multiracial Society." *Journal of Marriage and Family* 74 (October 2011): 1065–84.

Raley, Sara B., Marybeth J. Mattingly, and Suzanne M. Bianchi. "How Dual are Dual-Income Couples? Documenting Change From 1970 to 2001." *Journal of Marriage and Family* 68 (February 2006): 11–28.

Raymo, James M. "Later Marriages or Fewer? Changes in the Marital Behavior of Japanese Women." *Journal of Marriage and Family* 60 (November 1998): 1023–34.

Raymo, James M., and Miho Iwasawa. "Marriage Market Mismatches in Japan: An Alternative View of the Relationship Between Women's Education and Marriage." *American Sociological Review* 70 (October 2005): 801–22.

Sayer, Liana C., Paula England, Paul D. Allison, and Nicole Kangas. "She Left, He Left: How Employment and Satisfaction Affect Women's and Men's Decisions to Leave Marriages." *American Journal of Sociology* 116 (May 2011): 1982–2018.

Schwartz, Christine R. "Earnings Inequality and the Changing Association between Spouses' Earnings." *American Journal of Sociology* 115 (March 1, 2010): 1524–57.

Schwartz, Christine, and Nikki L. Graf. "Assortative Matching Among Same-Sex and Different-Sex Couples in the United States, 1990–2000." *Demographic Research* 21 (December 8, 2009): 843–78, available at www.demographic-research.org.

Schwartz, Christine R., and Robert D. Mare. "Trends in Educational Assortative Marriage from 1940 to 2003." *Demography* 42 (November 2005): 621–46.

Shafer, Emily Fitzgibbons. "Wives' Relative Wages, Husbands' Paid Work Hours, and Wives' Labor Force Exit." *Journal of Marriage and Family* 73 (February 2011): 250–63.

Smock, Pamela J., Wendy D. Manning, and Meredith Porter. " 'Everything's There Except Money': How Money Shapes Decisions to Marry Among Cohabitors." *Journal of Marriage and Family* 67 (August 2005): 680–96.

Spoor, Jennifer, and Michael Schmitt. " 'Things Are Getting Better' Isn't Always Better: Considering Women's Progress Affects Perceptions of and Reactions to Contemporary Gender Inequality." *Basic and Applied Social Psychology* 33 (2011): 24–36.

Stevenson, Betsey, and Justin Wolfers. "The Paradox of Declining Female Happiness." *American Economic Journal: Economic Policy* 1, no. 2 (2009): 190–255.

Stuart, H. Colleen, Sue Moon, and Tiziana Casciaro. "The Oscar Curse: Status Dynamics and Gender Differences in Marital Survival," *Social Science Research Network,* January 27, 2011, http://ssrn.com/abstract=1749612.

Sullivan, Oriel. "An End to Gender Display Through the Performance of Housework? A Review and Reassessment of the Quantitative Literature Using Insights from the Qualitative Literature." *Journal of Family Theory & Review* 3 (March 2011): 1–13.

Teachman, Jay. "Wives' Economic Resources and Risk of Divorce." *Journal of Family Issues* 31 (October 2010): 1305–23.

Tesser, Abraham, Murray Millar, and Janet Moore. "Some Affective Consequences of Social Comparison and Reflection Processes: The Pain and Pleasure of Being Close." *Journal of Personality and Social Psychology* 54 (1988): 49–61.

Tichenor, Veronica. "Maintaining Men's Dominance: Negotiating Identity and Power When She Earns More." *Sex Roles* 53 (August 2005): 191–205.

Waismel-Manor, Ronit, and Pamela Tolbert. "The Impact of Relative Earnings Among Dual-Earner Couples on Career Satisfaction and Family Satisfaction." Paper presented at the International Sociological Association meeting in Gothenburg, Sweden, July 2010.

Winkler, Anne E. "Earnings of Husbands and Wives in Dual-Earner Families." *Monthly Labor Review* (April 1998): 42–48.

Selected Government and Other Reports

Autor, David. "The Polarization of Job Opportunities in the U.S. Labor Market: Implications for Employment and Earnings." The Hamilton Project and Center for American Progress, April 2010, www.brookings.edu/papers/2010/04_jobs_autor.aspx.

Barsh, Joanna, and Lareina Yee. "Unlocking the Full Potential of Women in the US Economy." McKinsey & Company, April 2011, available at www.mckinsey.com/client_service/organization/latest_thinking/unlocking_the_full_potential.aspx.

Cohn, D'Vera, and Richard Fry. "Women, Men, and the New Economics of Marriage." Pew Research Center, *Social and Demographic Trends Report* (Washington, D.C.: Pew Research Center, January 19, 2010), www.pewsocialtrends.org/2010/01/19/women-men-and-the-new-economics-of-marriage/.

Galinsky, Ellen, Kerstin Aumann, and James T. Bond. "Times Are Changing: Gender and Generation at Work and at Home." *Families and Work Institute National Study of the Changing Workforce 2008*, www.familiesandwork.org.

Getz, David M. "Men's and Women's Earnings for States and Metropolitan Statistical Areas: 2009." *U.S. Census Bureau American Community Survey Briefs* (September 2010).

Goldin, Claudia, and Lawrence F. Katz. "The Career Cost of Family." Paper prepared for the Sloan Conference Focus on Flexibility, Washington, D.C., November 30, 2010.

Lacey, T. Alan, and Benjamin Wright. "Occupational Employment Projections to 2018." *Monthly Labor Review* (November 2009): 82–123, bls.gov/opub/mlr/2009/11/art5full.pdf.

Laughlin, Lynda. "Maternity Leave and Employment Patterns: 1961–2008." *U.S. Census Bureau Current Population Reports* (October 2011), 14, www.census.gov/prod/2011pubs/p70-128.pdf.

Pew Social Trends Staff. *The Decline of Marriage and Rise of New Families* (Washington, D.C.: Pew Research Center, November 18, 2010), www.pewsocialtrends.org/2010/11/18/the-decline-of-marriage-and-rise-of-new-families/2/#ii-overview.

Smith, Kristin. "Increased Reliance on Wives as Breadwinners During the First Year of the Recession." Carsey Institute, Issue Brief 9, Fall 2009.

———. "Wives as Breadwinners: Wives' Share of Family Earnings Hits Historic High During the Second Year of the Great Recession." Carsey Institute, Fact Sheet 20, Fall 2010.

Stewart, Jay. "What Do Male Nonworkers Do?" U.S. Bureau of Labor Statistics, Working Paper 371, April 2004, www.bls.gov/osmr/pdf/ec040010.pdf.

Toossi, Mitra. "A Behavioral Model for Projecting the Labor Force Participation Rate." *Monthly Labor Review*, May 2011, 31–32, www.bls.gov/opub/mlr/2011/05/art3full.pdf.

———. "Labor Force Projections to 2018: Older Workers Staying More Active." *Monthly Labor Review*, November 2009, bls.gov/opub/mlr/2009/11/art3full.pdf.

U.S. Bureau of Labor Statistics. "Highlights of Women's Earnings in 2010." Report 1031, July 2011, 2, www.bls.gov/cps/cpswom2010.pdf.

———. "Spotlight on Statistics: Women at Work" (March 2011). www.bls.gov/spotlight/2011/women.

———. *Women in the Labor Force: A Databook, 2010.* www.bls.gov/cps/wlf-databook2010.htm.

U.S. Centers for Disease Control and Prevention. "Percent of Live Births to Un-married Mothers: United States, Each State, Preliminary 2009." *Stats of the States, 2009,* www.cdc.gov/nchs/pressroom/stats_states.htm.

Wang, Wendy, and Kim Parker. "Women See Value and Benefits of College: Man Lag on Both Fronts, Survey Finds." Social and Demographic Trends Report. Washington, D.C.: Pew Research Center, August 17, 2011, www.pewsocial trends.org/2011/08/17/women-see-value-and-benefits-of-college-men-lag-on -both-fronts-survey-finds/.

Acknowledgments

Talk about riches. I have many people to thank who helped bring this book to fruition. First and foremost I would like to thank my editor, Priscilla Painton, without whose exuberant encouragement, perceptive analysis, unflagging support, and unfailing willingness to take phone calls it would never have happened. I wake up in the morning wondering what I ever did to be lucky enough to work with her. At Simon & Schuster, I would also like to thank Jonathan Karp for his support and wise counsel; Michael Szczerban, for cheerfully making sure things went smoothly; Anne Tate and Nina Pajak, for getting the word out; Fred Chase, for heroic copyediting; Nancy Inglis, for care and oversight; Arthur Hochstein, for such an elegant cover that it made me want to own that purse; Nancy Singer for her lovely design; Emily Remes; Richard Rhorer; Jackie Seow; Irene Kheradi; Gina DiMascia; and John Wahler. I would also like to thank my agent, Todd Shuster, for his attention and good counsel.

Many people tapped into extensive personal and professional networks to help find sources to interview, not because they knew me but because they believed in the topic and out of the goodness of their hearts. Jillian Blackwell is chief among these. A Michigan mother with her own inspiring life story, she designed an eye-popping listserv announcement for the women in her network. For the same reasons,

I thank Donna Brazile and Lavonia Perryman Fairfax. Also James Melton and Terry Barclay at Inforum Michigan, who approached their executive women membership. Also Andrea Messinger who put me in touch with many people at Michigan Works!, and Amaya Tune at the AFL-CIO. I also thank Melody Collins and the staff members at Michigan Works who shared their insights. I also would like to thank alumni networks for Boston University, Howard University, Florida International University, the University of North Carolina at Chapel Hill, the University of California-Los Angeles, and especially the University of Texas Pan-American. And the estimable Leah Nylen for providing research assistance that helped me get started. Donna Zerwitz and Tim Page kindly gave me access to the National Bureau of Economic Research electronic archives. I also thank the staff and membership of the National Council on Family Relations.

I would like to say special thanks to those respected colleagues who not only provided counsel but read the manuscript with their wealth of knowledge and a keen editing eye: Naomi Cahn and D'Vera Cohn and James Chung, thank you so much. Other experts who read all or portions include Elizabeth McClintock, Anne McDaniel, Justin Garcia, Lamar Pierce, Abraham Tesser, Albert Esteve, Liana Sayer, Christy Spivey, Mary Bowler, Hyunok Lee and Ran Abramitzky. They were so generous, and I am so grateful. Just because they read it does not mean they agree with all my arguments.

Many distinguished academics were willing to give up an hour, or more, out of their busy schedules for an interview about their work as it pertained to the topic of women and earnings. I learned so much from them. In addition to the expert readers mentioned above, those who gave interviews or other help include Gary Becker, Claudia Goldin, David Autor, Fran Blau, Anne Winkler, Pamela Tolbert, Shelly Lundberg, Souha Ezzedeen, Jay Teachman, Jerry Suls, Betsey Stevenson, Maria Cancian, Heather Boushey, Christine Schwartz, Sonia Goltz, Karen Nussbaum, Elaina Rose, Lee Badgett, Kristin Smith, Sanjiv Gupta, Viviana Zelizer, Sam Yagan, Whitney Casey, Thomas Blume, Helen Fisher, Carmen Knudson-Martin, Philip Cohen, Naveen Jonathan, Magdalena Hinojosa, Judy Kuriansky, Brad Wilcox, Anju Malhotra, Byram Karasu, Joan Garcia, Iñaki Permanyer, Atsushi

Nishiguchi, Yukari Hirakawa, Toko Shirakawa, Masahiro Yamada, Yosuke Shionagi, Mira Kirshenbaum, Patti Giglio, Andrew Cherlin, Michelle Hindin, Margaret Greene, Markie Blumer, Hajj Flemings, Catalyst, and Rebecca Glade. At the Bureau of Labor Statistics, special thanks to Mary Bowler, Alan Lacey, and Mitra Toossi.

For Chapter Eleven, on international trends, I was fortunate to have the support of a fellowship from the Japan Society, for six weeks of interviews in Japan. I am grateful to Ruri Kawashima, Betty Borden, Tomoko Nagai, and two interpreters who were so fun to work with: Miyako Yoshida and David d'Heilly. David was also kind enough to read the chapter and provide his expert take on Japanese gender relations.

I am also grateful to the New America Foundation, which has proved such a valuable professional perch. This book benefited greatly from the inexhaustible talents of Caroline Esser, who provided research assistance, fact-checking, and so much more. I also thank Marie Lawrence for her painstaking fact-checking—any remaining errors are my own—as well as Andrés Martinez and Steve Coll for their guidance and support. I thank Faith Smith and Sabrini Siddiqui for their smart and energetic help in promotion. At the Washington Post, I thank Lynda Robinson, Sydney Trent, David Rowell, Lynn Medford, Nicole Arthur, Peter Perl, and Marcus Brauchli, for being so supportive. Thanks to Becky Gardiner at *The Guardian* for publishing some early thoughts and to Double X editors Jessica Grose and Kate Julian for doing the same. Thanks, Emily Yoffe. And Jack Shafer. And Kris McMenamin.

The best part of book writing is getting out and talking to people, and I thank the far-flung group of men and women who shared their reflections and experiences. Many of their stories appear in these pages, and others contributed to my—and readers'—overall understanding. More than a few were unforgettable. I particularly thank the gracious and extended Hawkins family, who combine good sense and good humor. I also thank, the many women in South Texas who came forward to tell their stories, and the men.

I especially want to thank Margaret Talbot and Nell Minow, cherished friends who are always there: to listen, to lunch, to read, to improve. And my own family: Mark, who knows what it's like, and Anna and Robin, who always cheerlead and never complain. And my mother and father, siblings, and many family members who tolerate a writing relative who spends too much time at the desk, away from them. And thanks to Daisy and Doug Layman, for all that driving.

Index

.